SEVEN SEAS ENTERTAINMENT PRESENTS

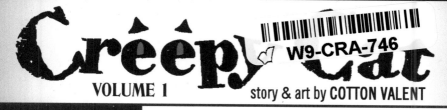

Creepy Cat

VOLUME 1

story & art by COTTON VALENT

TRANSLATION
Alethea & Athena Nibley

ADAPTATION
David Lumsdon

LETTERING
Karis Page

COVER DESIGN
Nicky Lim

COPY EDITOR
Dawn Davis

EDITOR
Nick Mamatas

PREPRESS TECHNICIAN
Rhiannon Rasmussen-Silverstein

PRODUCTION ASSOCIATE
Christa Miesner

PRODUCTION MANAGER
Lissa Pattillo

MANAGING EDITOR
Julie Davis

ASSOCIATE PUBLISHER
Adam Arnold

PUBLISHER
Jason DeAngelis

CreepyCat Neko to Watashi no Kimyouna Seikatsu Vol. 1

Original Japanese edition published by Star Seas Company.
English publishing rights arranged with Star Seas Company
through KODANSHA LTD., Tokyo.

Seven Seas press and purchase enquiries can be sent to Marketing Manager Lianne Sentar at press@gomanga.com. Information regarding the distribution and purchase of digital editions is available from Digital Manager CK Russell at digital@gomanga.com.

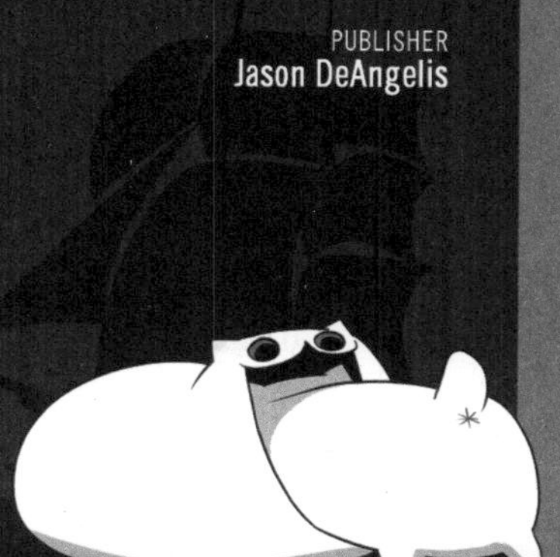

ISBN: 978-1-64827-787-0
Printed in Canada
First Printing: October 2021
10 9 8 7 6 5 4 3 2 1

READING DIRECTIONS

This book reads from ***right to left***, Japanese style. If this is your first time reading manga, you start reading from the top right panel on each page and take it from there. If you get lost, just follow the numbered diagram here. It may seem backwards at first, but you'll get the hang of it! Have fun!!

1
2
3
4
5
6
7
8
9

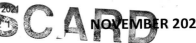

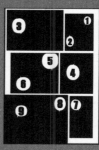

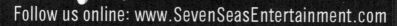

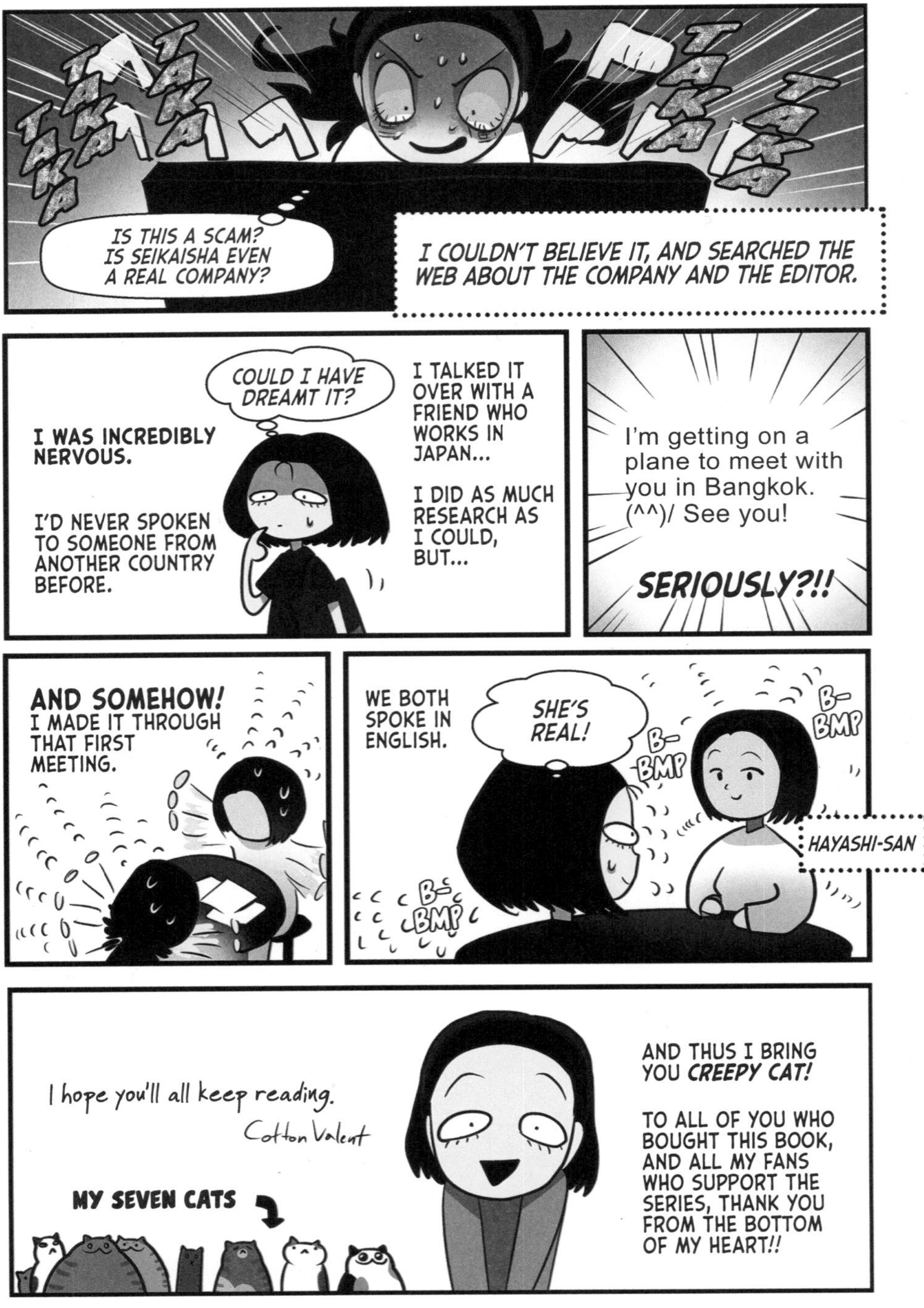
TAKA TAKA TAKA TAKA
IS THIS A SCAM? IS SEIKAISHA EVEN A REAL COMPANY?
I COULDN'T BELIEVE IT, AND SEARCHED THE WEB ABOUT THE COMPANY AND THE EDITOR.
I WAS INCREDIBLY NERVOUS.
I'D NEVER SPOKEN TO SOMEONE FROM ANOTHER COUNTRY BEFORE.
COULD I HAVE DREAMT IT?
I TALKED IT OVER WITH A FRIEND WHO WORKS IN JAPAN...
I DID AS MUCH RESEARCH AS I COULD, BUT...
I'm getting on a plane to meet with you in Bangkok. (^^)/ See you!
SERIOUSLY?!!
AND SOMEHOW! I MADE IT THROUGH THAT FIRST MEETING.
WE BOTH SPOKE IN ENGLISH.
SHE'S REAL!
B-BMP
B-BMP
B-BMP
HAYASHI-SAN
I hope you'll all keep reading.
Cotton Valent
MY SEVEN CATS
AND THUS I BRING YOU CREEPY CAT!
TO ALL OF YOU WHO BOUGHT THIS BOOK, AND ALL MY FANS WHO SUPPORT THE SERIES, THANK YOU FROM THE BOTTOM OF MY HEART!!

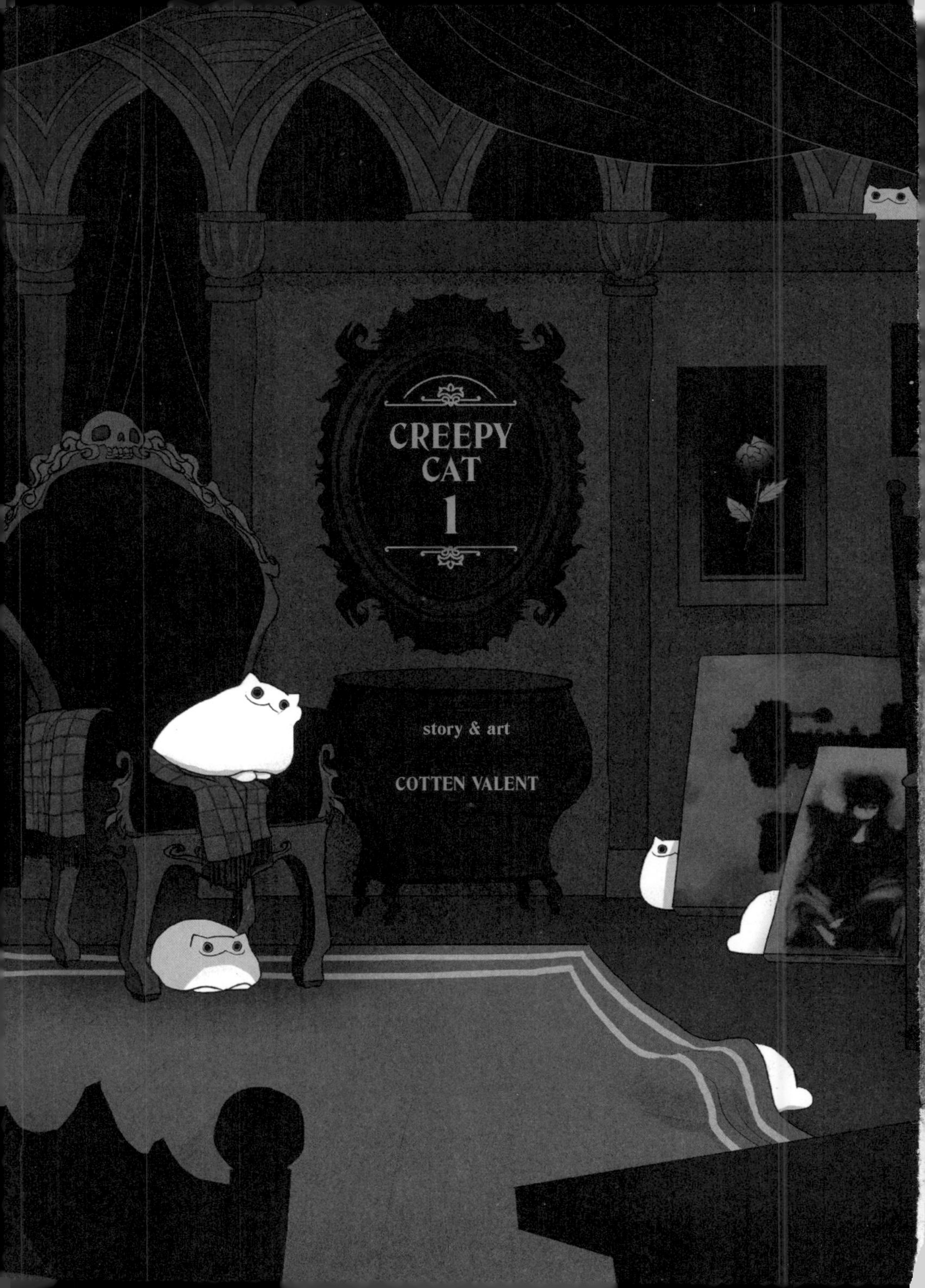
CREEPY
CAT
1
story & art
COTTEN VALENT

Creepy Cat

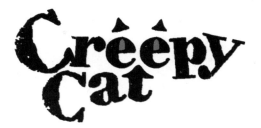

INTRUDER

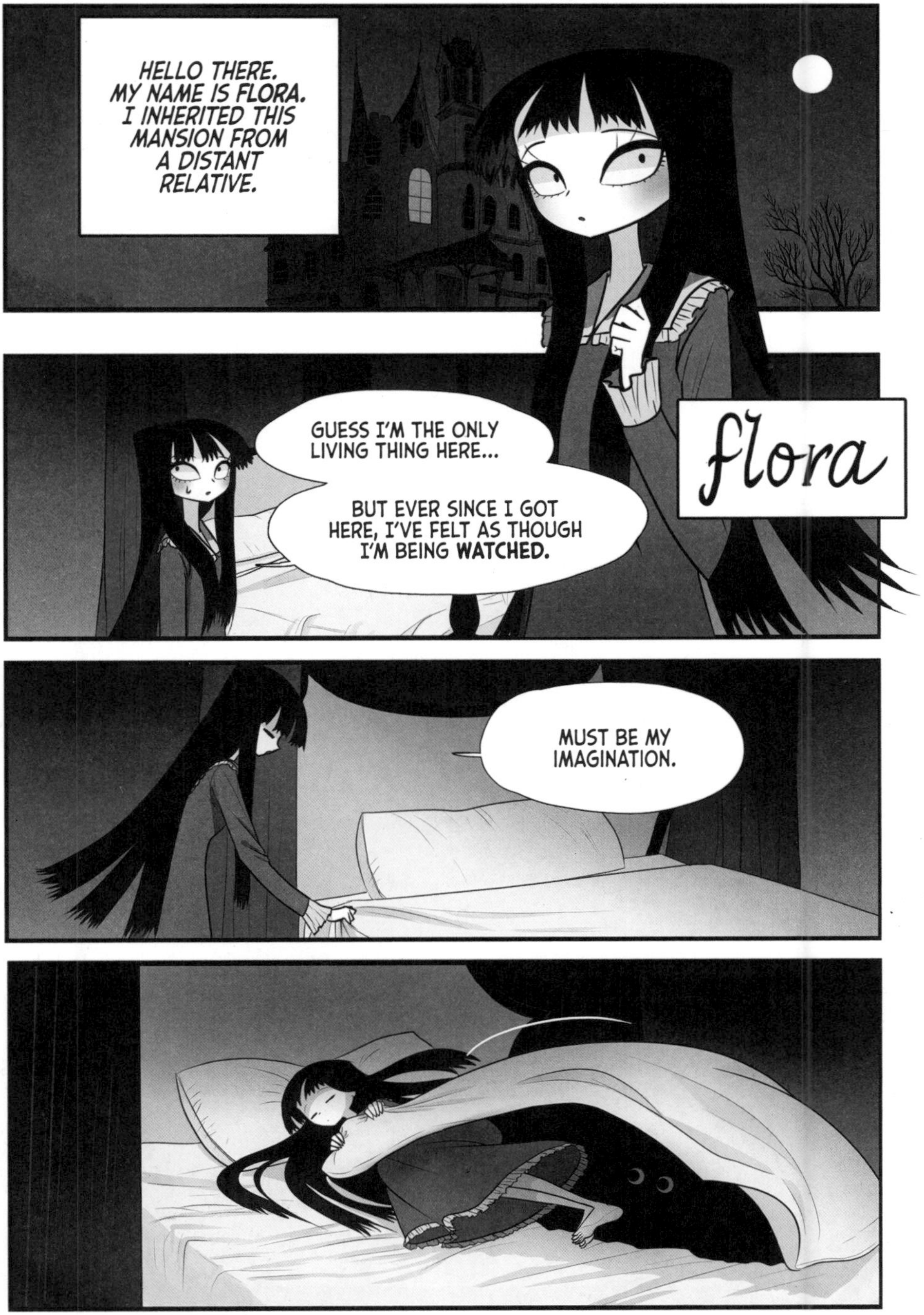
HELLO THERE. MY NAME IS FLORA. I INHERITED THIS MANSION FROM A DISTANT RELATIVE.
GUESS I'M THE ONLY LIVING THING HERE...
BUT EVER SINCE I GOT HERE, I'VE FELT AS THOUGH I'M BEING **WATCHED.**
flora
MUST BE MY IMAGINATION.

HEAVY

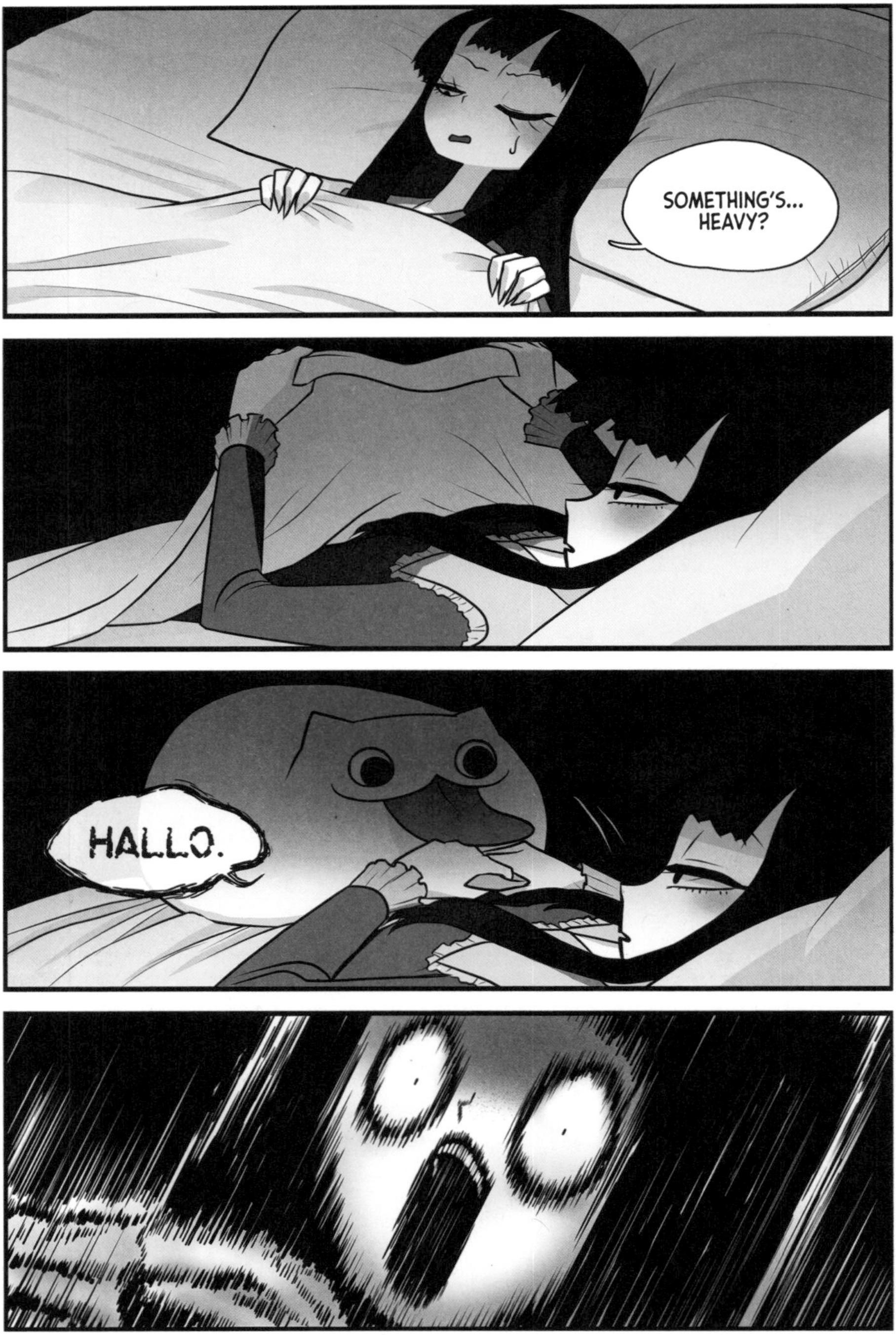
SOMETHING'S... HEAVY?
HALLO.

A CAT?

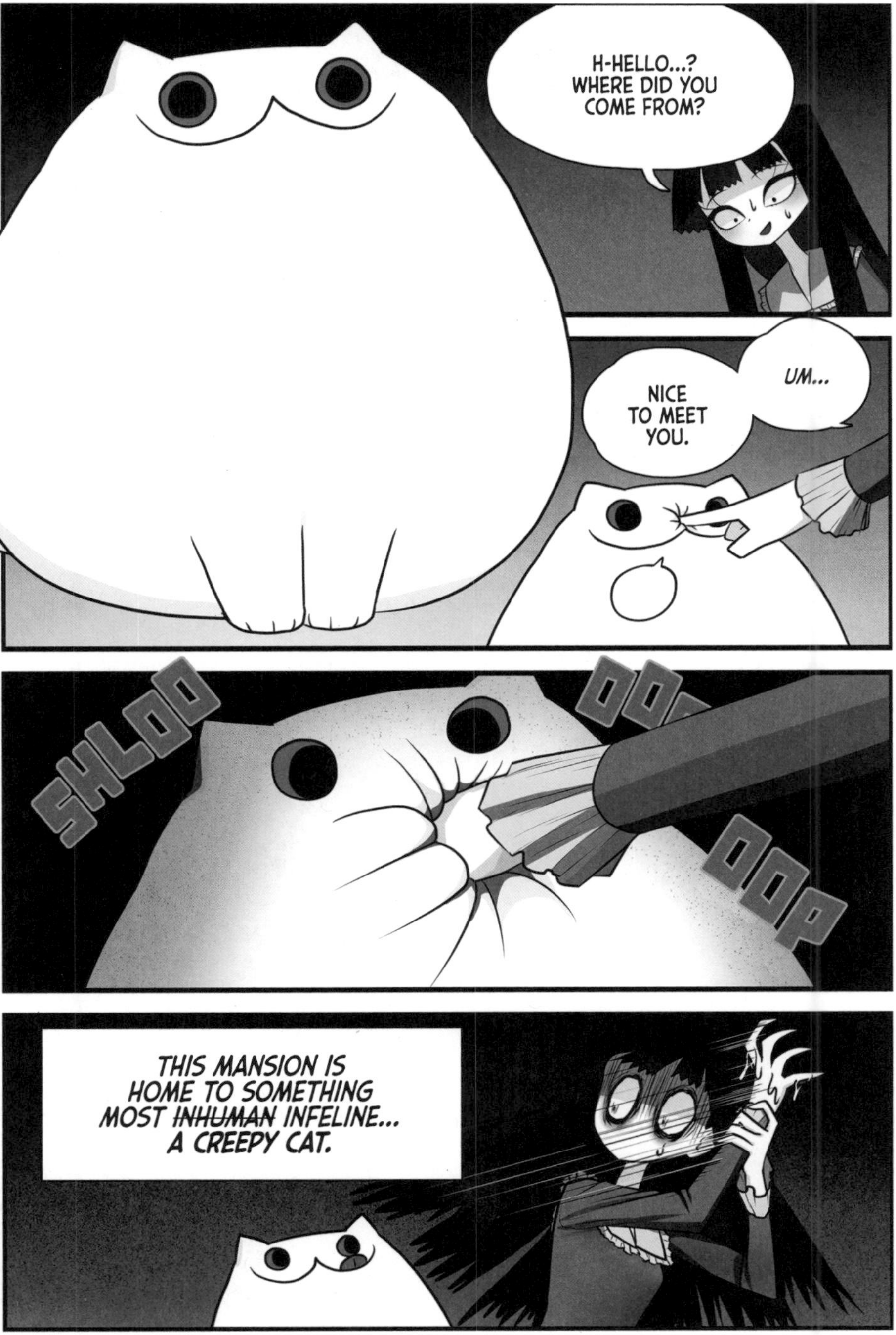
H-HELLO...? WHERE DID YOU COME FROM?
UM...
NICE TO MEET YOU.
SHLOO
OOO
OOP
THIS MANSION IS HOME TO SOMETHING MOST ~~INHUMAN~~ INFELINE... A CREEPY CAT.

CREEPY CAT

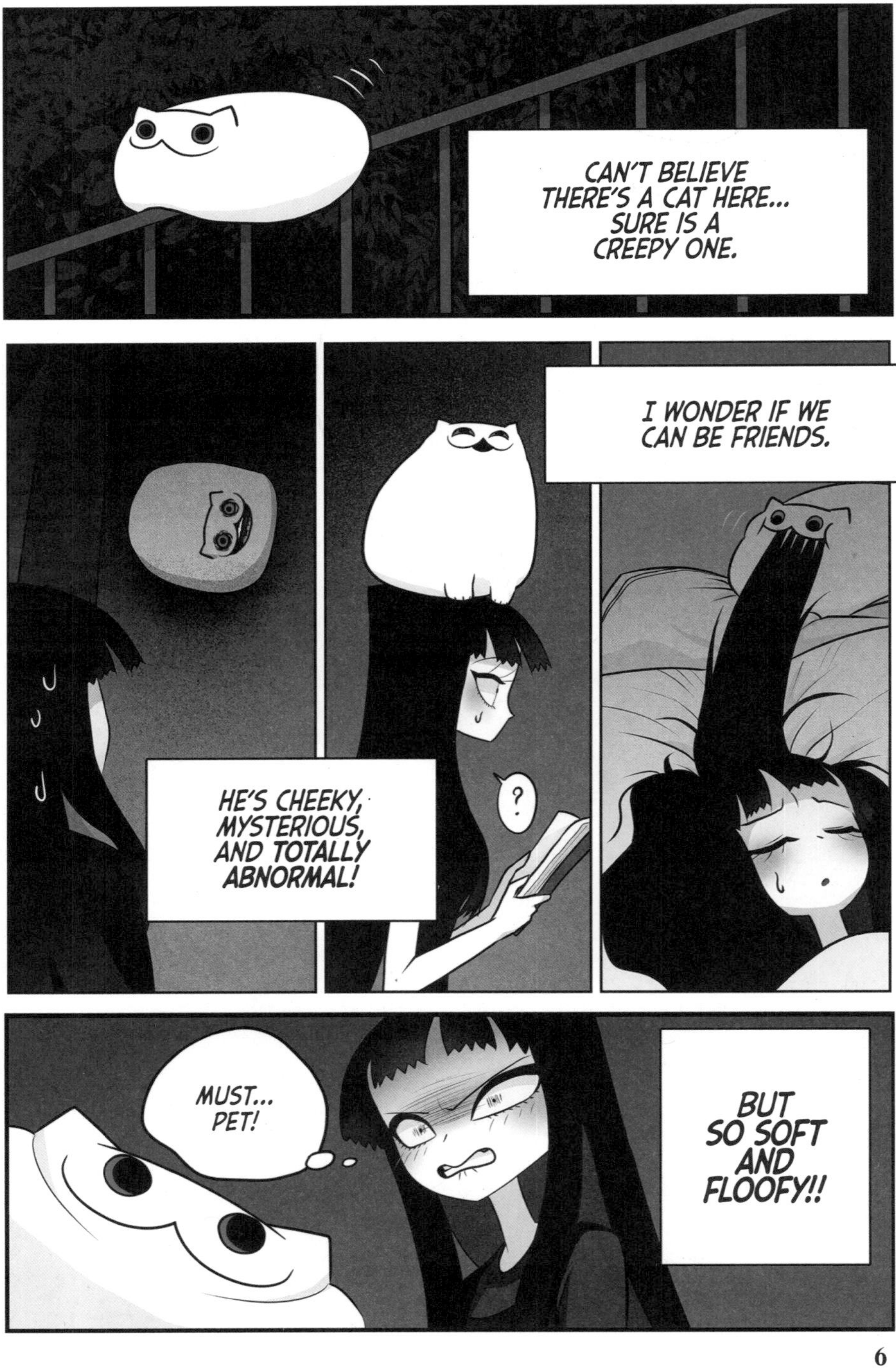
CAN'T BELIEVE THERE'S A CAT HERE... SURE IS A CREEPY ONE.
HE'S CHEEKY, MYSTERIOUS, AND TOTALLY ABNORMAL!
?
I WONDER IF WE CAN BE FRIENDS.
MUST... PET!
BUT SO SOFT AND FLOOFY!!

SNACK ATTACK

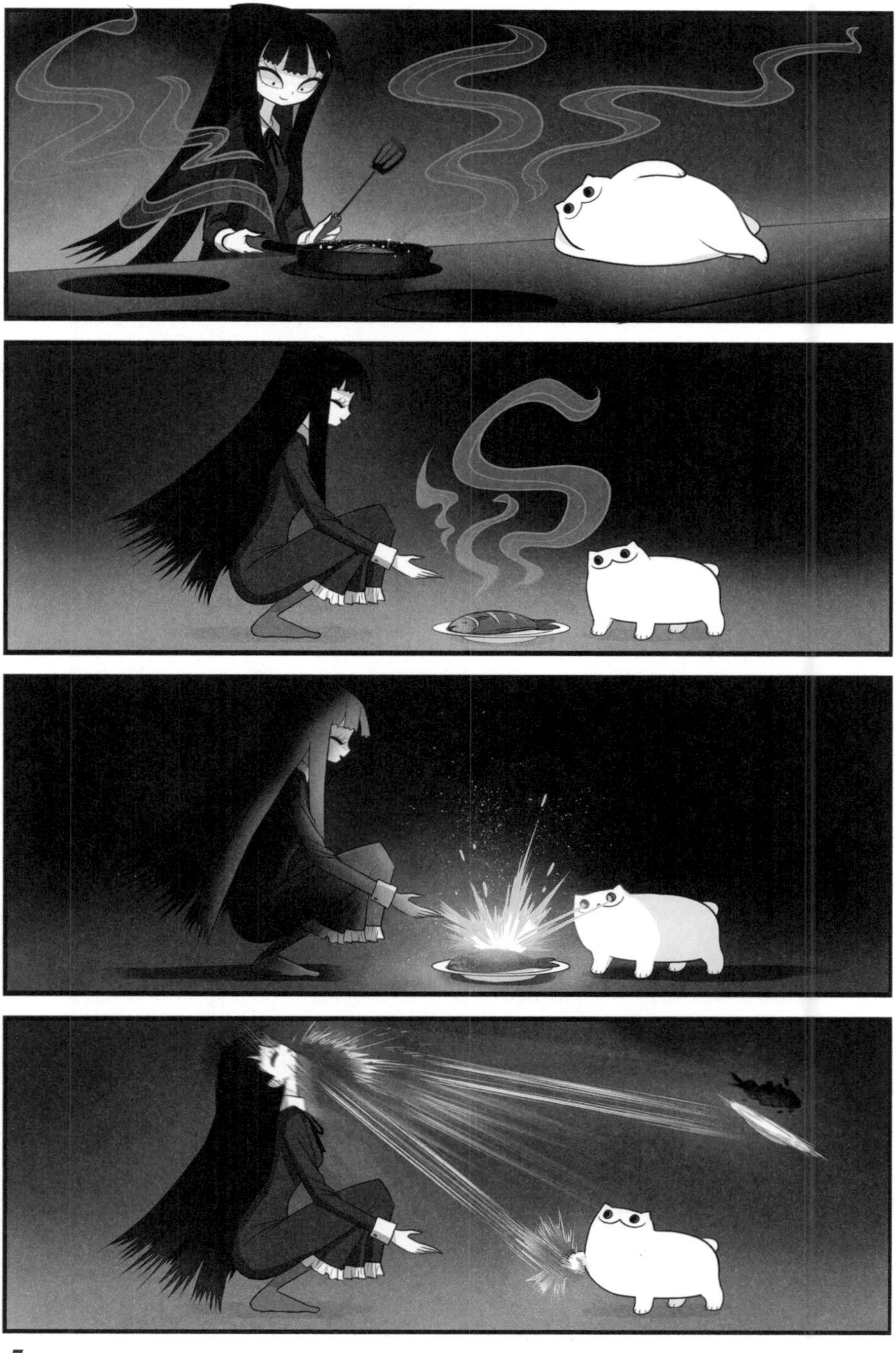

YES WE CAN!

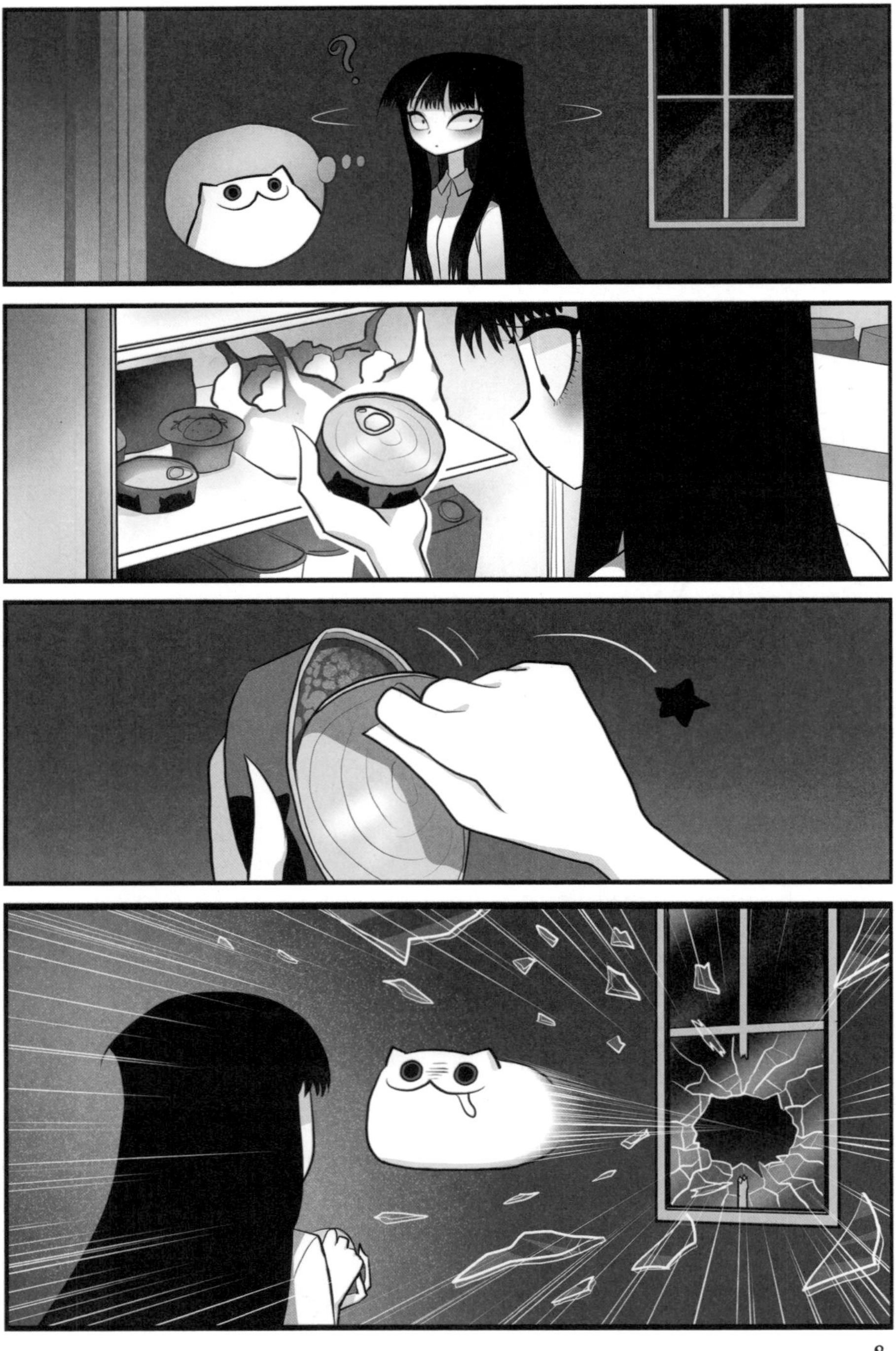
?

PICKLE TRICK

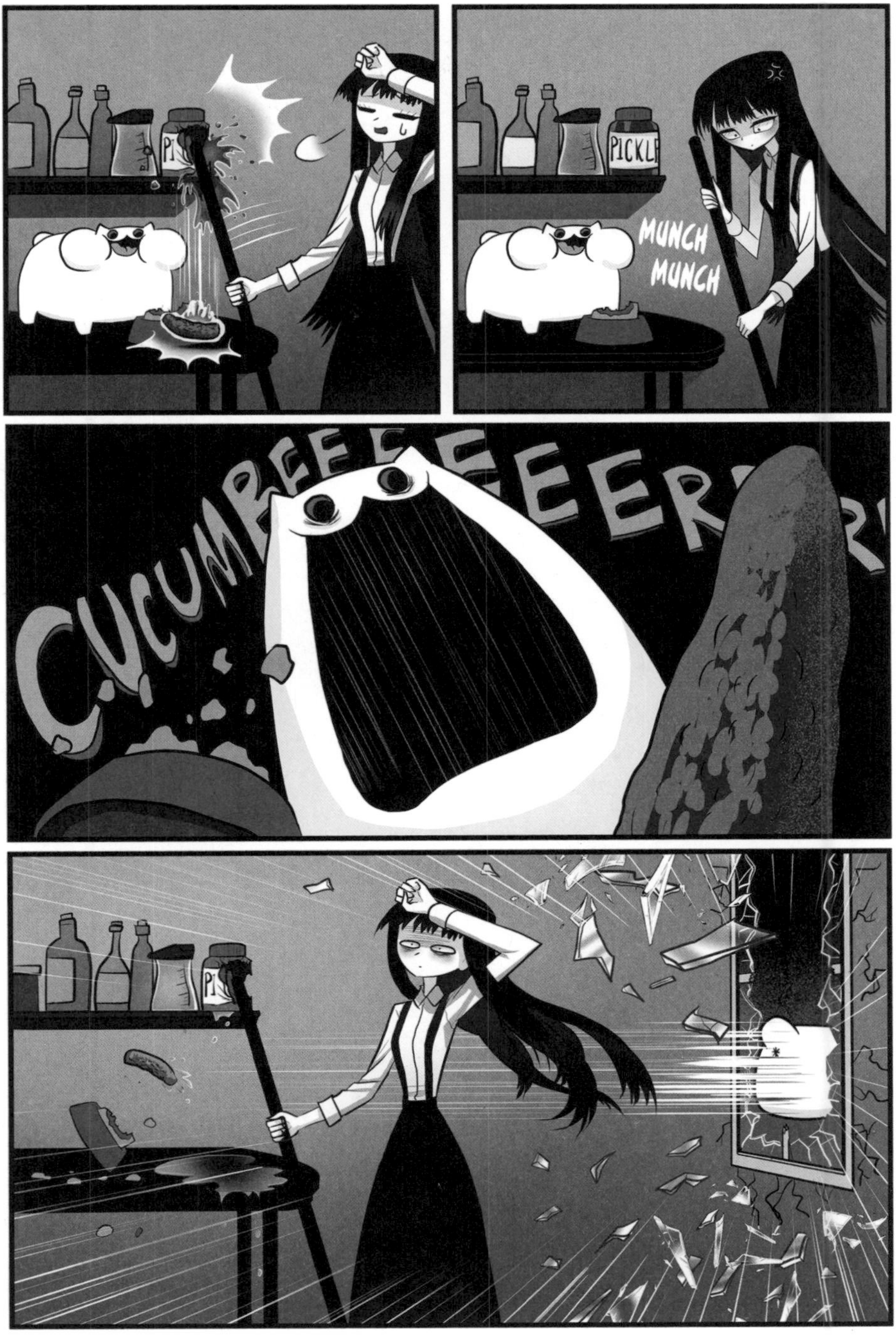
MUNCH
MUNCH
CUCUMBEEEEERR

THE VETERINARIAN

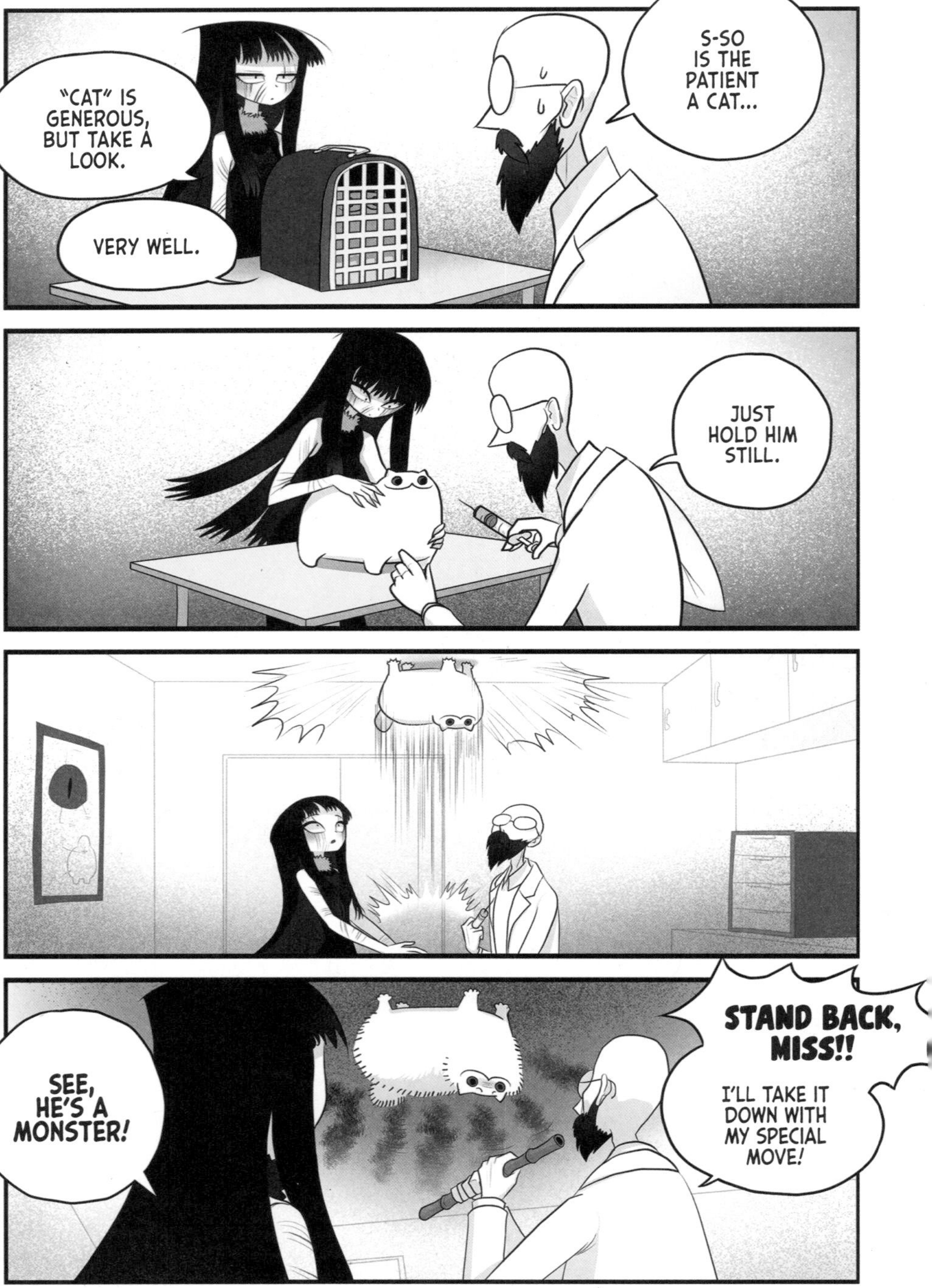

"CAT" IS GENEROUS, BUT TAKE A LOOK.
S-SO IS THE PATIENT A CAT...
VERY WELL.
JUST HOLD HIM STILL.
SEE, HE'S A MONSTER!
STAND BACK, MISS!!
I'LL TAKE IT DOWN WITH MY SPECIAL MOVE!

HE'S WATCHING

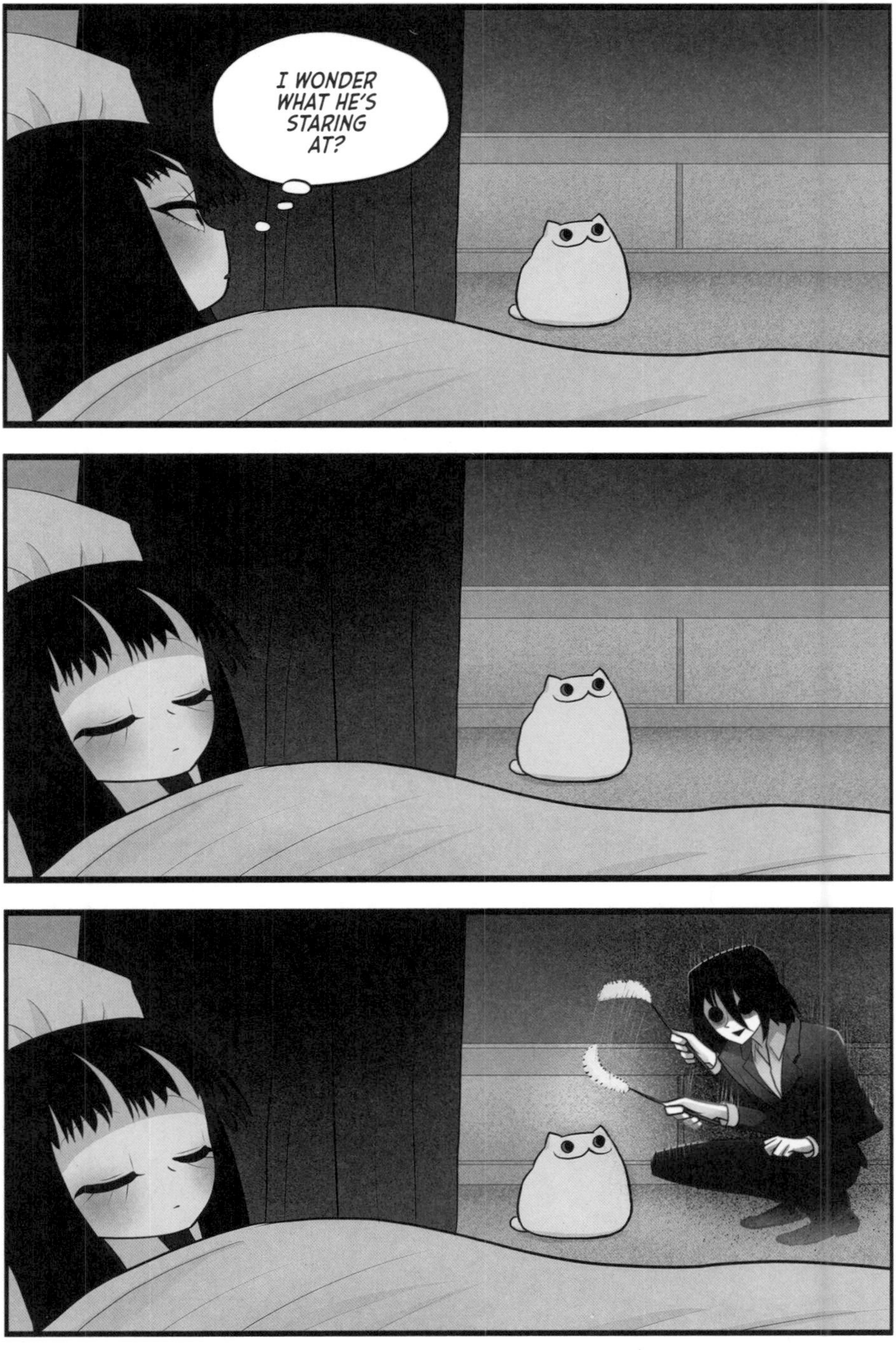

I WONDER WHAT HE'S STARING AT?

PRESS PAWS

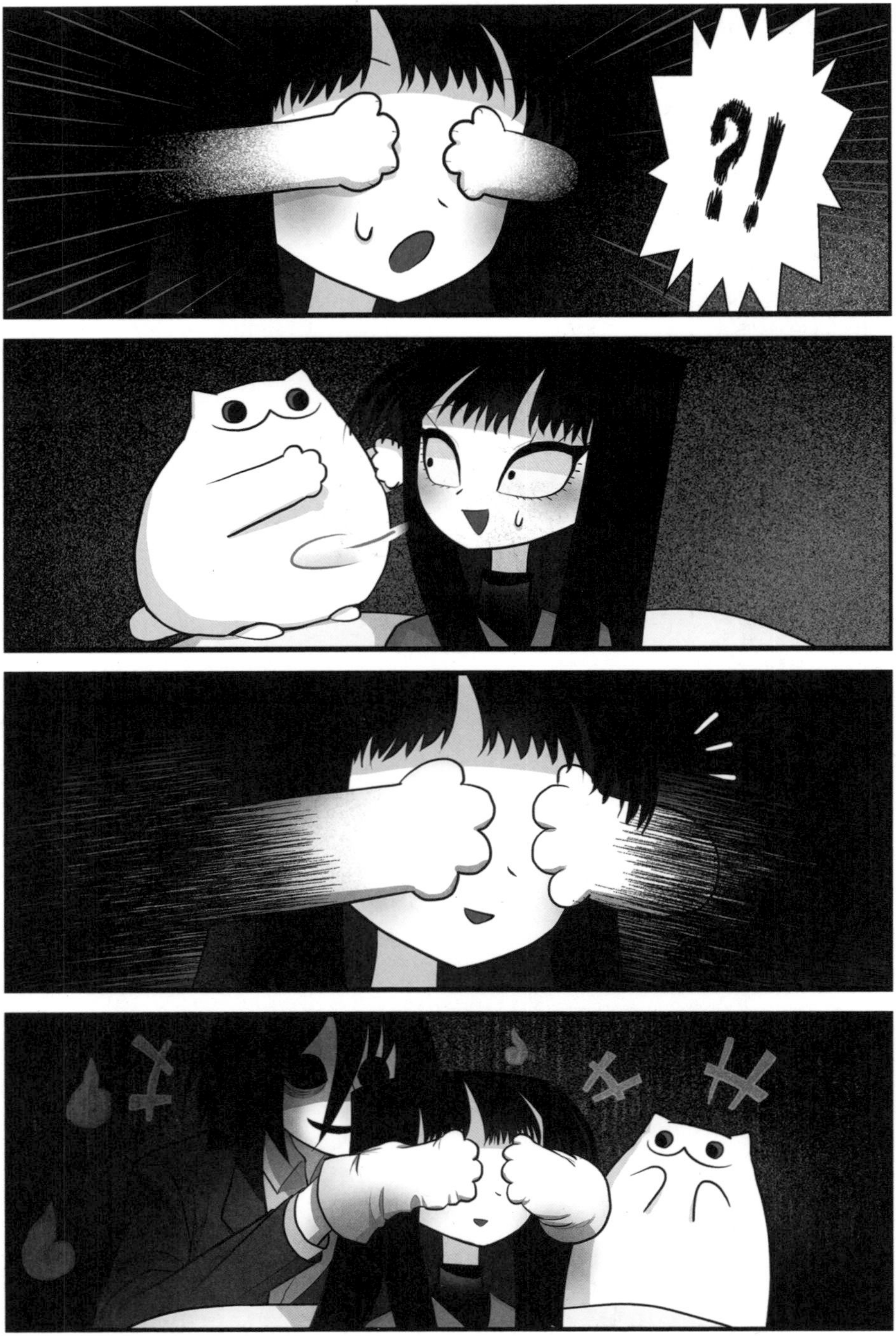
?!

COINCIDENCE

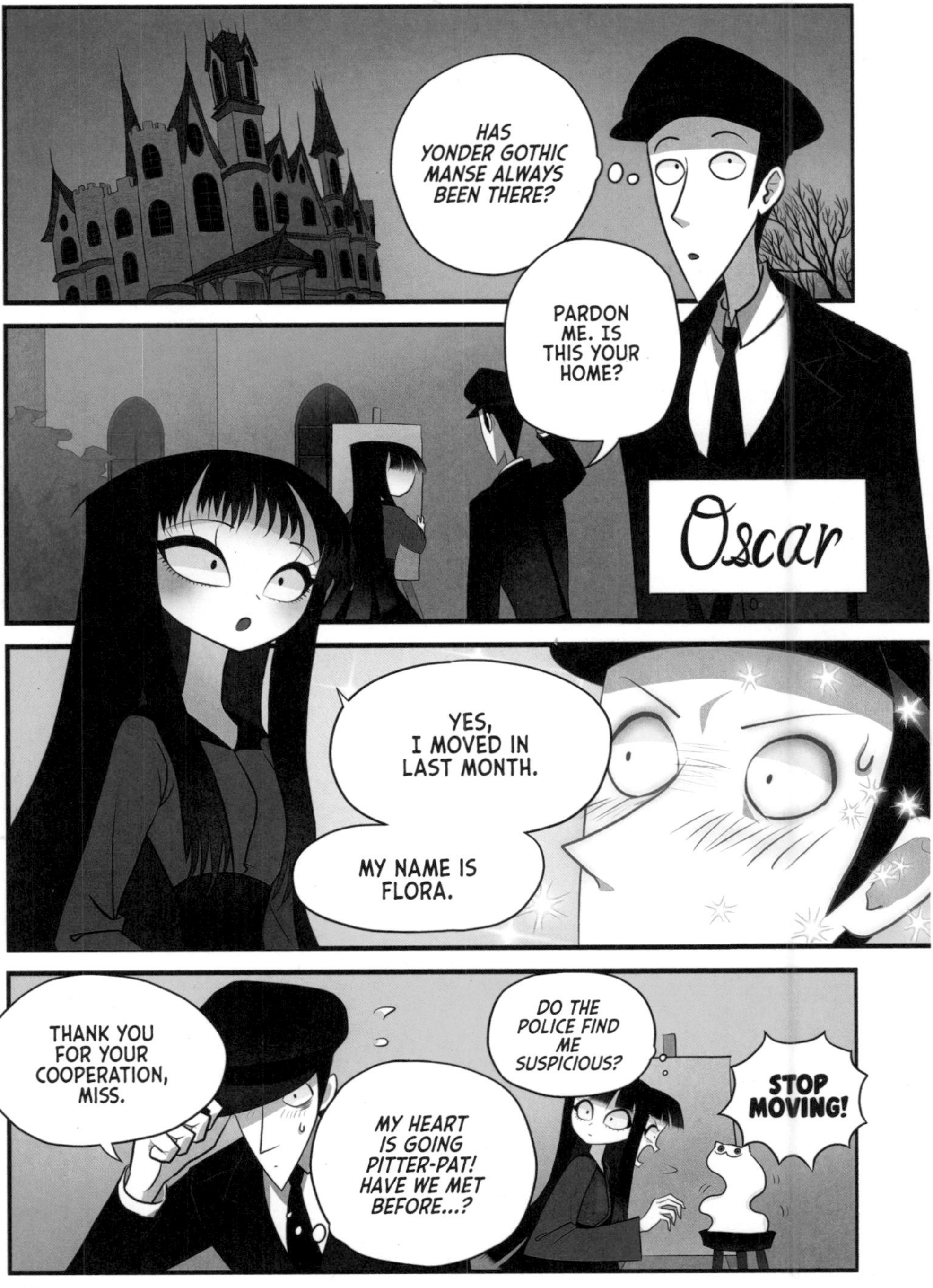
HAS YONDER GOTHIC MANSE ALWAYS BEEN THERE?
PARDON ME. IS THIS YOUR HOME?
Oscar
YES, I MOVED IN LAST MONTH.
MY NAME IS FLORA.
THANK YOU FOR YOUR COOPERATION, MISS.
MY HEART IS GOING PITTER-PAT! HAVE WE MET BEFORE...?
DO THE POLICE FIND ME SUSPICIOUS?
STOP MOVING!

A HAIR-RAISING TRUTH

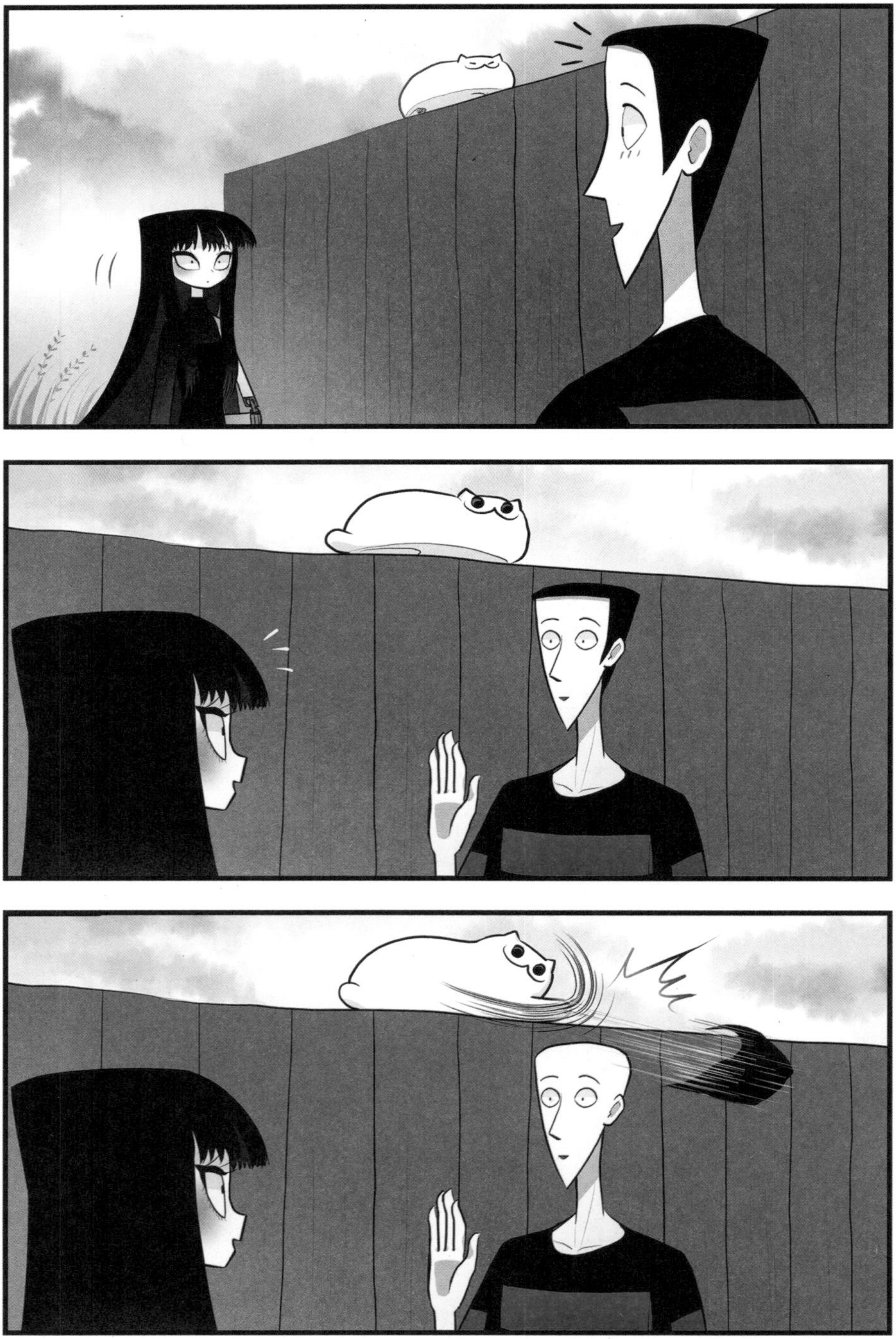

HAIRY SITUATION

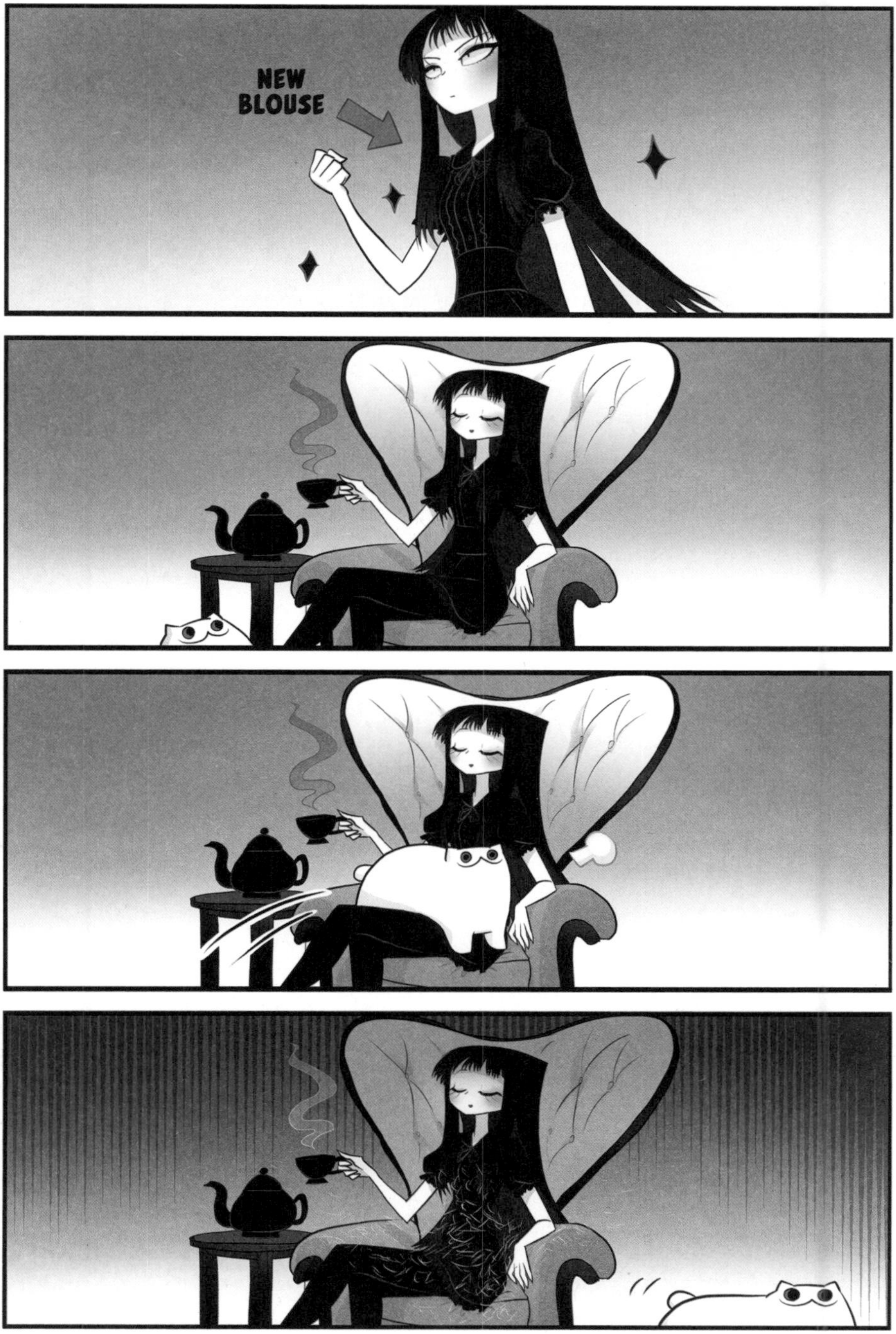
NEW
BLOUSE

STALKER

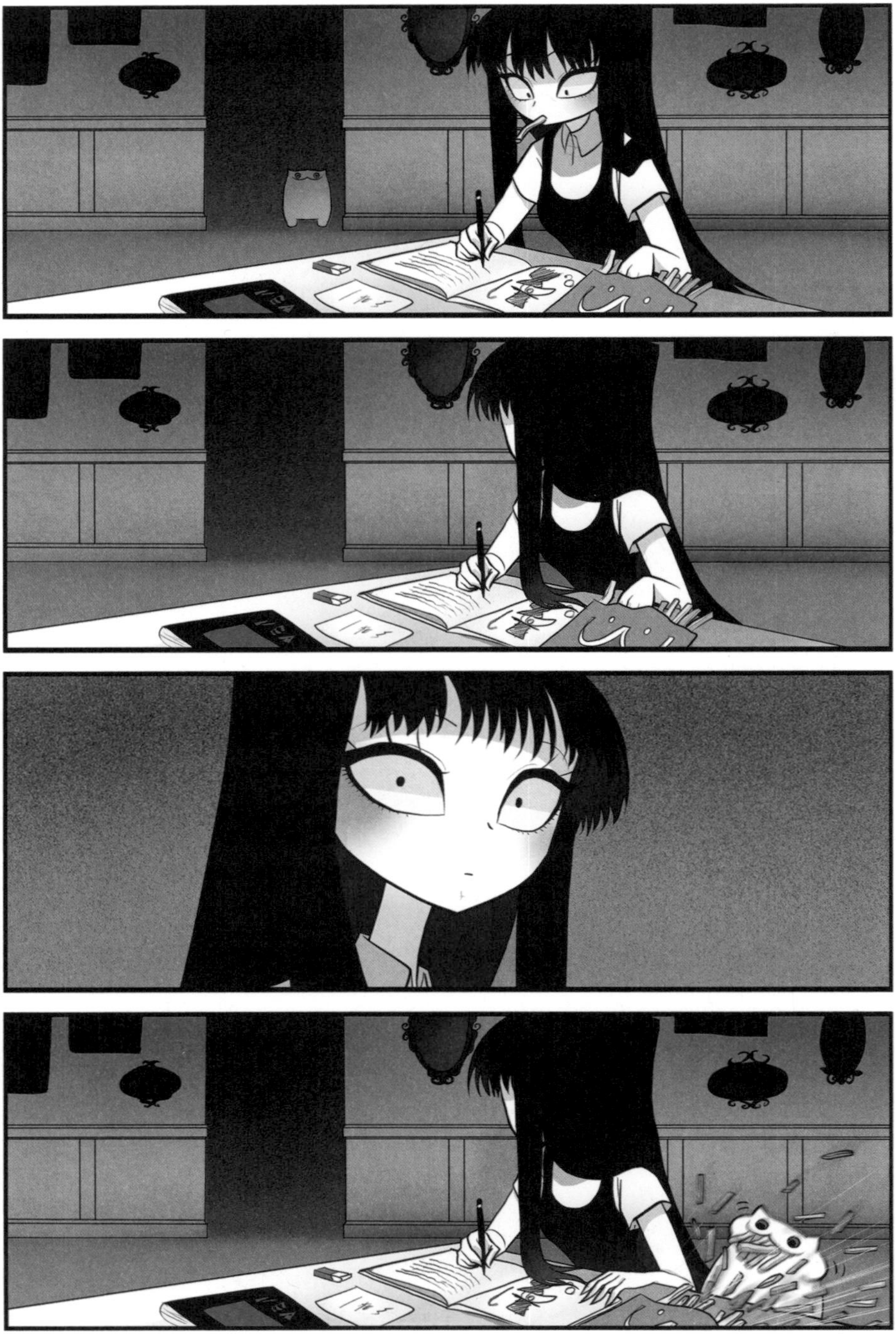

VAMPIRE

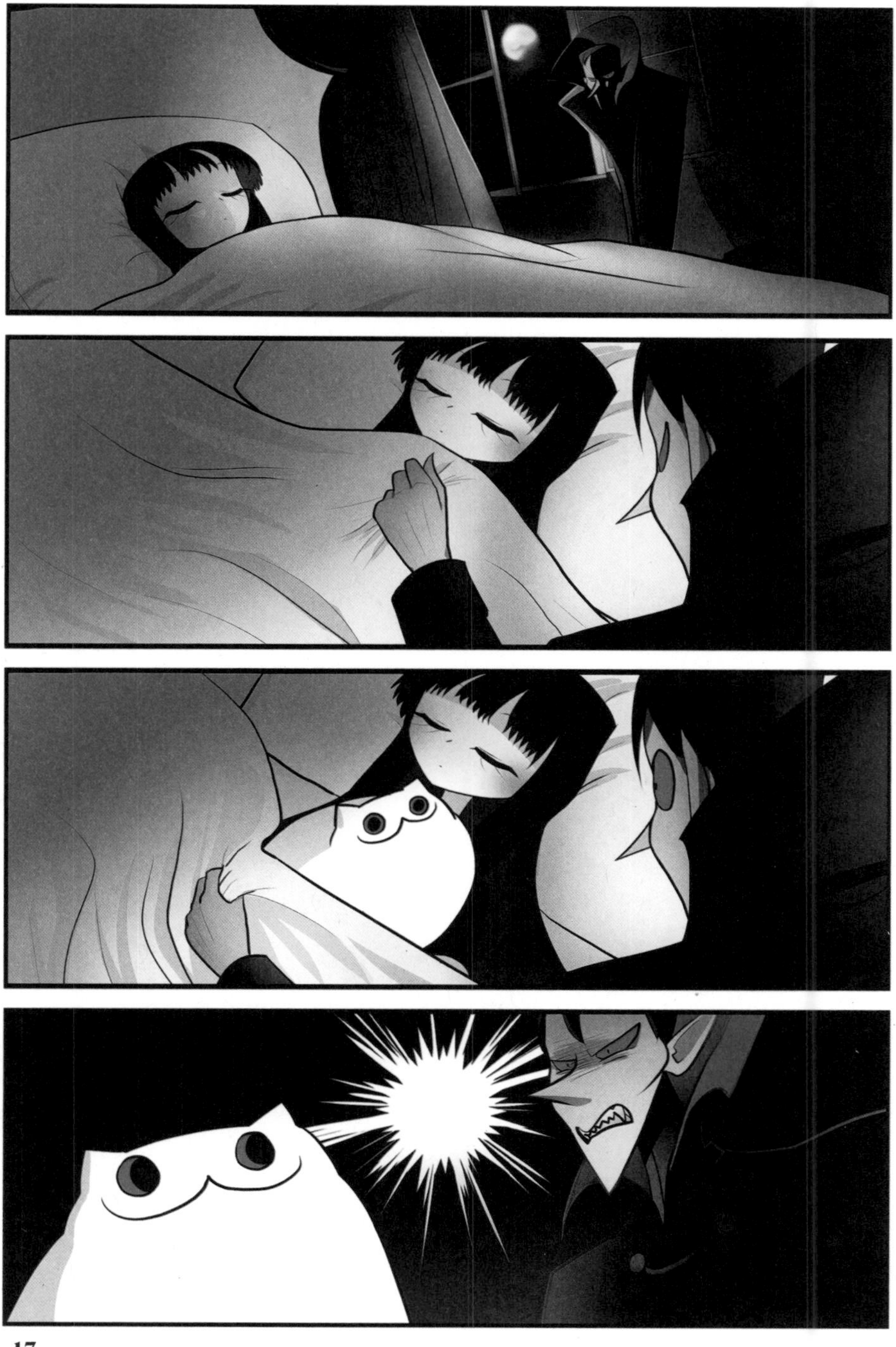

GRITTY LITTER

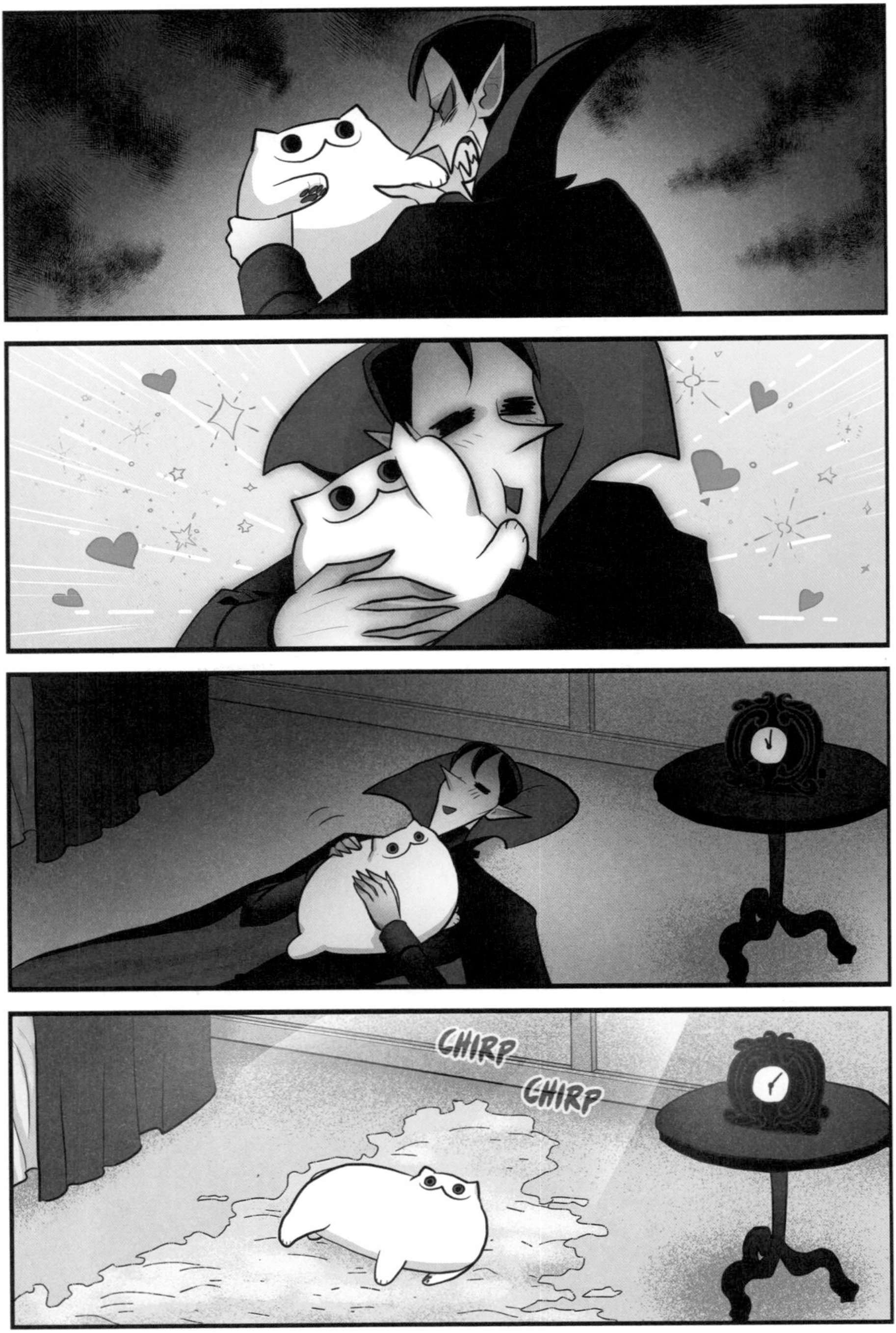
CHIRP
CHIRP

WALL

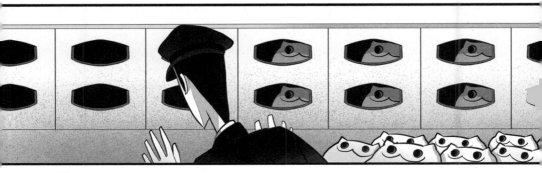

FRIENDS

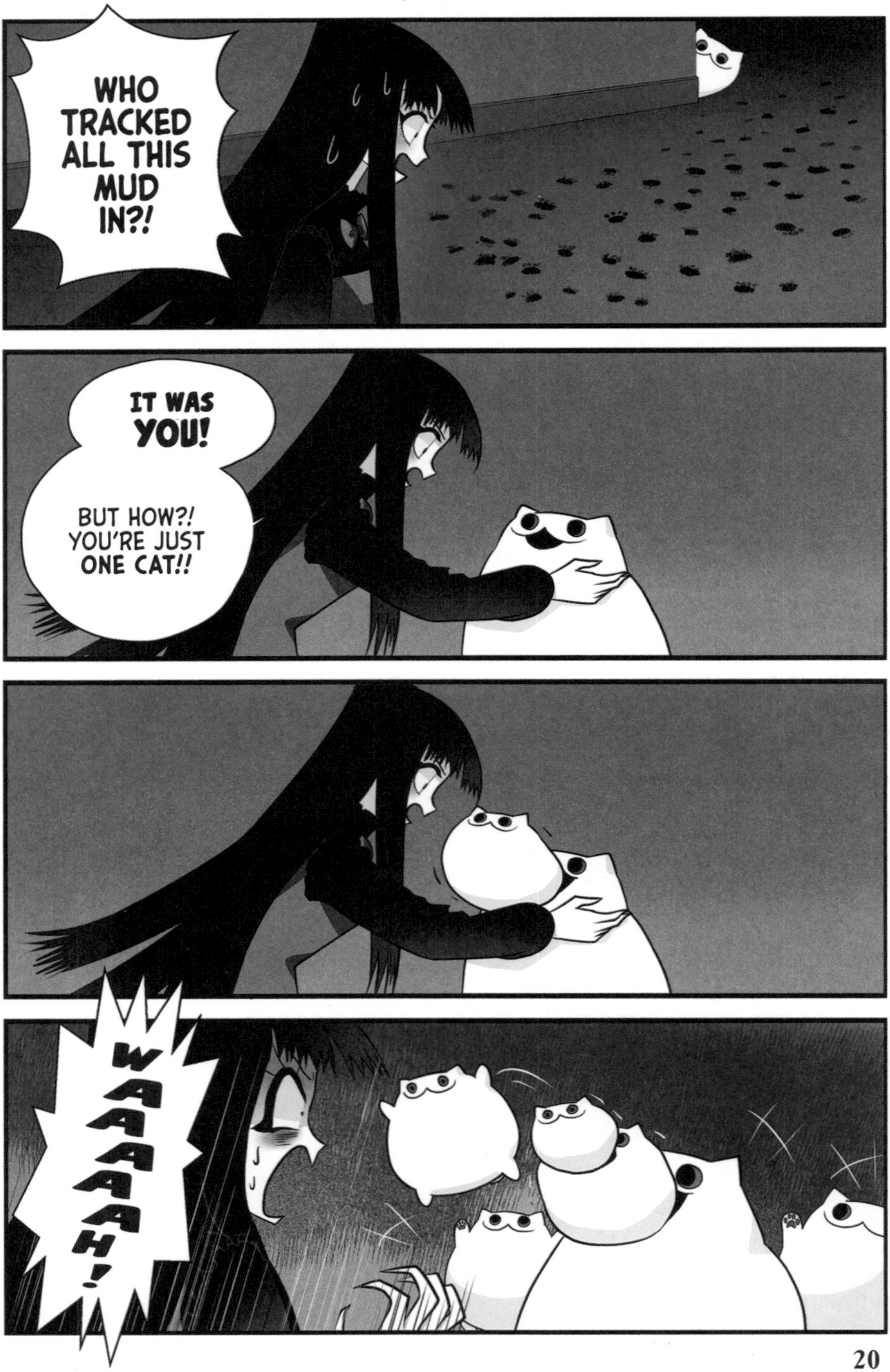
WHO TRACKED ALL THIS MUD IN?!
IT WAS YOU!
BUT HOW?! YOU'RE JUST ONE CAT!!
WAAAAAAH!

STANDING ROOM ONLY

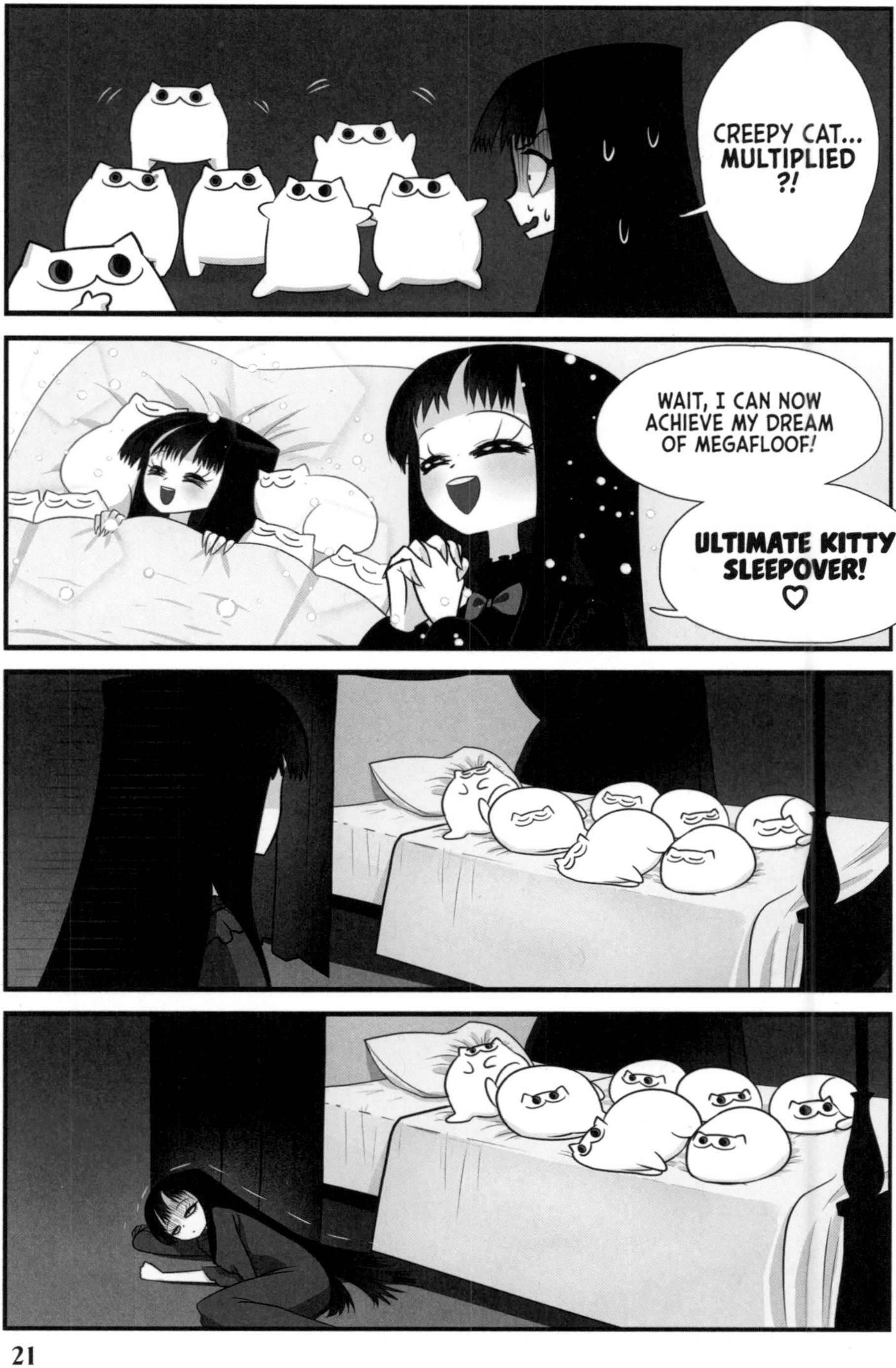
CREEPY CAT... MULTIPLIED ?!
WAIT, I CAN NOW ACHIEVE MY DREAM OF MEGAFLOOF!
ULTIMATE KITTY SLEEPOVER! ♡

MUNCH MUNCH

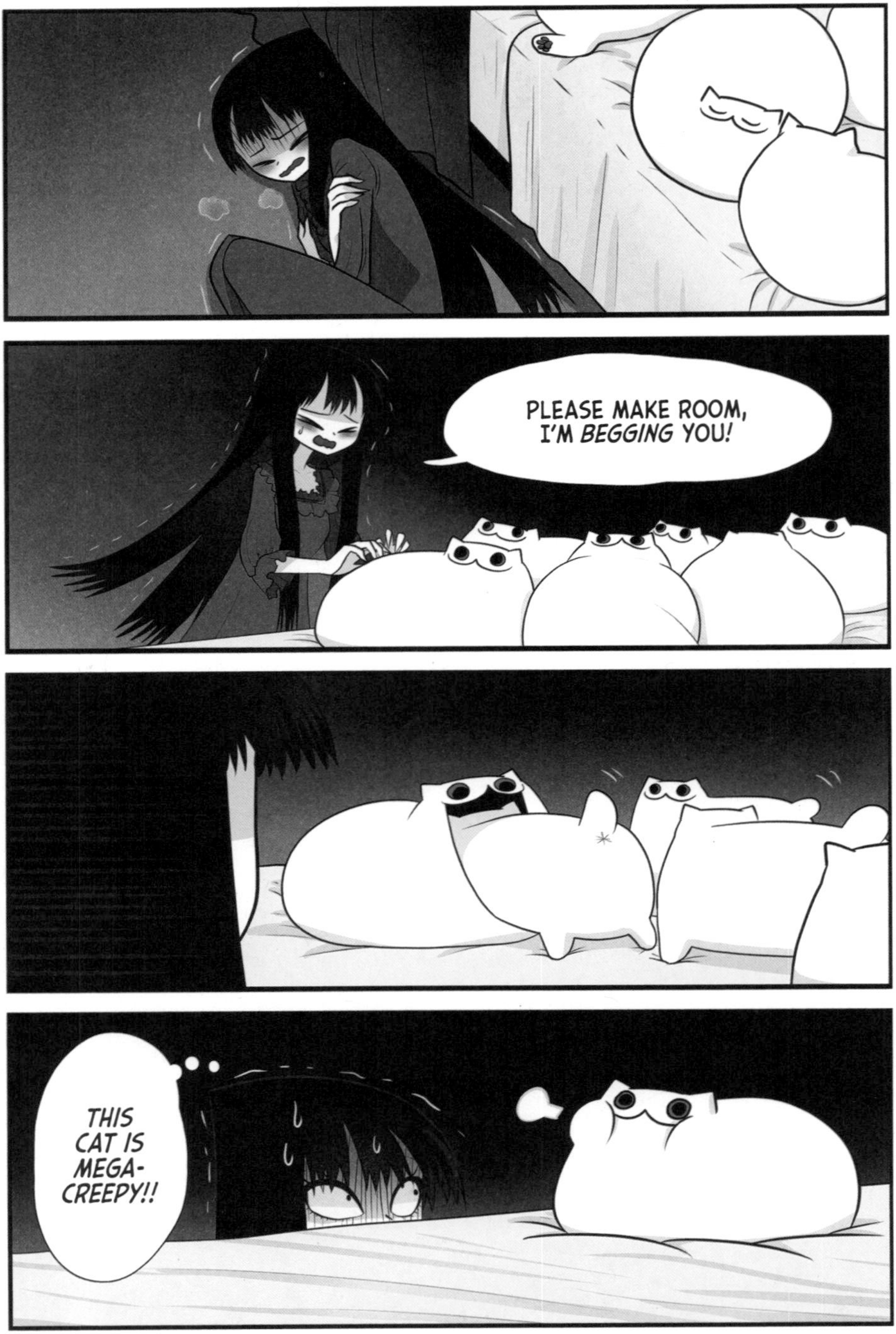
PLEASE MAKE ROOM, I'M *BEGGING* YOU!
THIS CAT IS MEGA-CREEPY!!

PIZZA

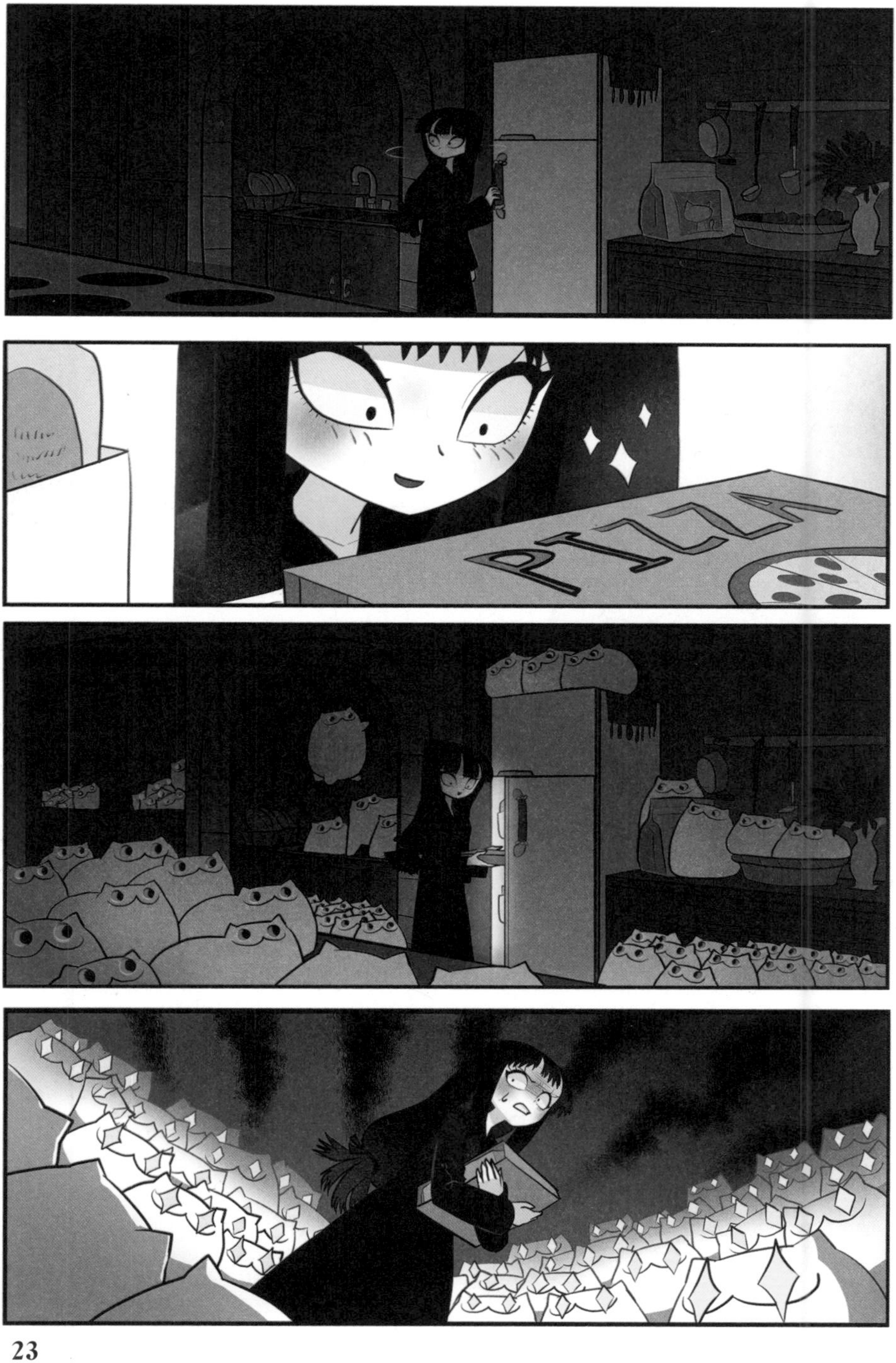
PIZZA

A GIFT

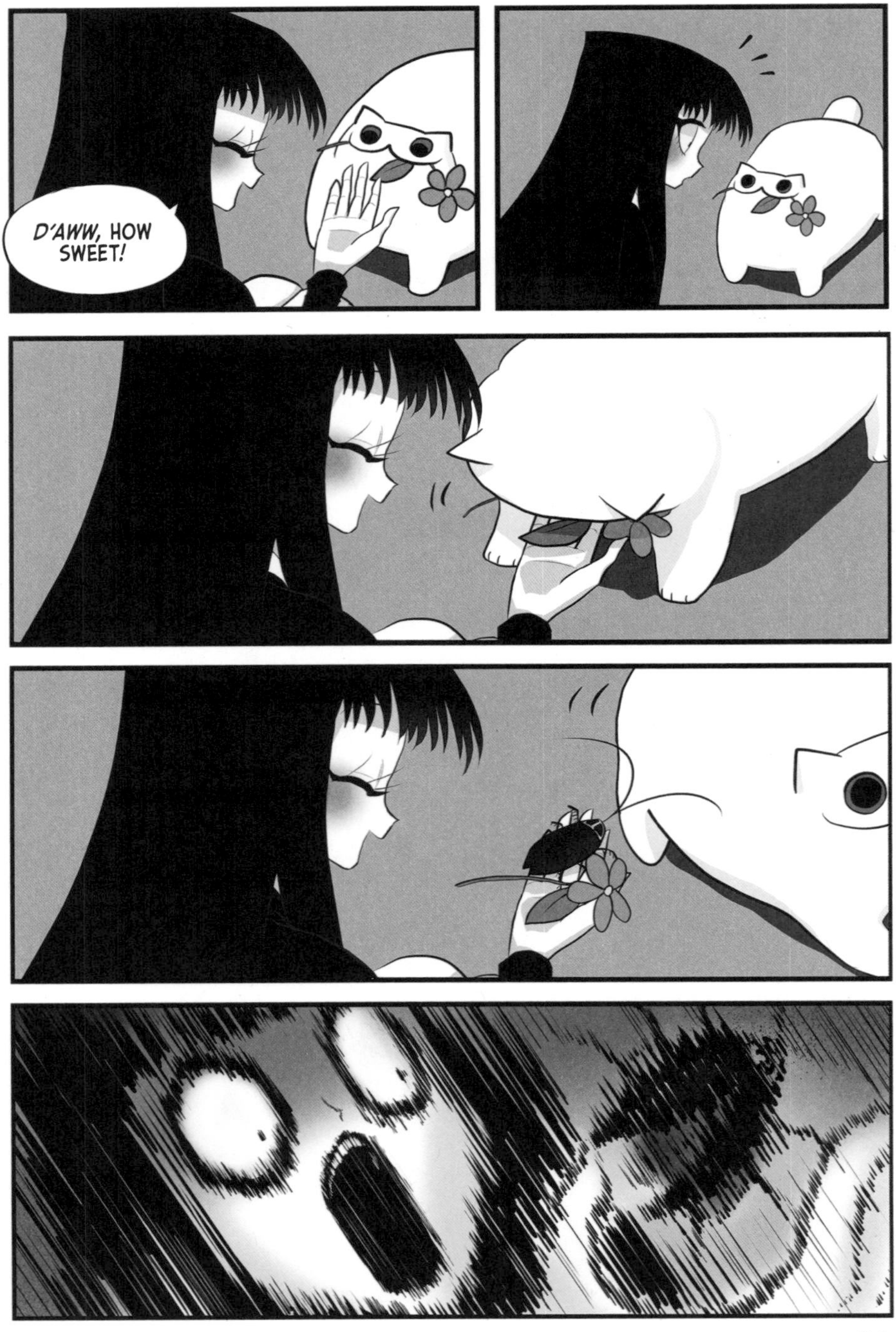
D'AWW, HOW SWEET!

PAWTH OF DESTRUCTION

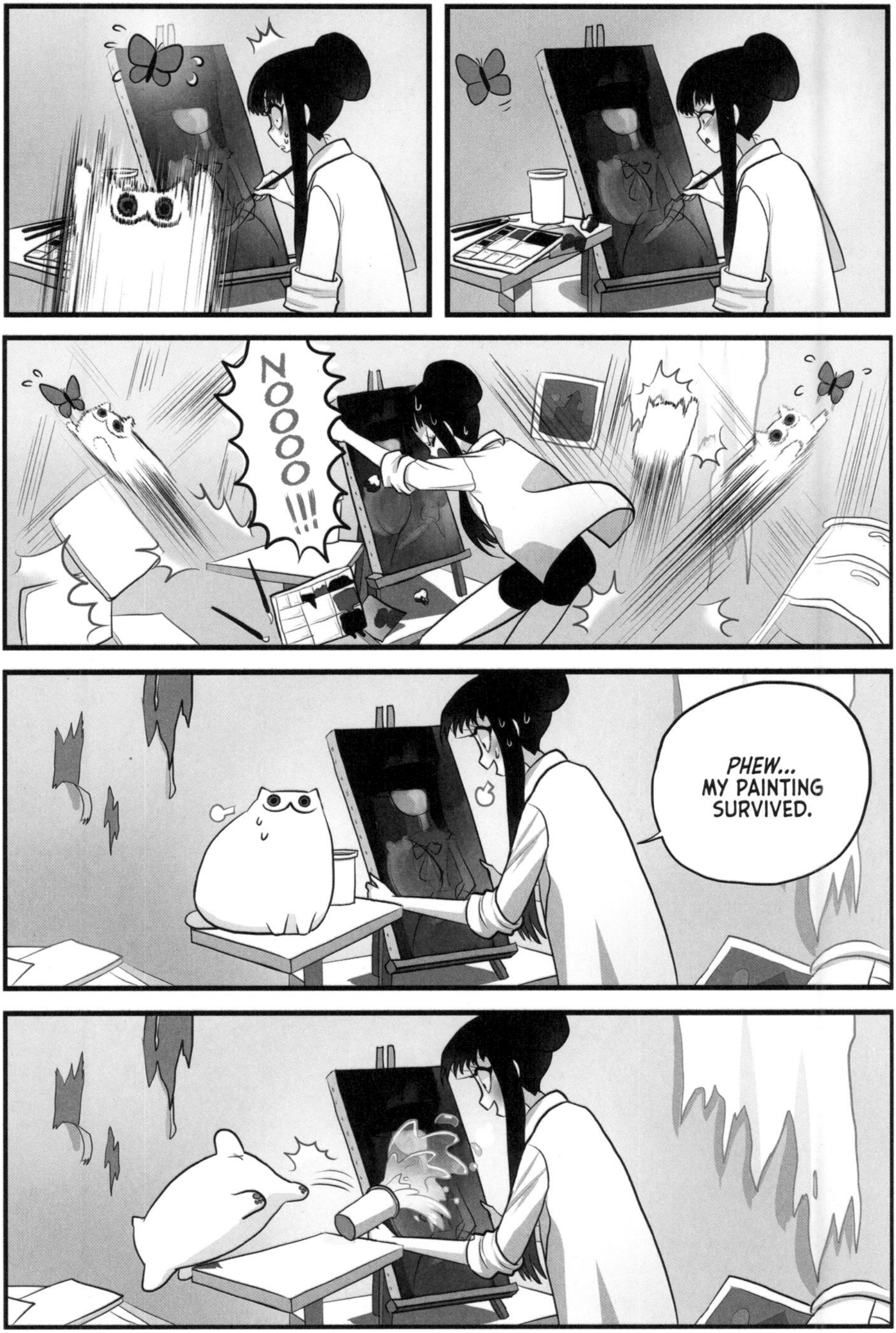
NOOOO!!!
PHEW... MY PAINTING SURVIVED.

SULKING

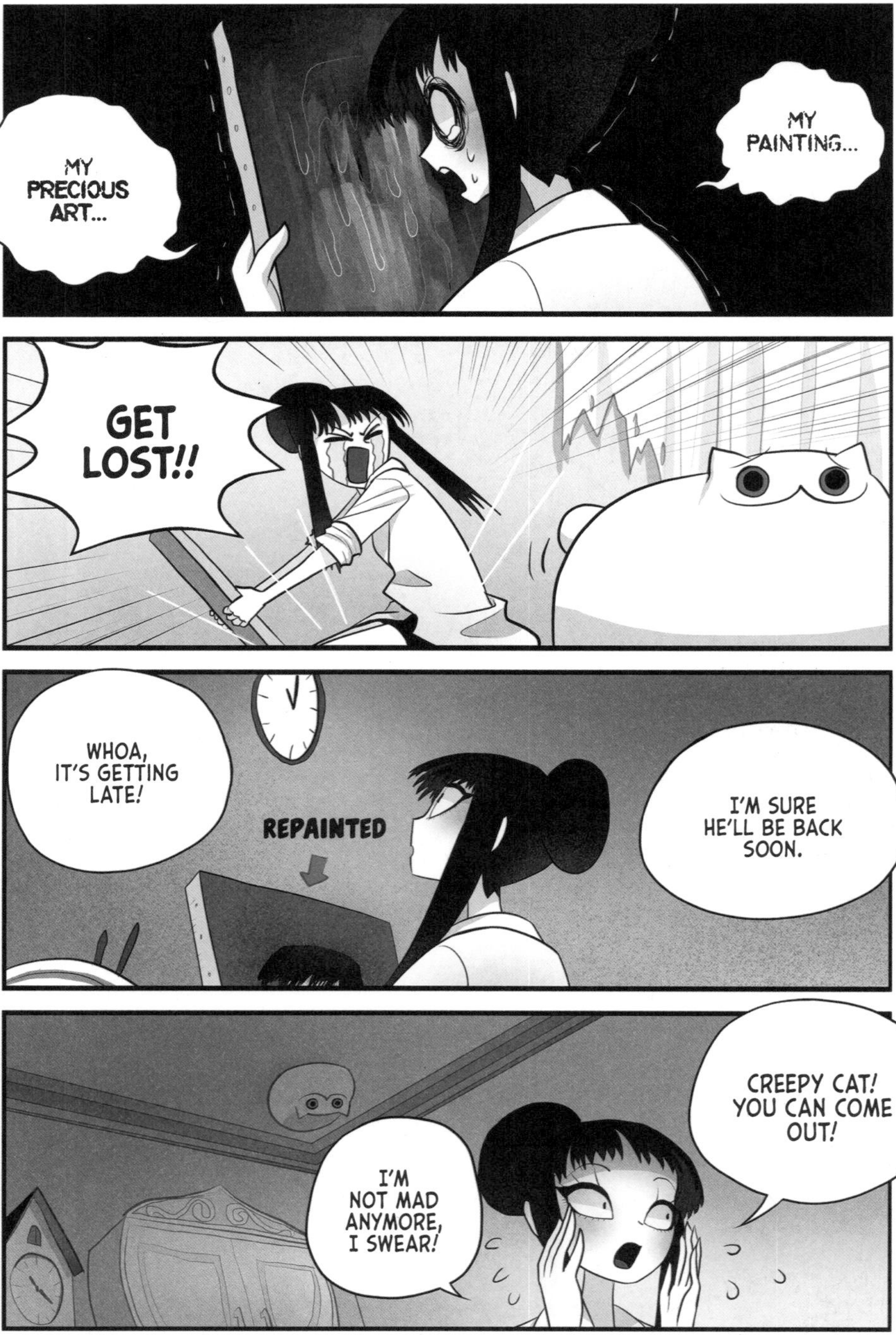
MY PRECIOUS ART...
MY PAINTING...
GET LOST!!
WHOA, IT'S GETTING LATE!
REPAINTED
I'M SURE HE'LL BE BACK SOON.
CREEPY CAT! YOU CAN COME OUT!
I'M NOT MAD ANYMORE, I SWEAR!

DISCOVERY

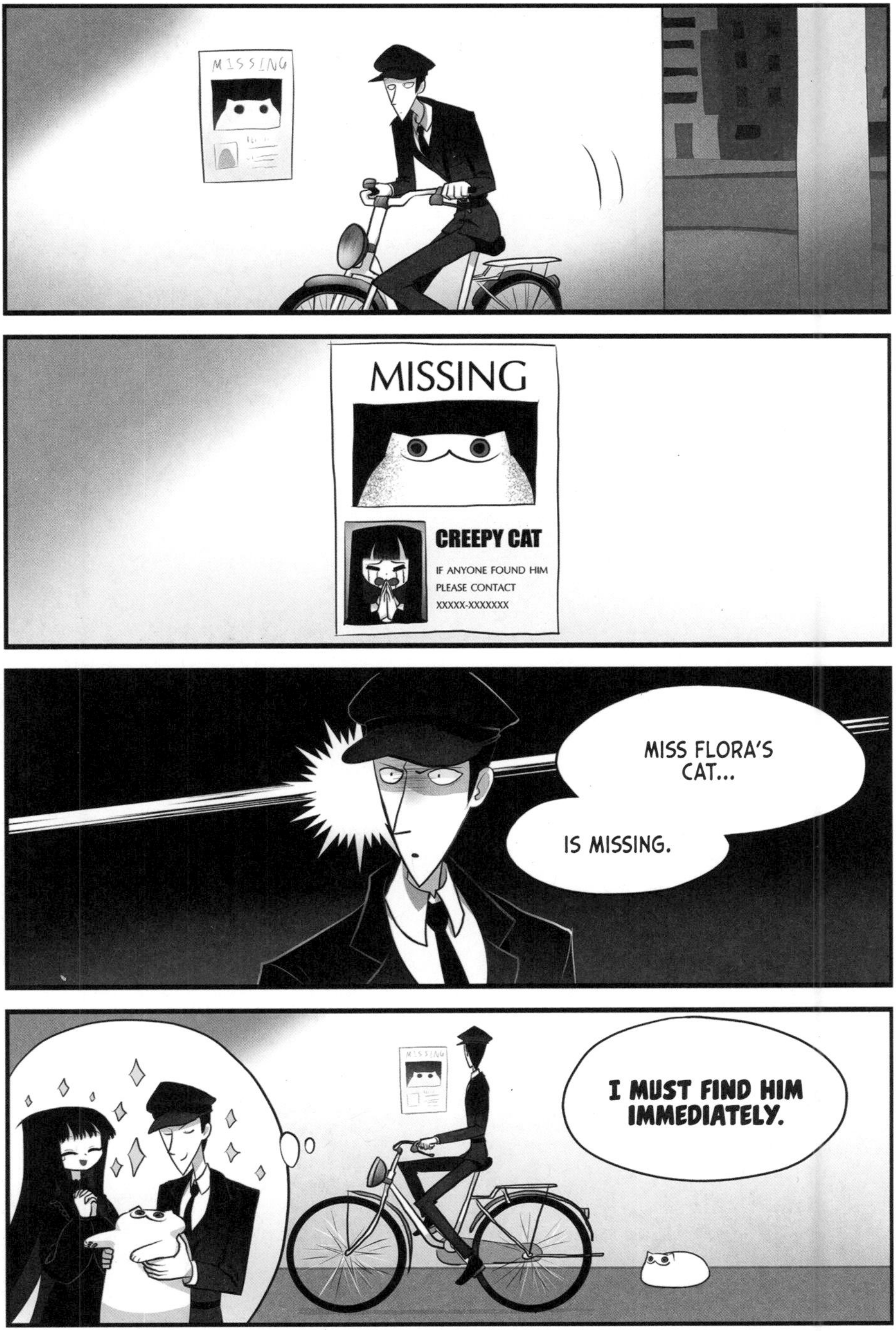
MISSING
CREEPY CAT
IF ANYONE FOUND HIM
PLEASE CONTACT
XXXXX-XXXXXXX
MISS FLORA'S CAT...
IS MISSING.
I MUST FIND HIM IMMEDIATELY.

WORRY

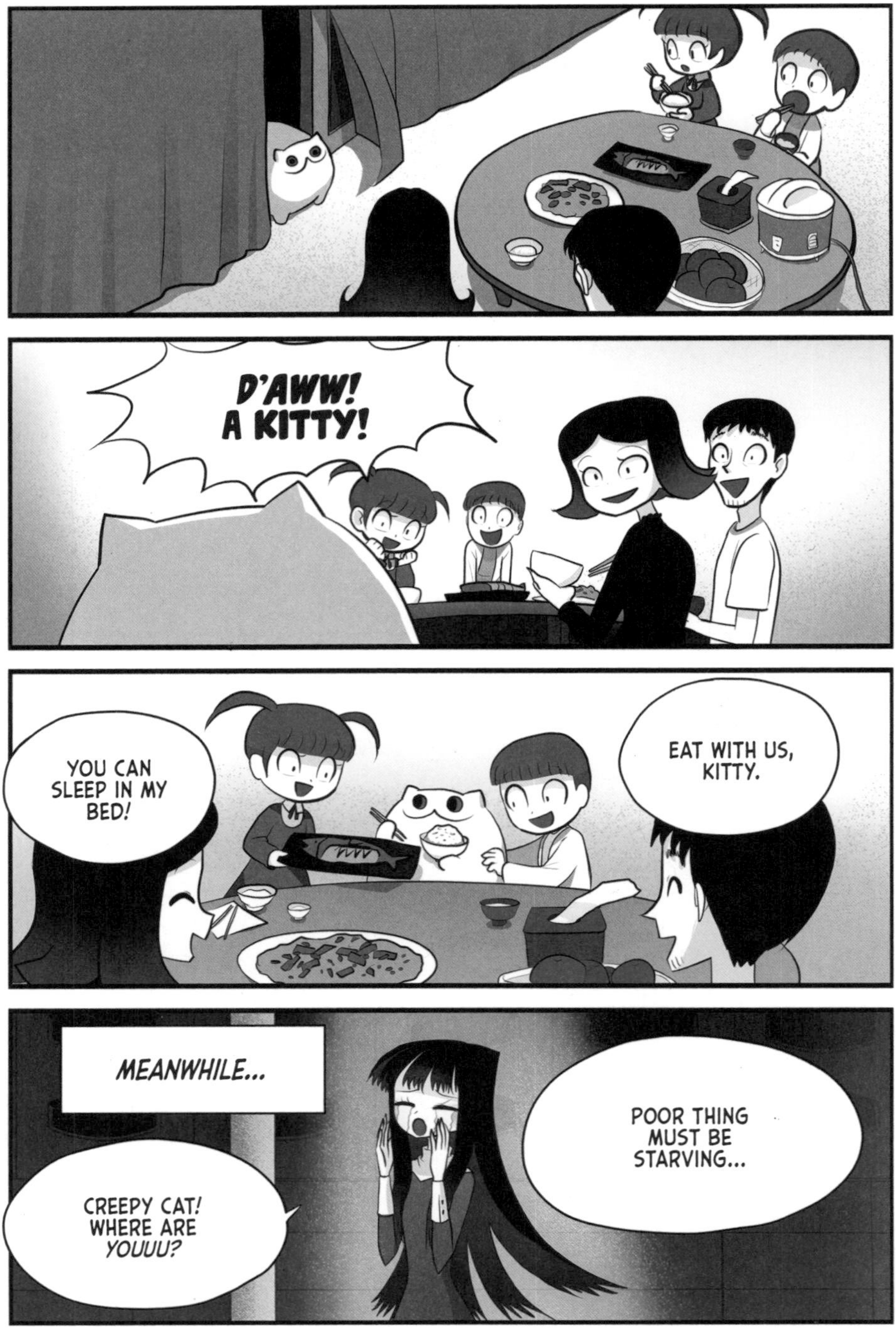
D'AWW! A KITTY!
YOU CAN SLEEP IN MY BED!
EAT WITH US, KITTY.
MEANWHILE...
POOR THING MUST BE STARVING...
CREEPY CAT! WHERE ARE YOUUU?

PAWSITIVE I.D.

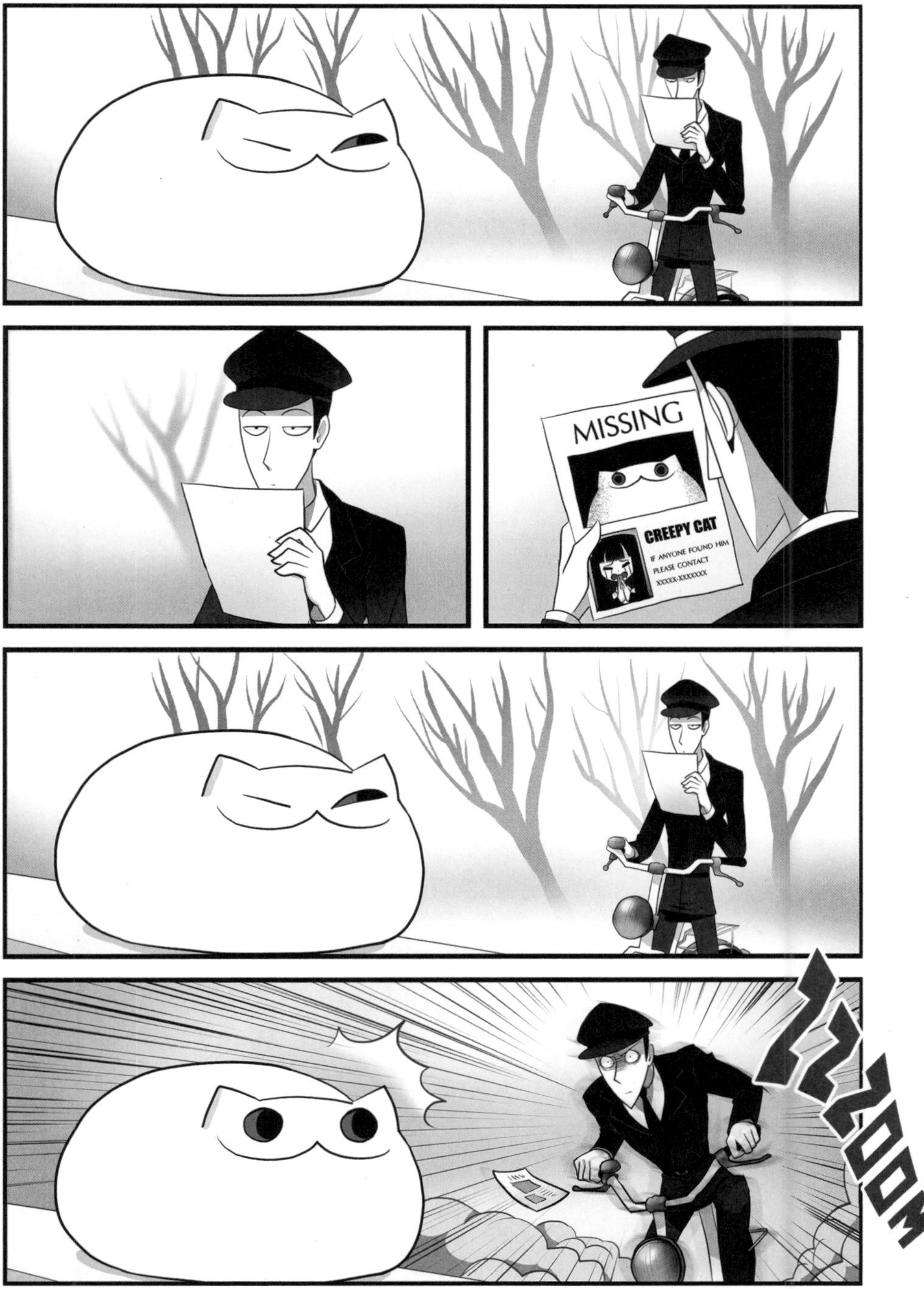
MISSING
CREEPY CAT
IF ANYONE FOUND HIM
PLEASE CONTACT
XXXXX-XXXXXXX
ZZZOOM

BEHIND YOU

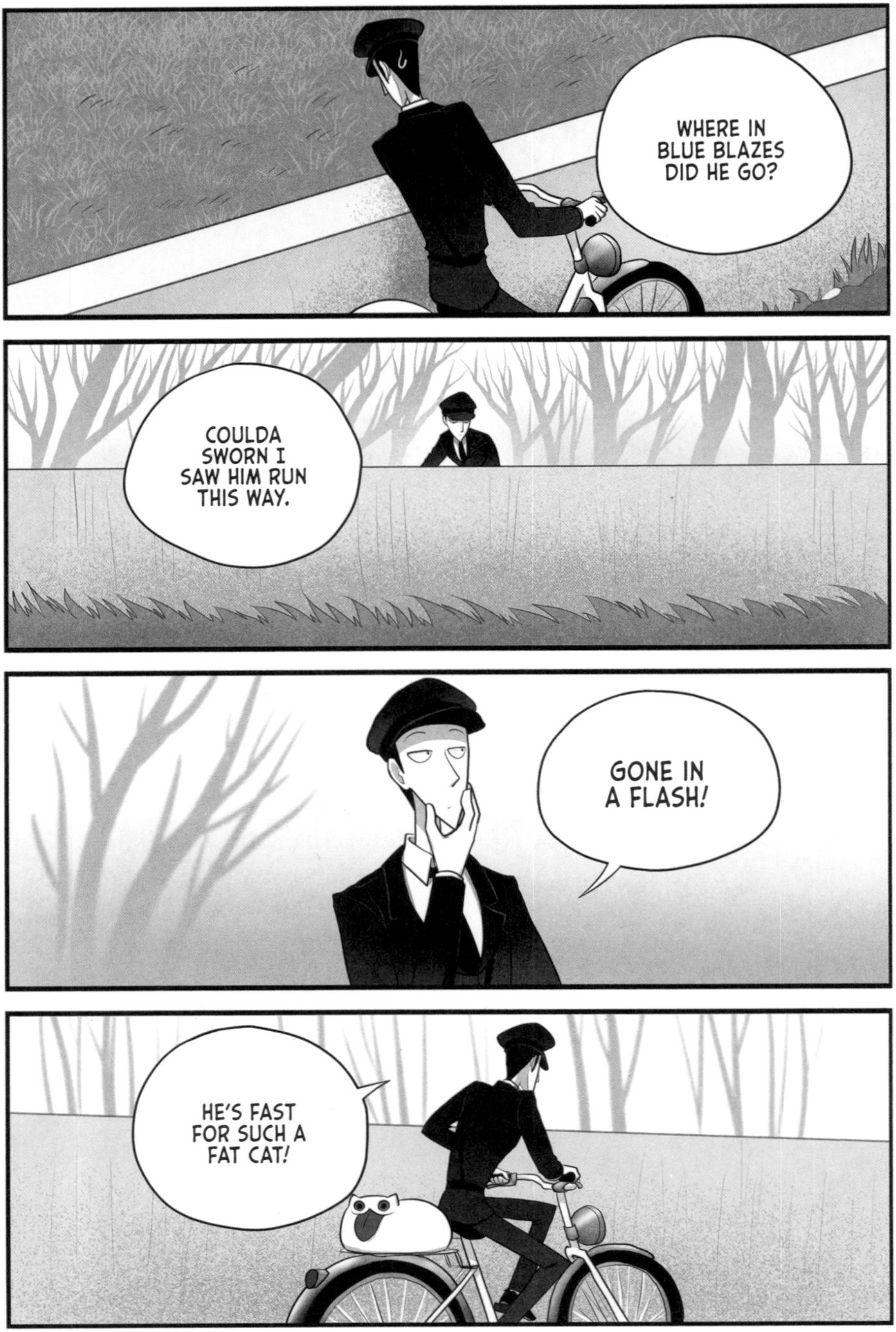
WHERE IN BLUE BLAZES DID HE GO?
COULDA SWORN I SAW HIM RUN THIS WAY.
GONE IN A FLASH!
HE'S FAST FOR SUCH A FAT CAT!

HOME AGAIN

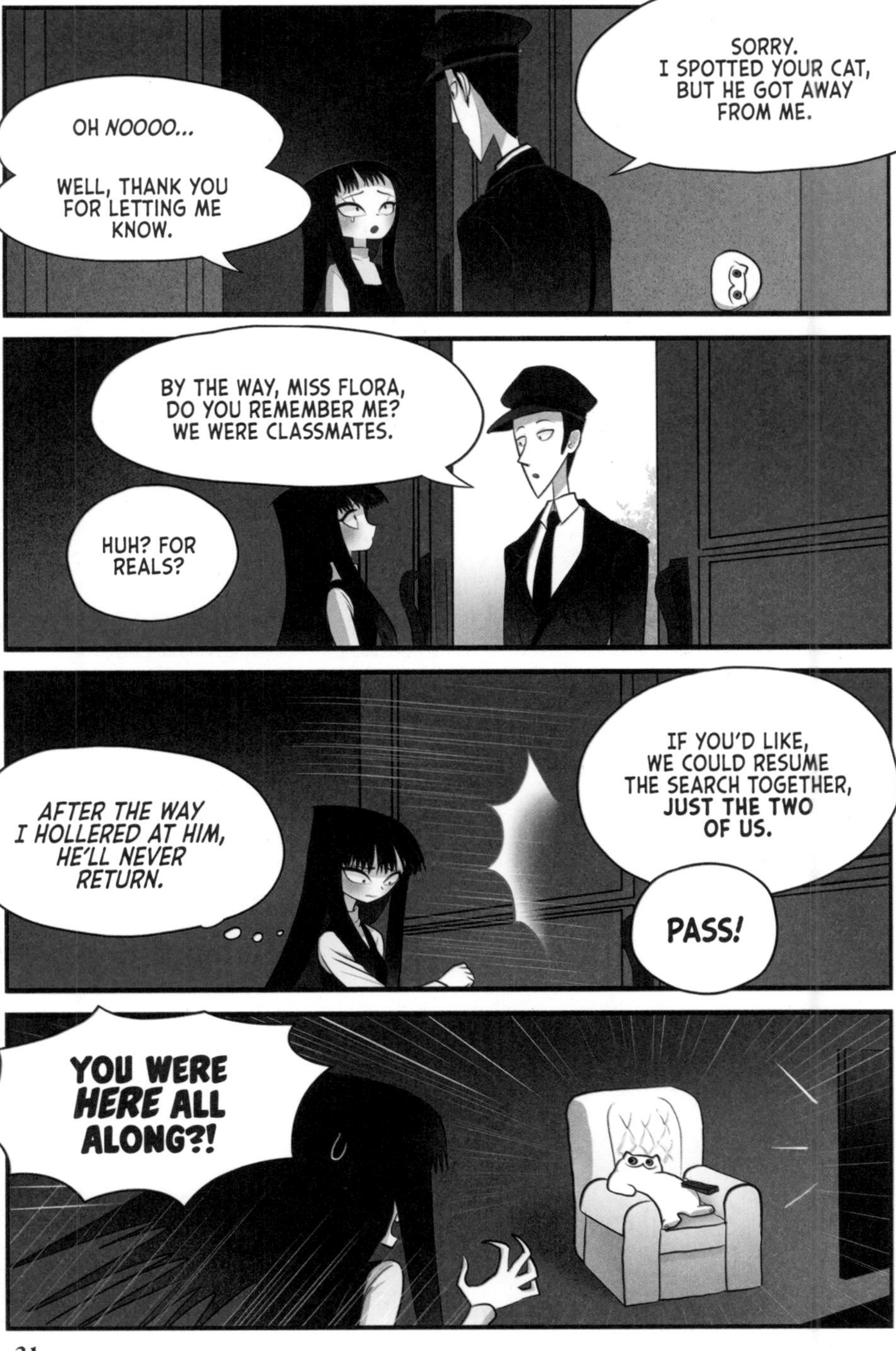
SORRY. I SPOTTED YOUR CAT, BUT HE GOT AWAY FROM ME.
OH *NOOOO...*
WELL, THANK YOU FOR LETTING ME KNOW.
BY THE WAY, MISS FLORA, DO YOU REMEMBER ME? WE WERE CLASSMATES.
HUH? FOR REALS?
IF YOU'D LIKE, WE COULD RESUME THE SEARCH TOGETHER, **JUST THE TWO OF US.**
AFTER THE WAY I HOLLERED AT HIM, HE'LL NEVER RETURN.
PASS!
YOU WERE *HERE* ALL ALONG?!

MEOWSTERPEICE

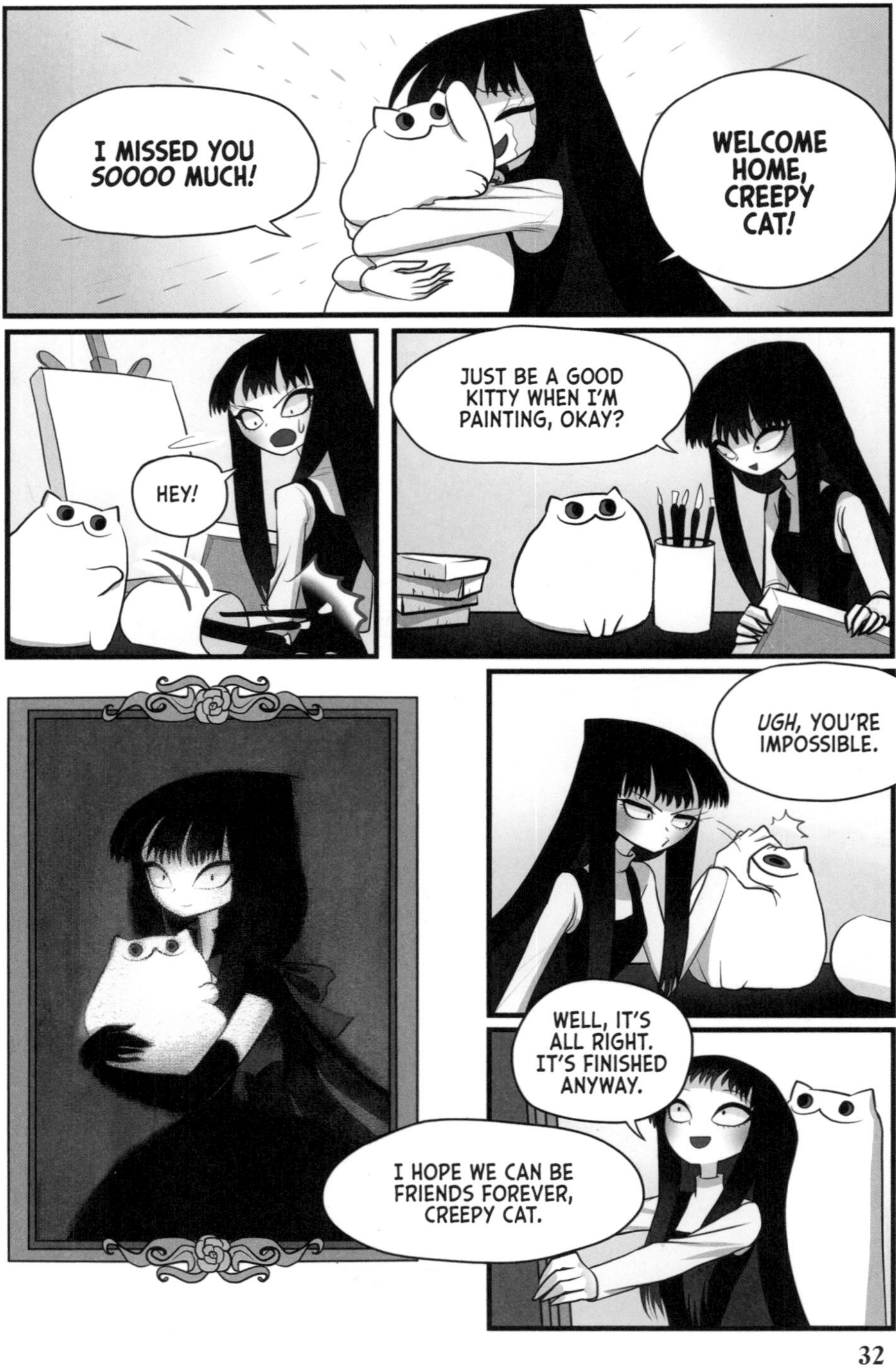
I MISSED YOU SOOOO MUCH!
WELCOME HOME, CREEPY CAT!
HEY!
JUST BE A GOOD KITTY WHEN I'M PAINTING, OKAY?
UGH, YOU'RE IMPOSSIBLE.
WELL, IT'S ALL RIGHT. IT'S FINISHED ANYWAY.
I HOPE WE CAN BE FRIENDS FOREVER, CREEPY CAT.

YOGA

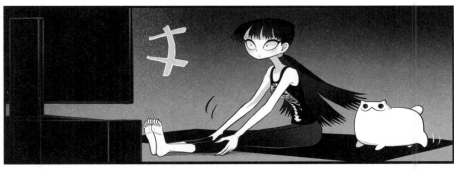

LIGHT HUMOR

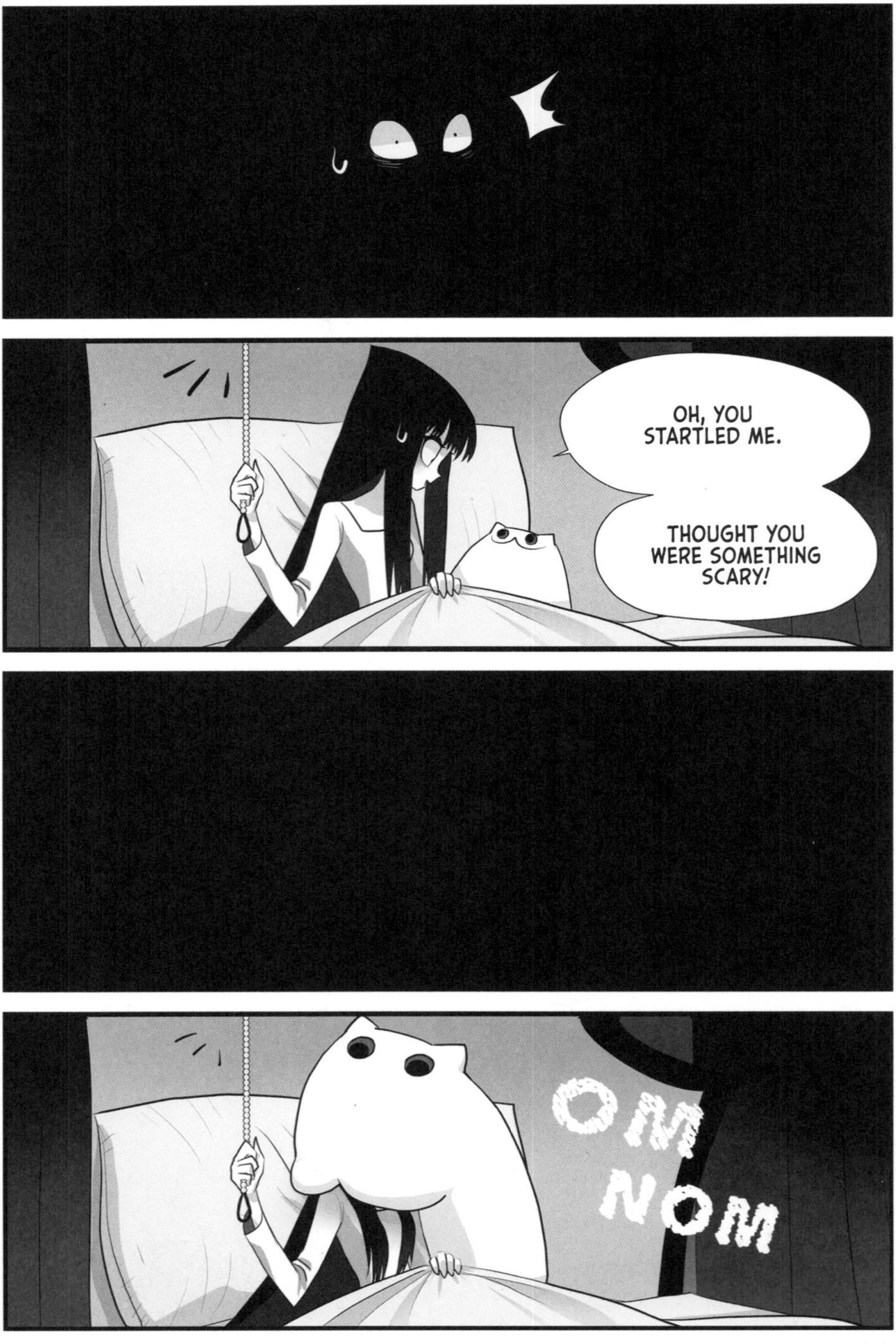

OH, YOU STARTLED ME.
THOUGHT YOU WERE SOMETHING SCARY!
OM NOM NOM

PHOTOGRAPHY

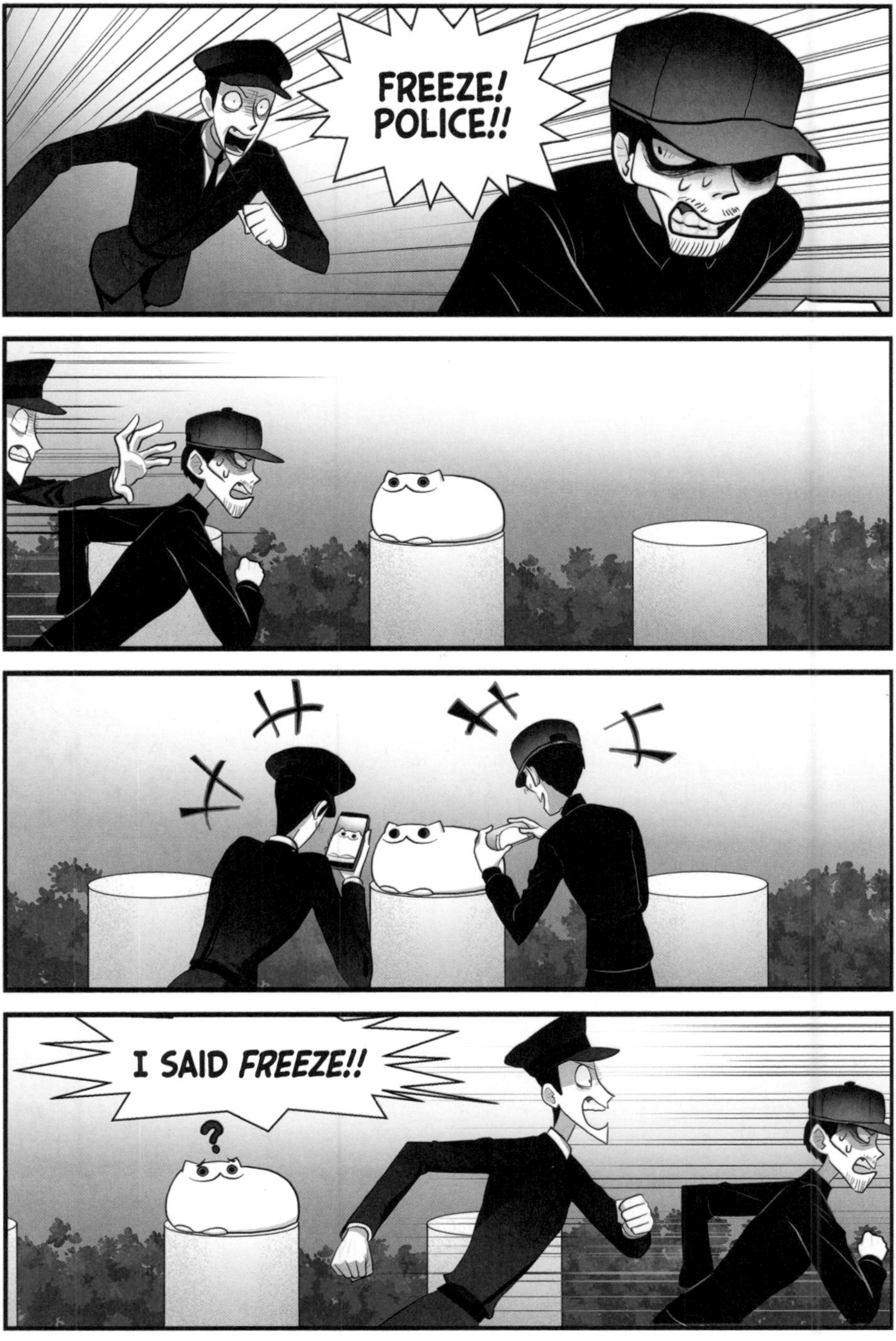

FREEZE! POLICE!!
I SAID FREEZE!!

SOLITUDE

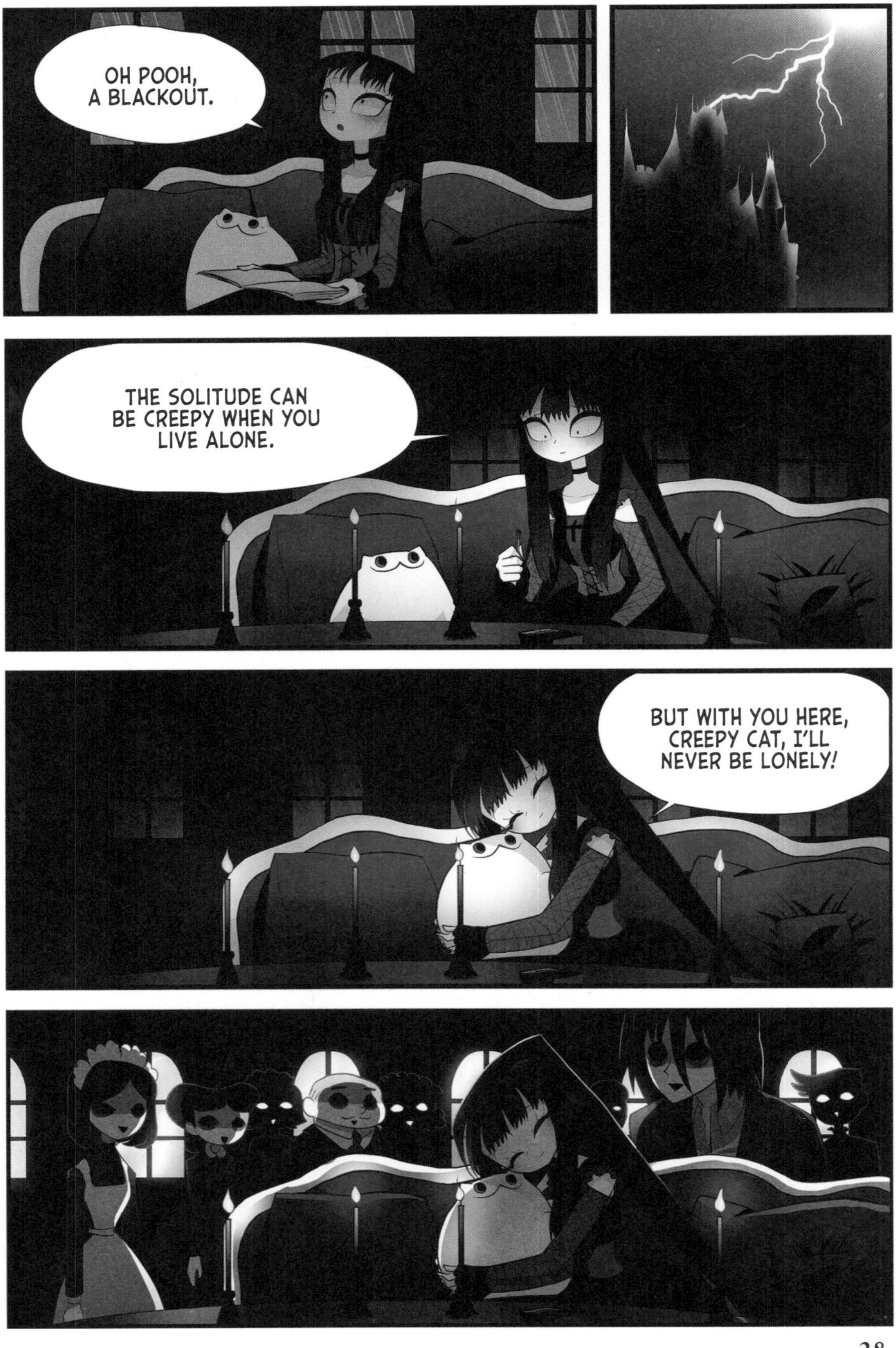
OH POOH, A BLACKOUT.
THE SOLITUDE CAN BE CREEPY WHEN YOU LIVE ALONE.
BUT WITH YOU HERE, CREEPY CAT, I'LL NEVER BE LONELY!

BED

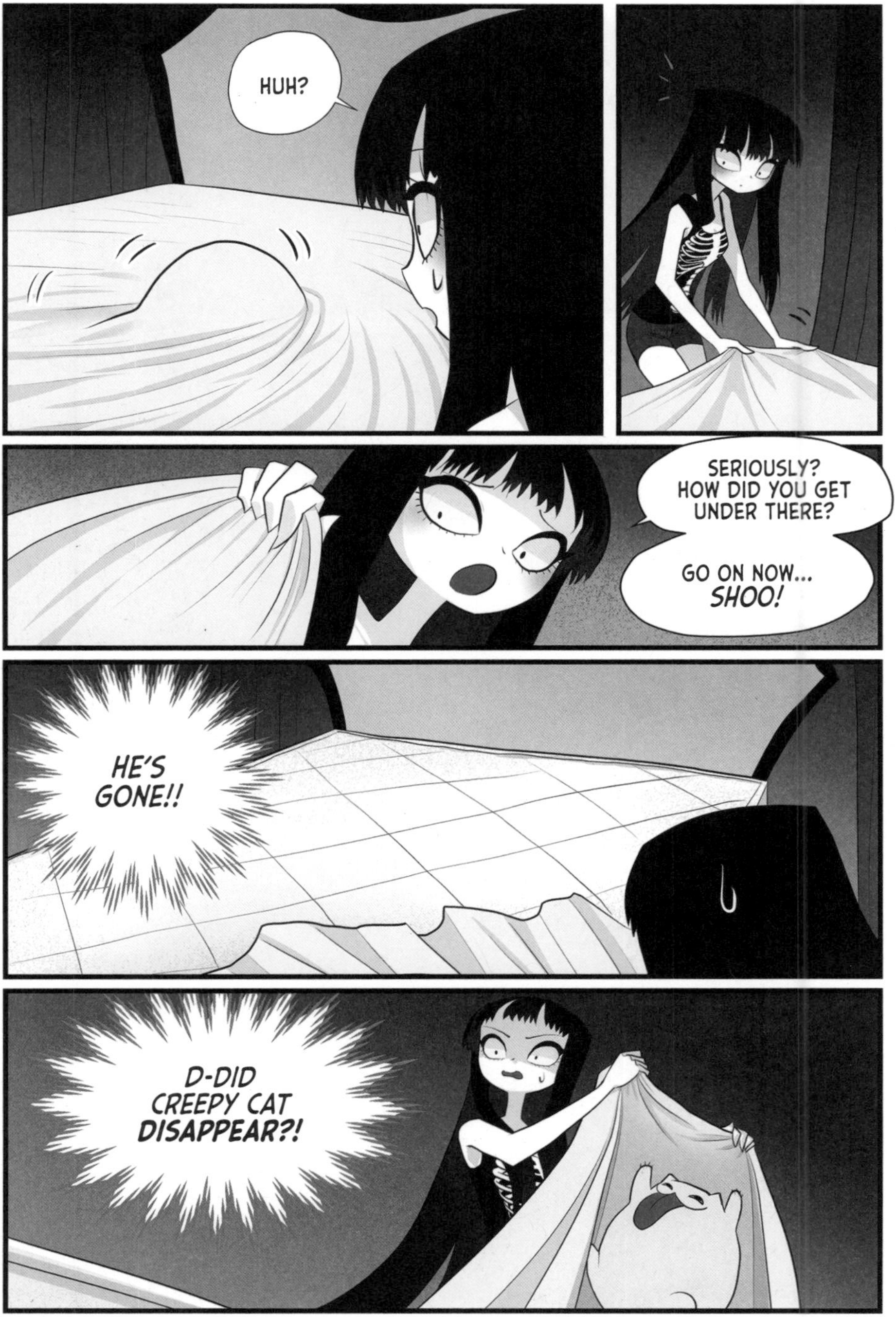

HUH?
SERIOUSLY? HOW DID YOU GET UNDER THERE?
GO ON NOW... SHOO!
HE'S GONE!!
D-DID CREEPY CAT DISAPPEAR?!

BOGEYMAN

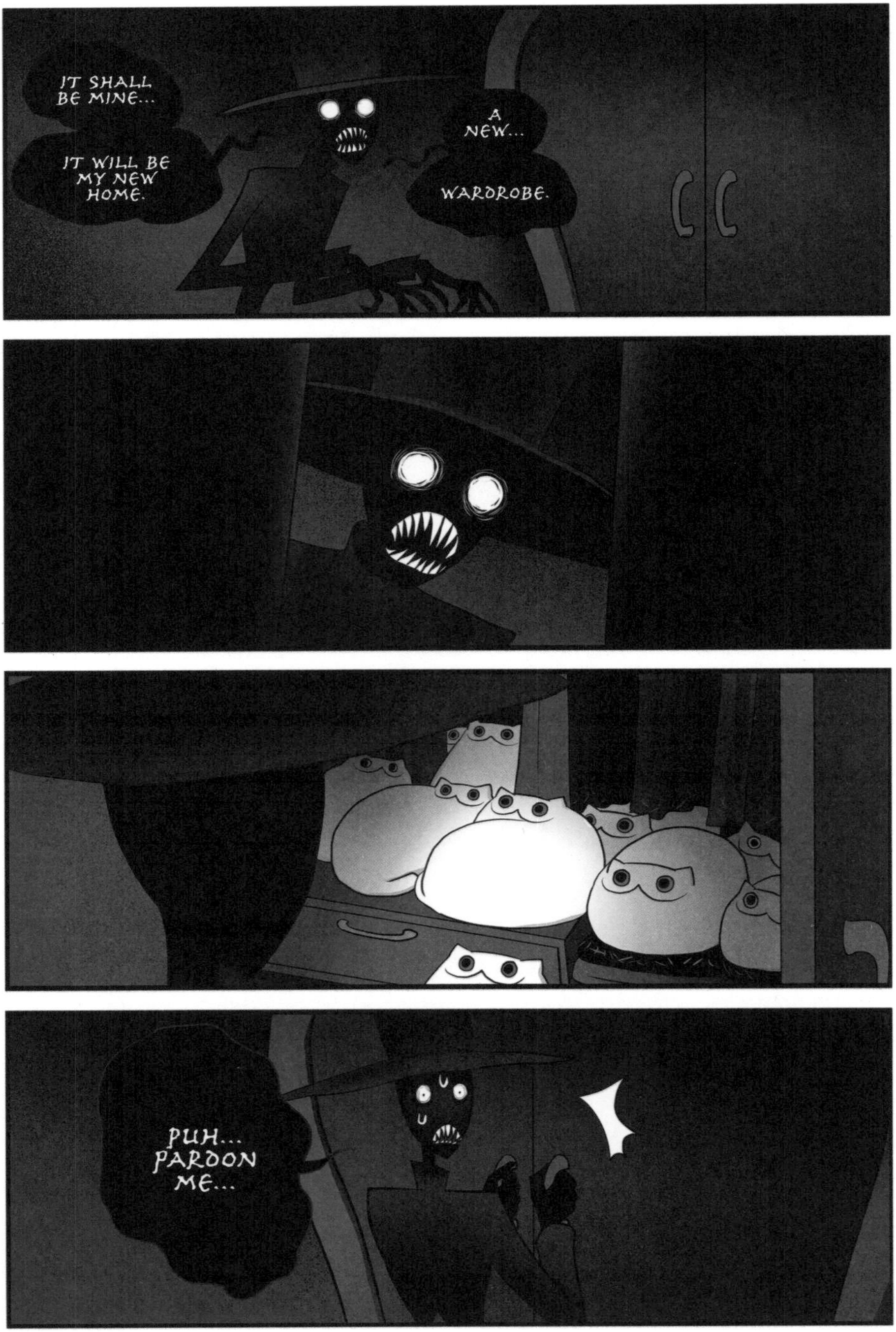
IT SHALL BE MINE...
IT WILL BE MY NEW HOME.
A NEW...
WARDROBE.
PUH... PARDON ME...

CHEEKY KITTIES

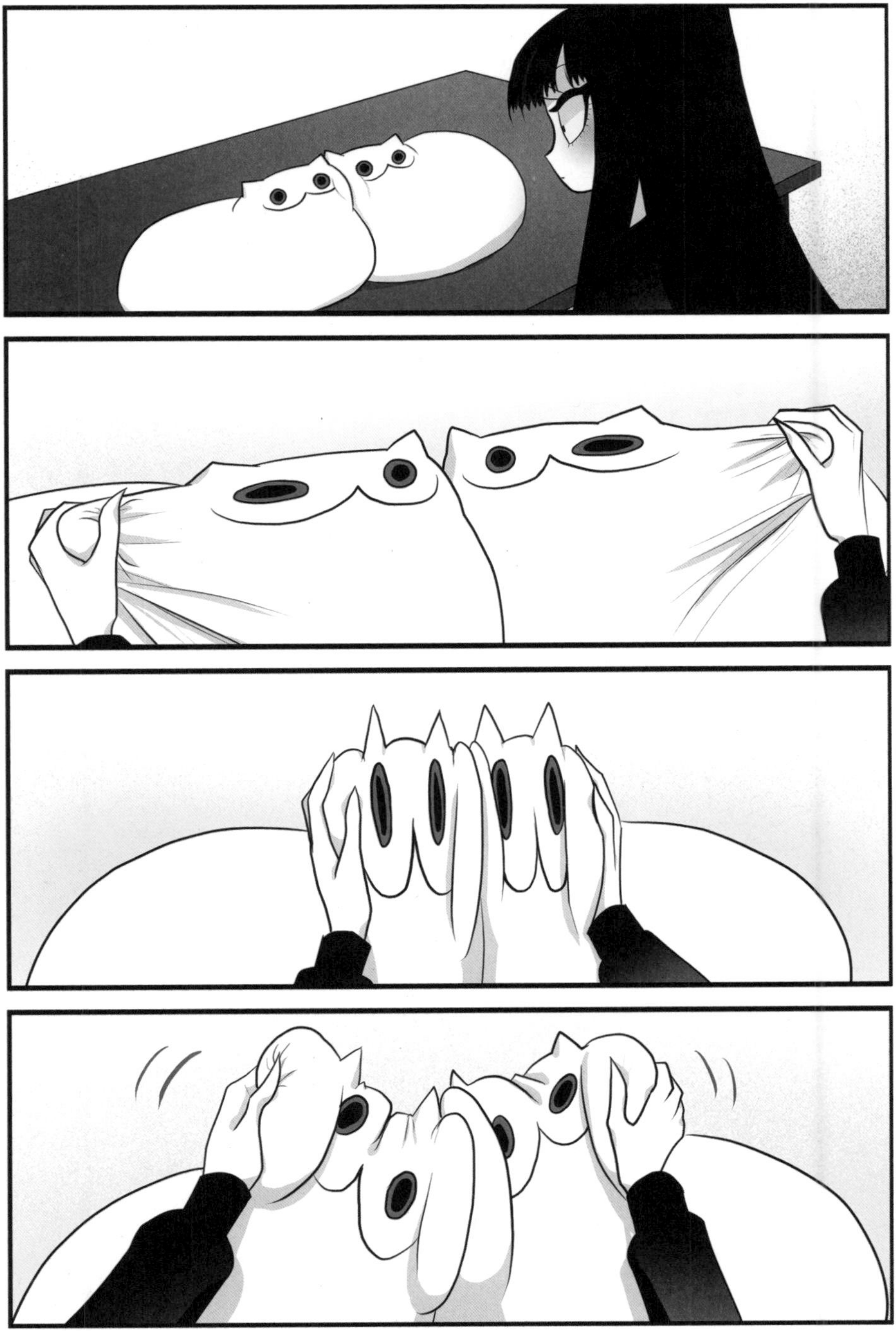

KEYBOARD

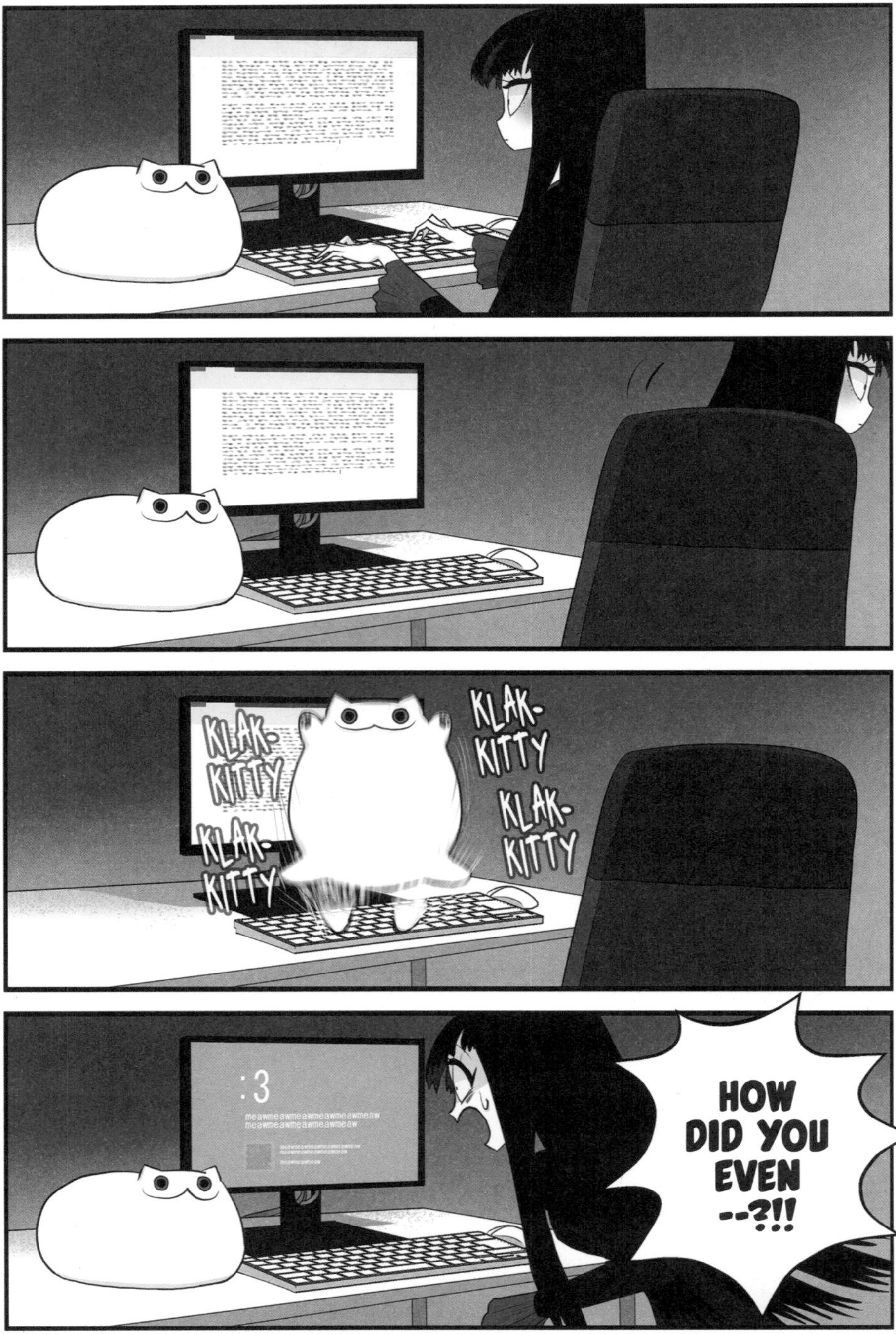
KLAK-KITTY
KLAK-KITTY
KLAK-KITTY
KLAK-KITTY
:3
HOW DID YOU EVEN --?!!

PAWS FOR ALARM

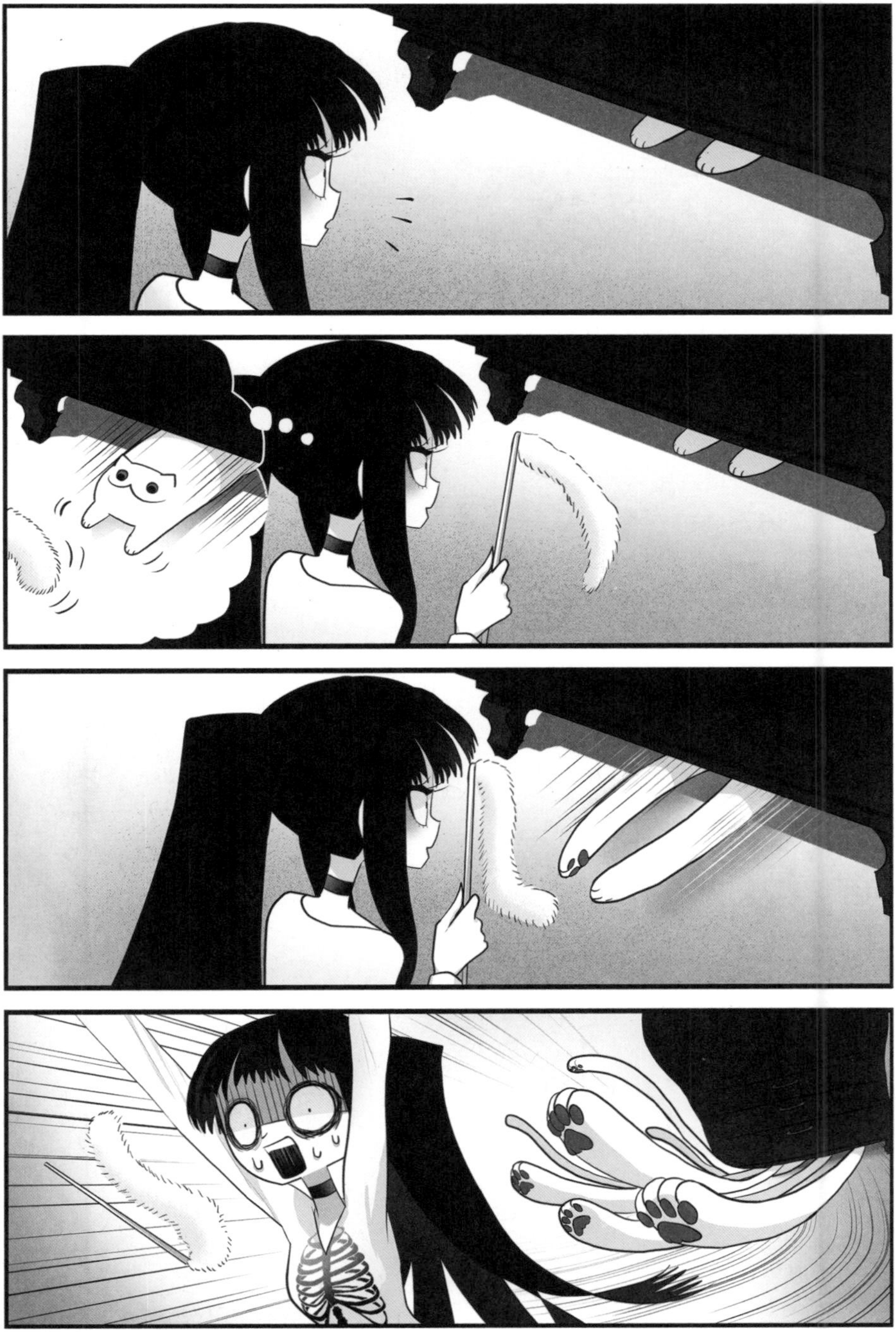

MEOWSSAGE

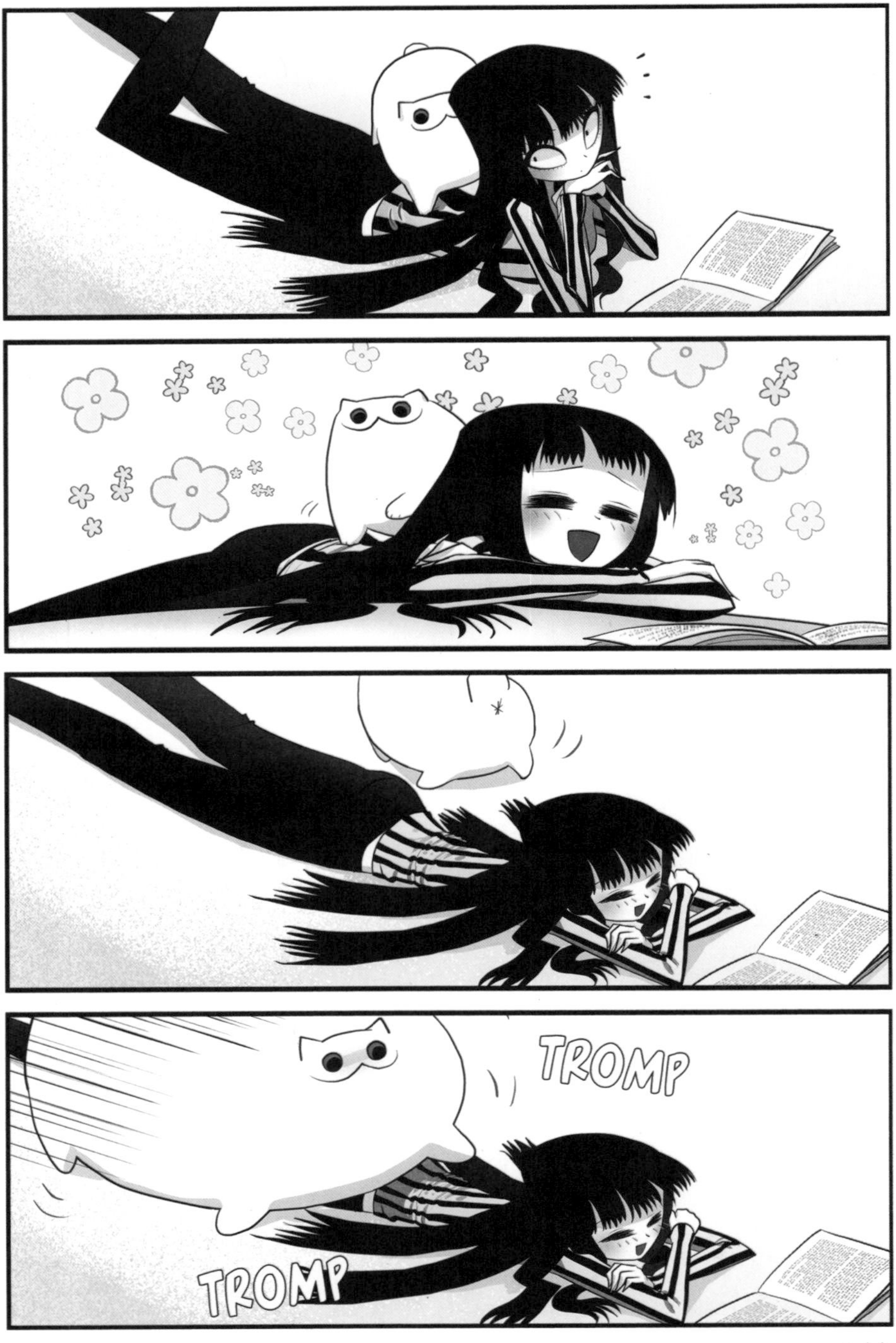
TROMP
TROMP

HAIR SCARE

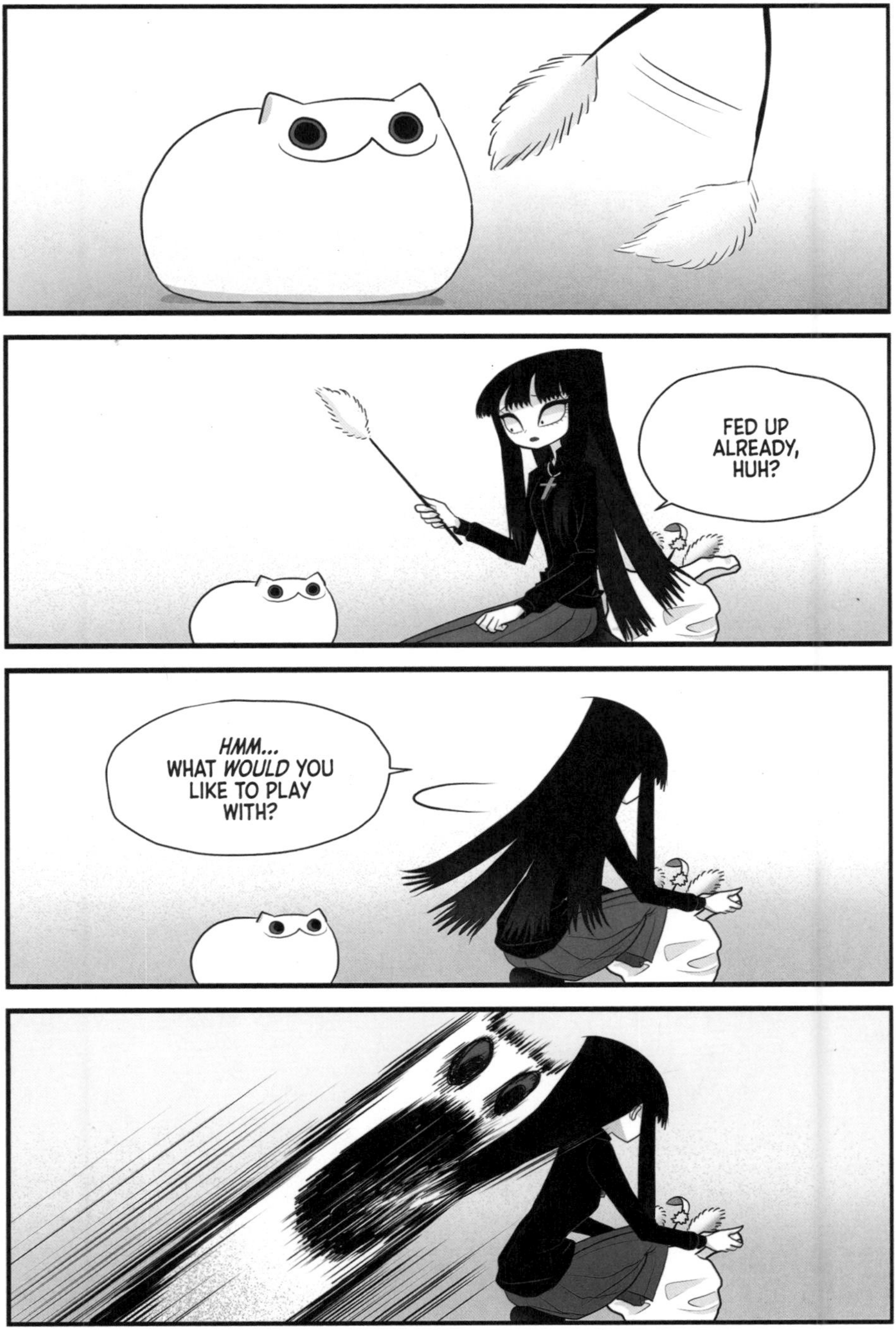
FED UP ALREADY, HUH?
HMM... WHAT WOULD YOU LIKE TO PLAY WITH?

KEY

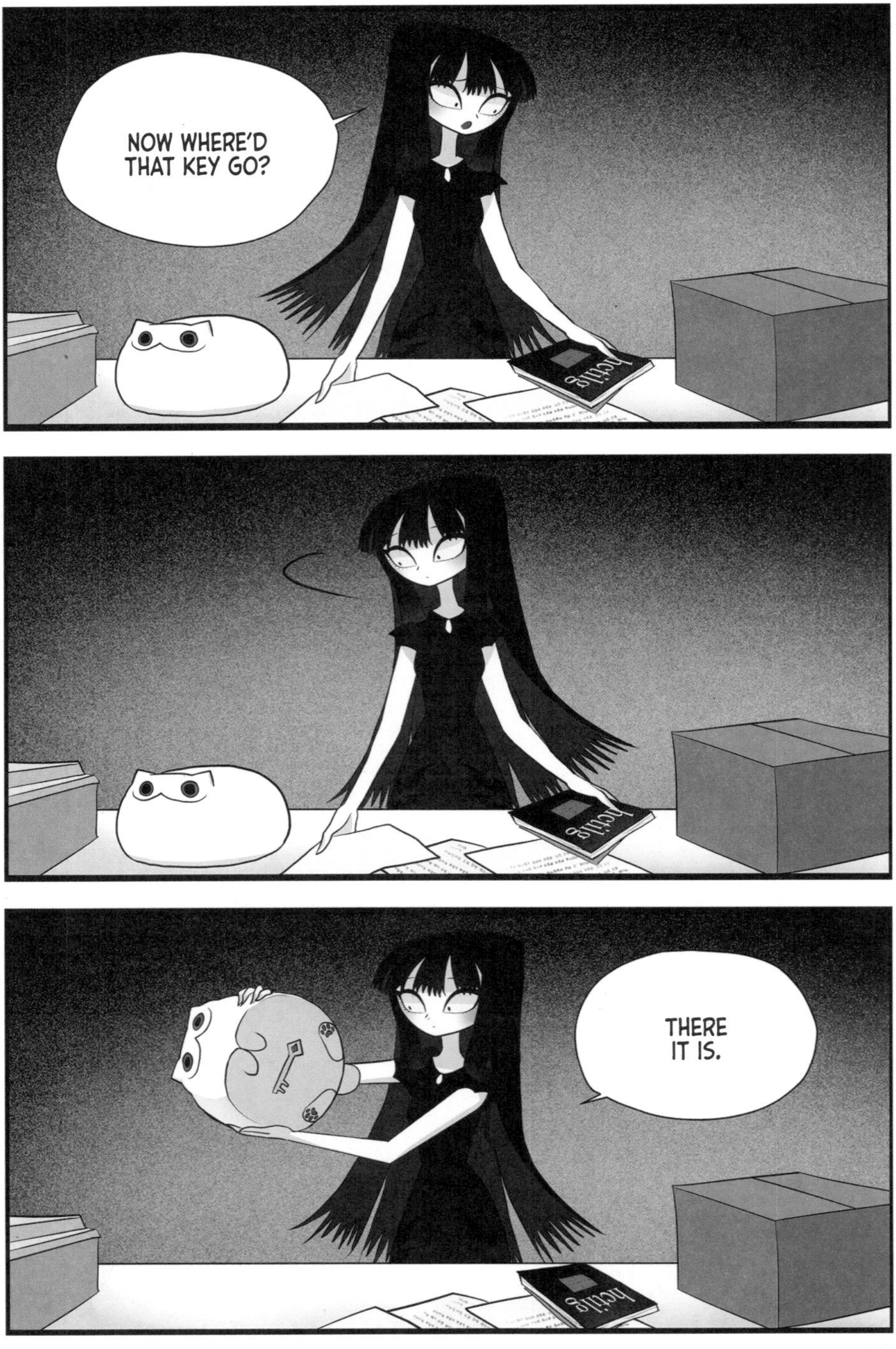
NOW WHERE'D THAT KEY GO?
THERE IT IS.

SWIPER NO SWIPING

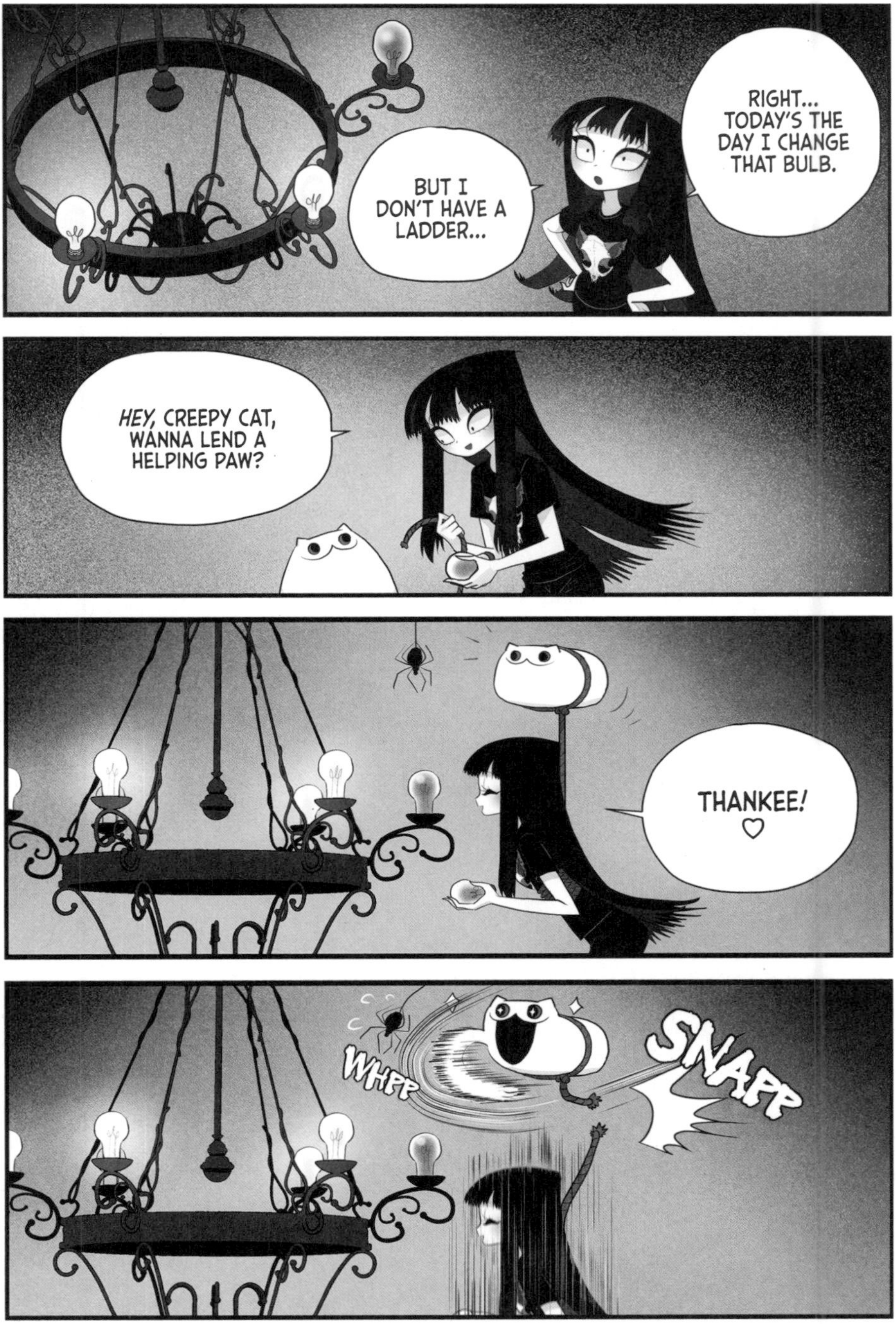
RIGHT... TODAY'S THE DAY I CHANGE THAT BULB.
BUT I DON'T HAVE A LADDER...
HEY, CREEPY CAT, WANNA LEND A HELPING PAW?
THANKEE! ♡
WHPP
SNAPP

PURRFECT FIT

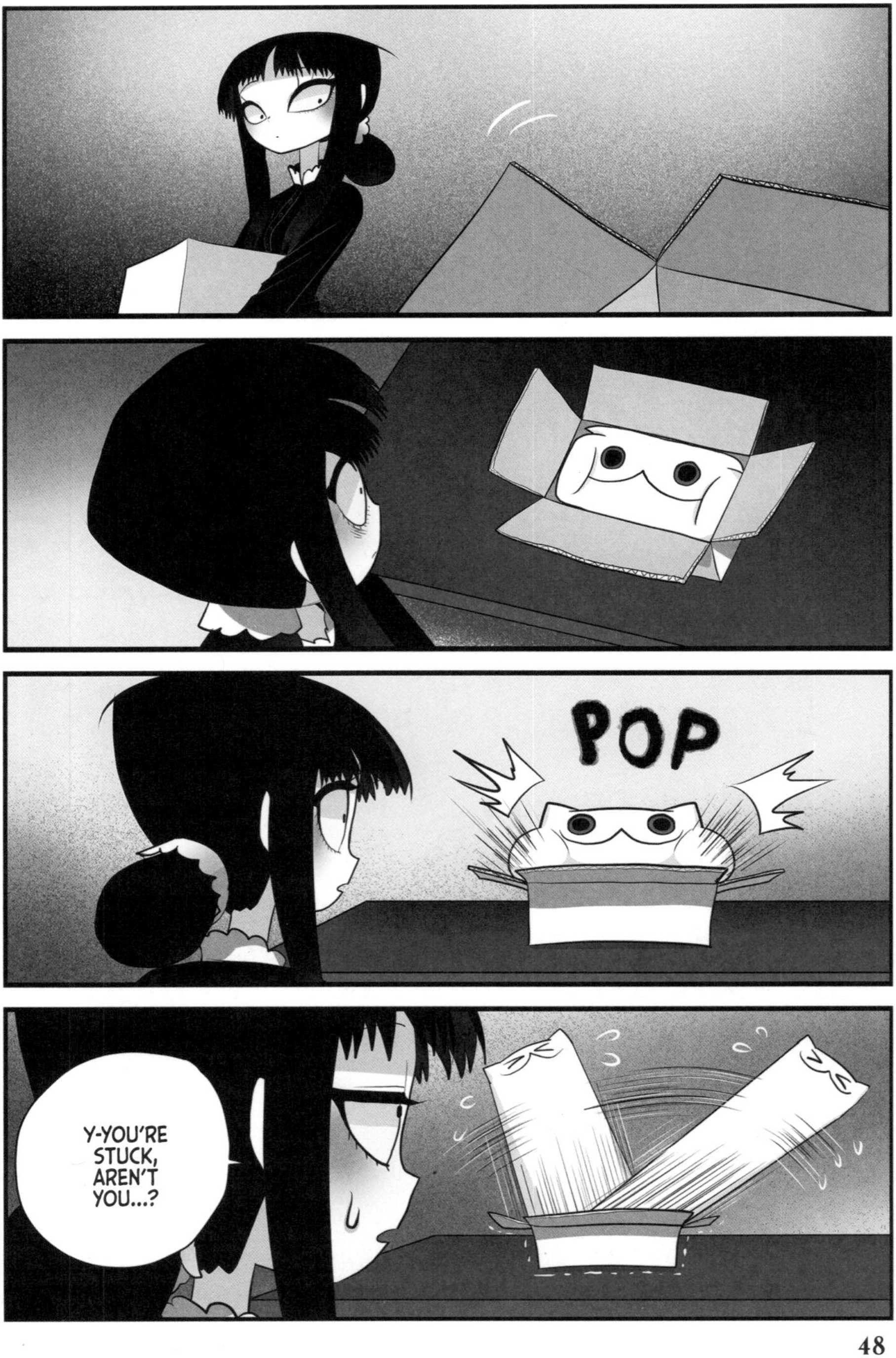

POP
Y-YOU'RE STUCK, AREN'T YOU...?

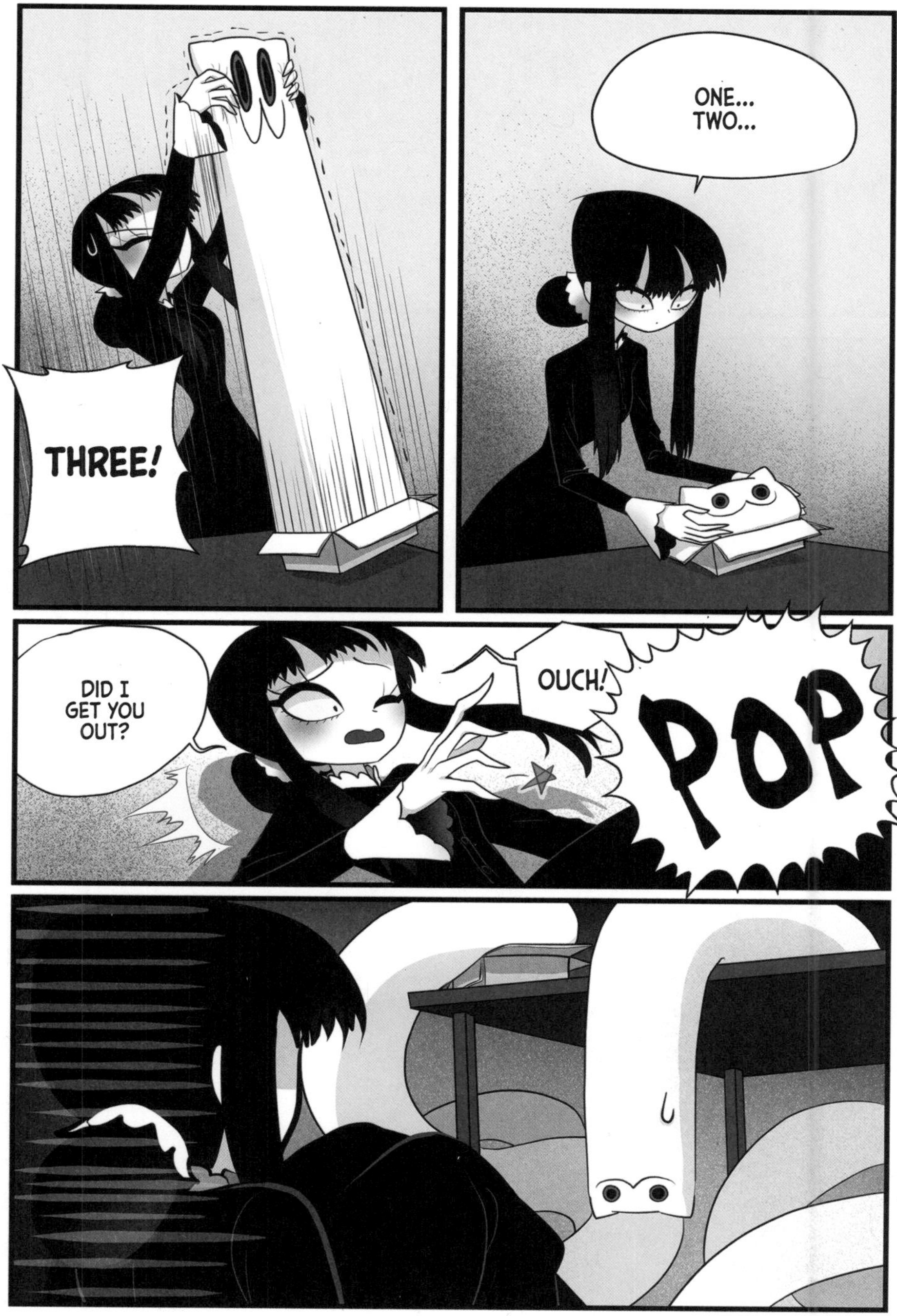
ONE...
TWO...
THREE!
DID I
GET YOU
OUT?
OUCH!
POP

LONG II

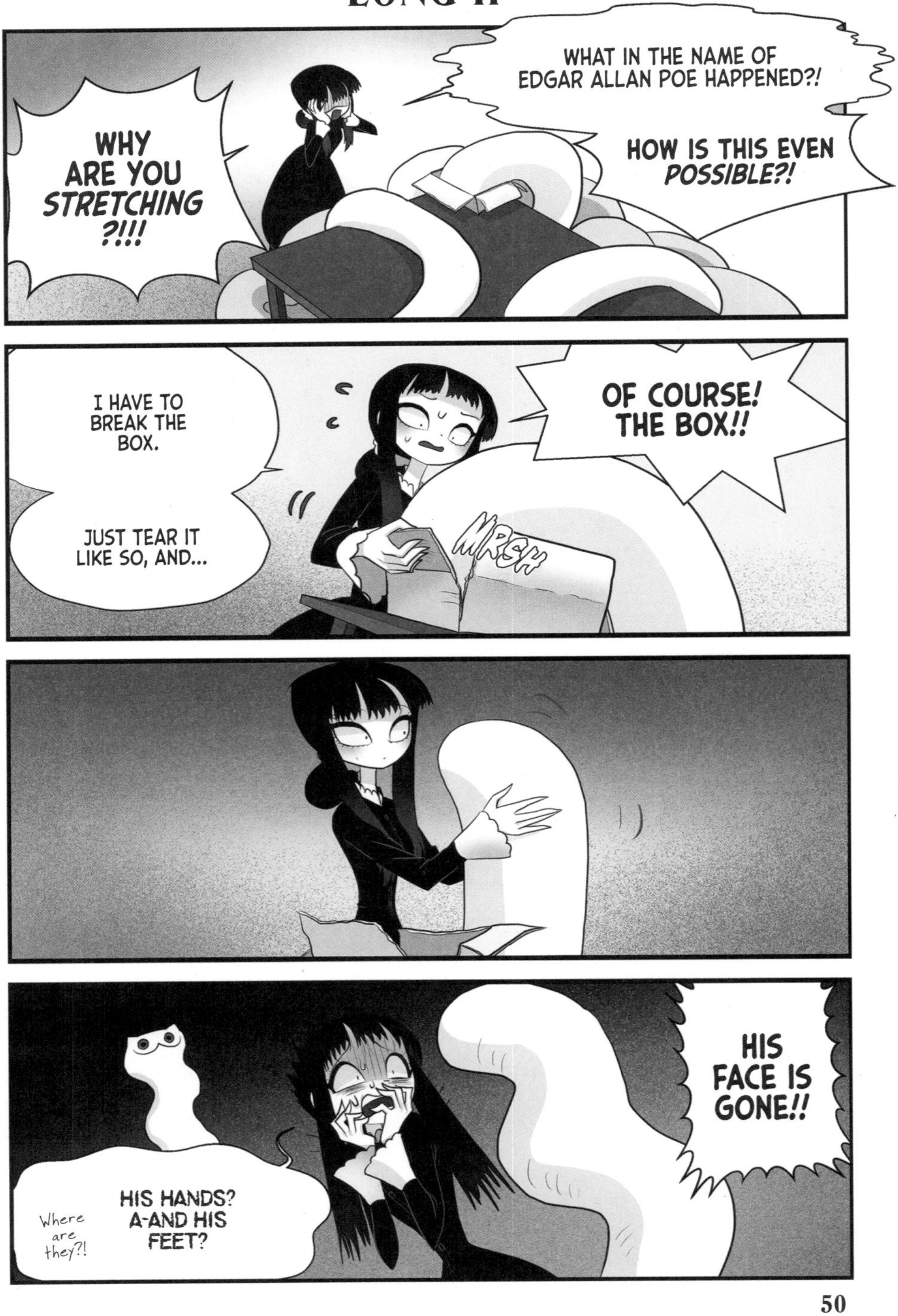
WHAT IN THE NAME OF EDGAR ALLAN POE HAPPENED?!
HOW IS THIS EVEN POSSIBLE?!
WHY ARE YOU STRETCHING ?!!!
OF COURSE! THE BOX!!
I HAVE TO BREAK THE BOX.
JUST TEAR IT LIKE SO, AND...
MRSH
HIS FACE IS GONE!!
HIS HANDS? A-AND HIS FEET?
Where are they?!

LONG III

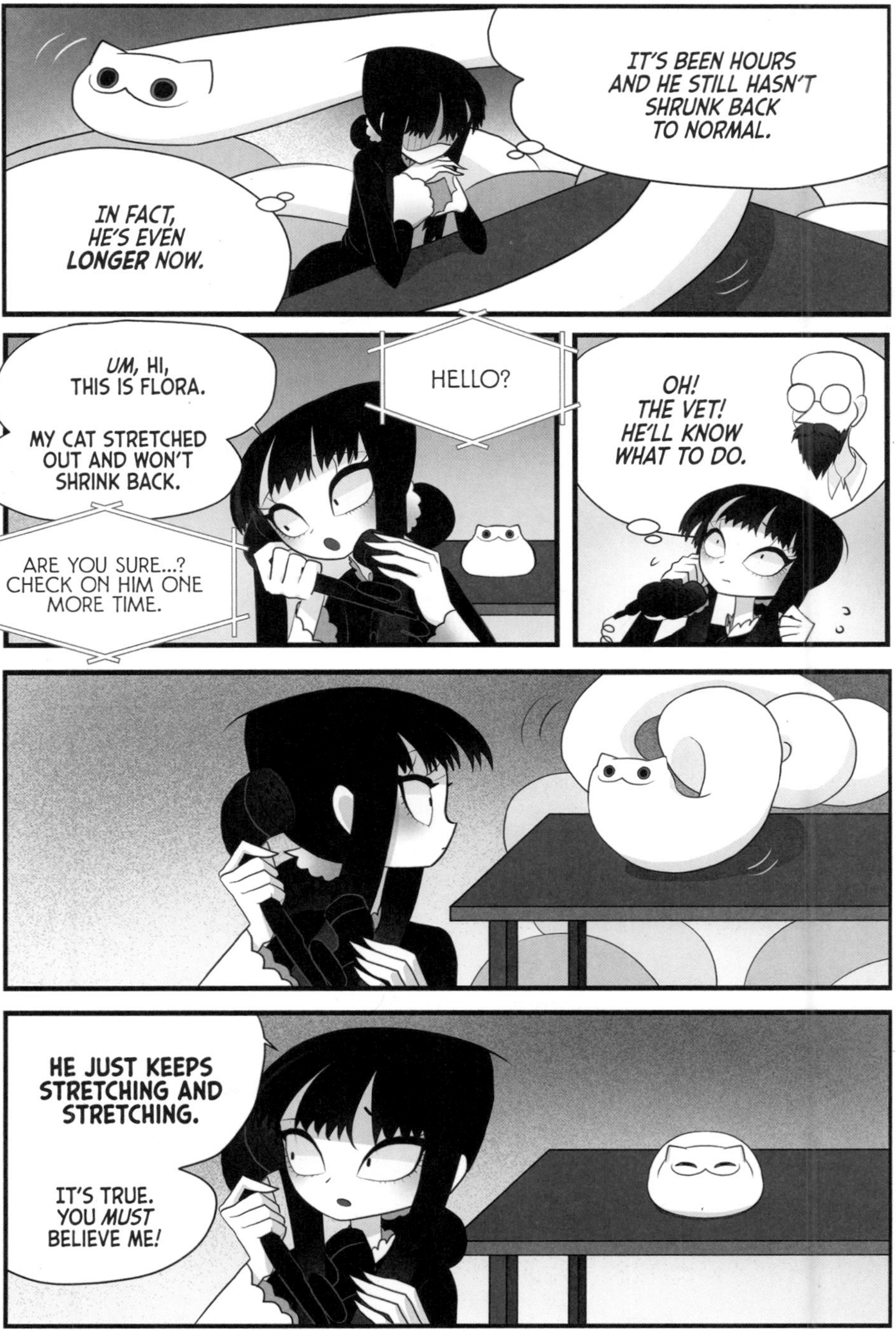

IT'S BEEN HOURS AND HE STILL HASN'T SHRUNK BACK TO NORMAL.
IN FACT, HE'S EVEN *LONGER* NOW.
OH! THE VET! HE'LL KNOW WHAT TO DO.
HELLO?
UM, HI, THIS IS FLORA.
MY CAT STRETCHED OUT AND WON'T SHRINK BACK.
ARE YOU SURE...? CHECK ON HIM ONE MORE TIME.
HE JUST KEEPS STRETCHING AND STRETCHING.
IT'S TRUE. YOU *MUST* BELIEVE ME!

PHONE CALL

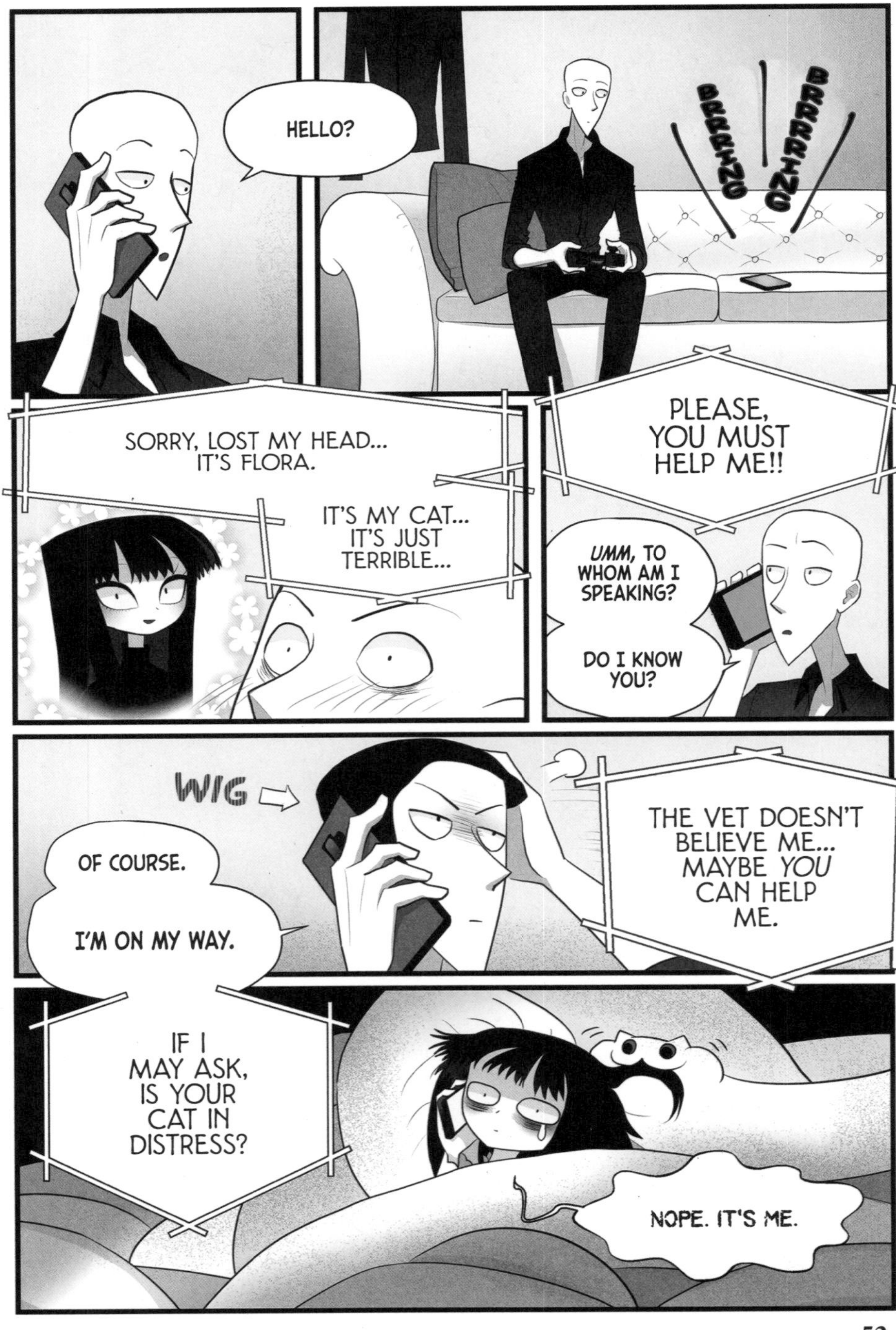
BRRRING BRRRING
HELLO?
SORRY, LOST MY HEAD... IT'S FLORA.
IT'S MY CAT... IT'S JUST TERRIBLE...
PLEASE, YOU MUST HELP ME!!
UMM, TO WHOM AM I SPEAKING?
DO I KNOW YOU?
WIG
THE VET DOESN'T BELIEVE ME... MAYBE YOU CAN HELP ME.
OF COURSE.
I'M ON MY WAY.
IF I MAY ASK, IS YOUR CAT IN DISTRESS?
NOPE. IT'S ME.

TELEPHONE NUMBER

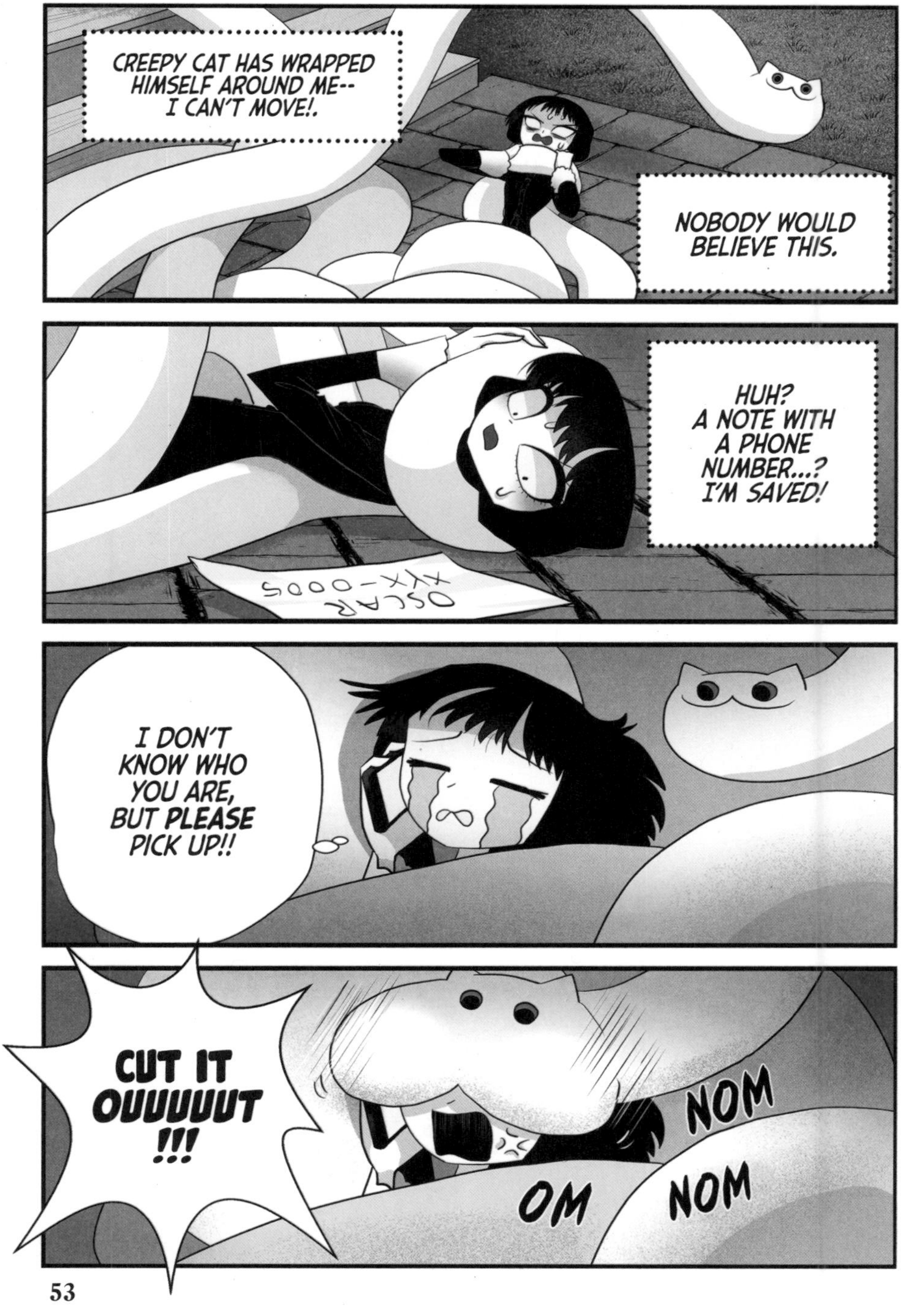
CREEPY CAT HAS WRAPPED HIMSELF AROUND ME-- I CAN'T MOVE!.
NOBODY WOULD BELIEVE THIS.
HUH? A NOTE WITH A PHONE NUMBER...? I'M SAVED!
OSCAR
XXX-0005
I DON'T KNOW WHO YOU ARE, BUT PLEASE PICK UP!!
CUT IT OUUUUUT !!!
NOM
OM
NOM

HIDDEN FROM SIGHT

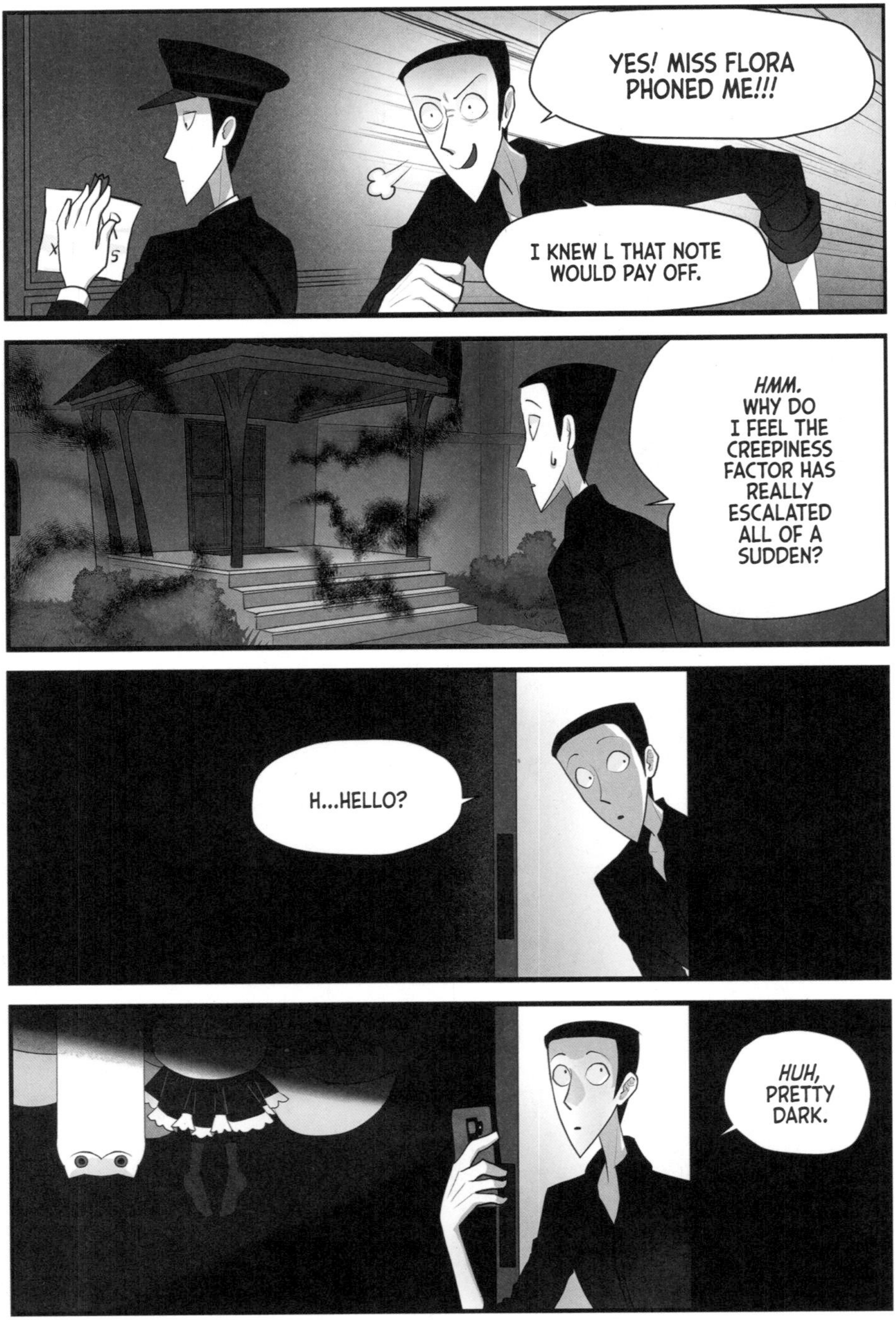
YES! MISS FLORA PHONED ME!!!
I KNEW L THAT NOTE WOULD PAY OFF.
HMM. WHY DO I FEEL THE CREEPINESS FACTOR HAS REALLY ESCALATED ALL OF A SUDDEN?
H...HELLO?
HUH, PRETTY DARK.

SOFT WALL

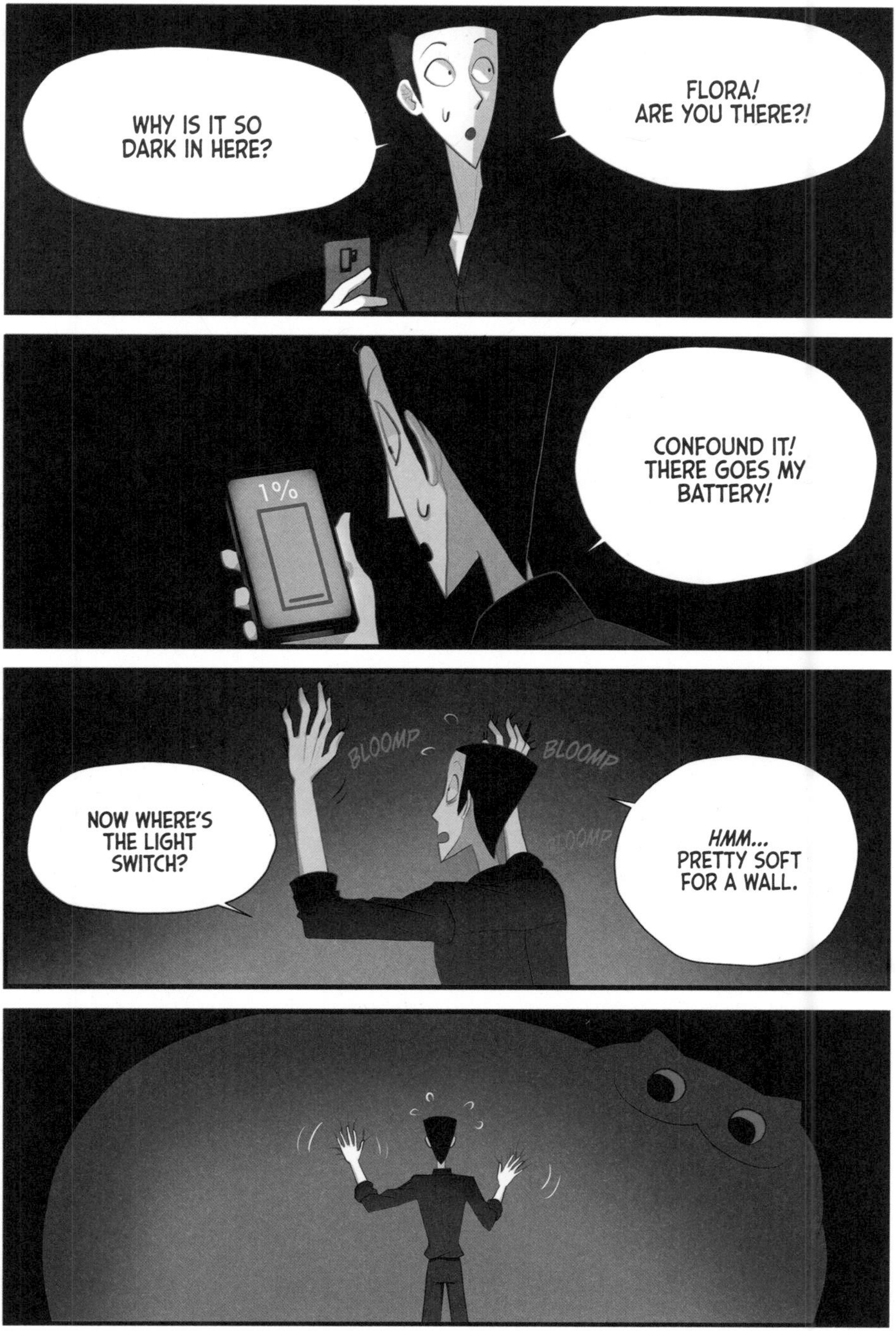
WHY IS IT SO DARK IN HERE?
FLORA! ARE YOU THERE?!
1%
CONFOUND IT! THERE GOES MY BATTERY!
BLOOMP
BLOOMP
NOW WHERE'S THE LIGHT SWITCH?
BLOOMP
HMM... PRETTY SOFT FOR A WALL.

MIRROR

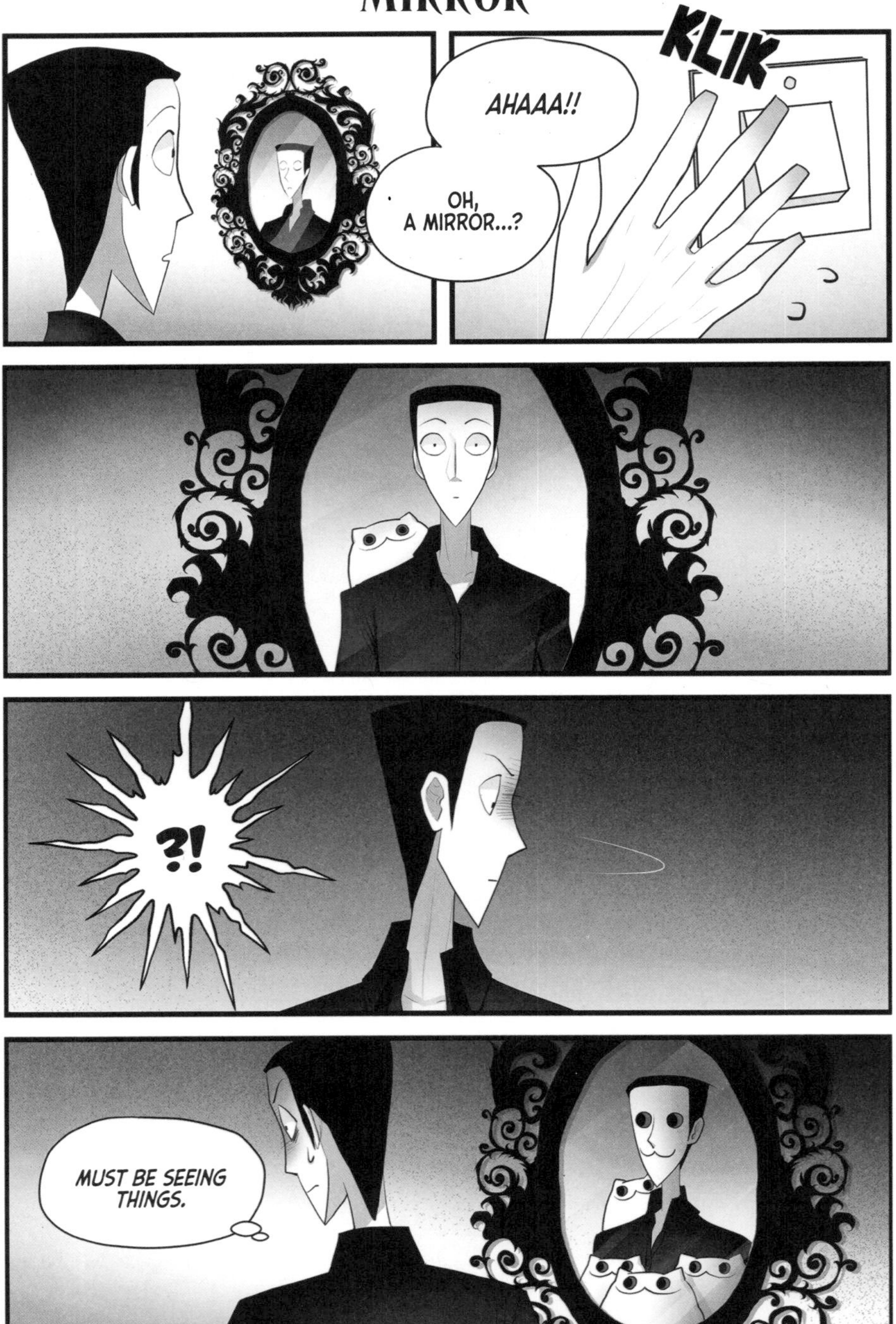
KLIK
AHAAA!!
OH, A MIRROR...?
?!
MUST BE SEEING THINGS.

CRAMPED

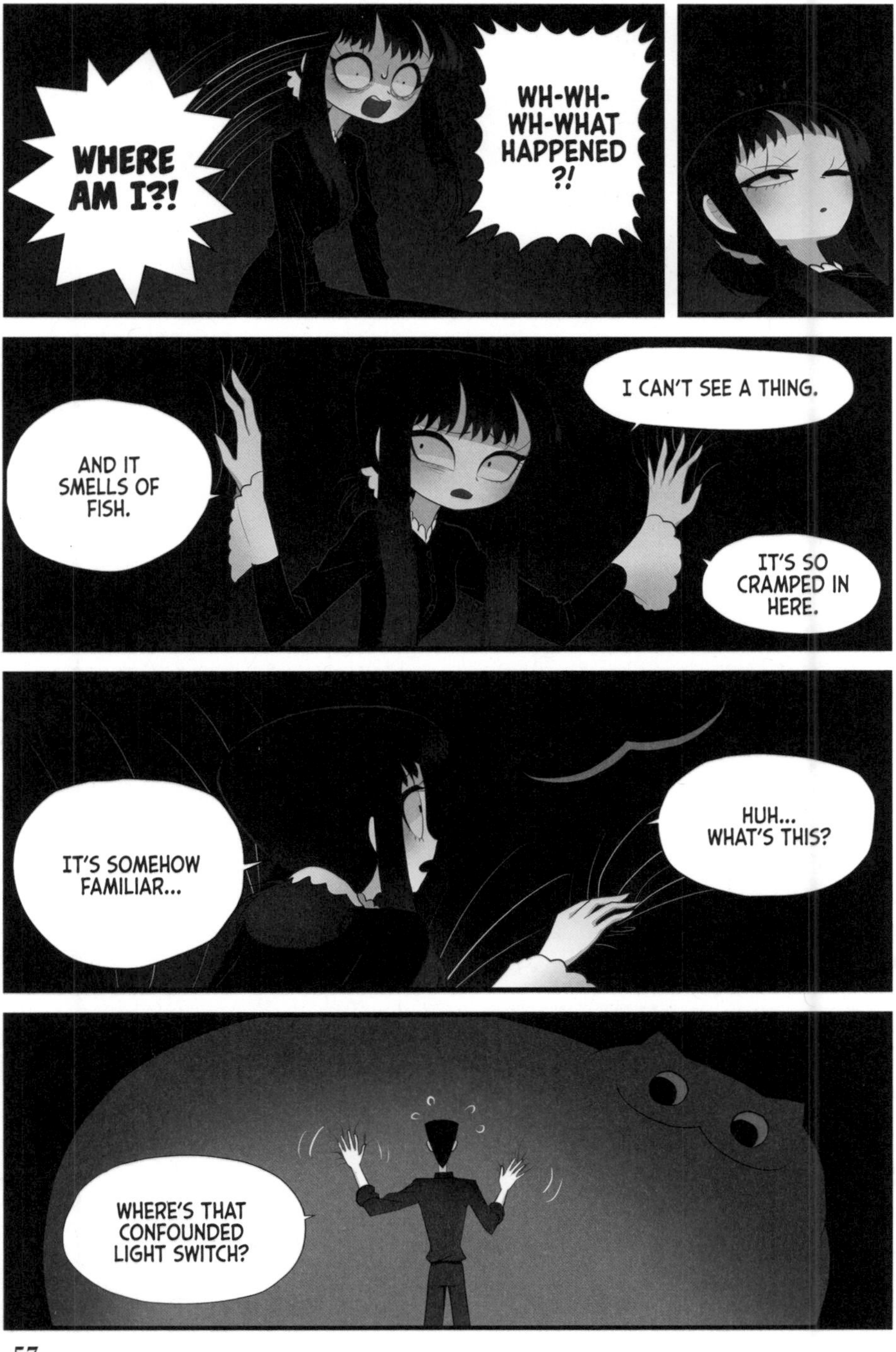
WHERE AM I?!
WH-WH-WH-WHAT HAPPENED ?!
I CAN'T SEE A THING.
AND IT SMELLS OF FISH.
IT'S SO CRAMPED IN HERE.
HUH... WHAT'S THIS?
IT'S SOMEHOW FAMILIAR...
WHERE'S THAT CONFOUNDED LIGHT SWITCH?

COSTUME I

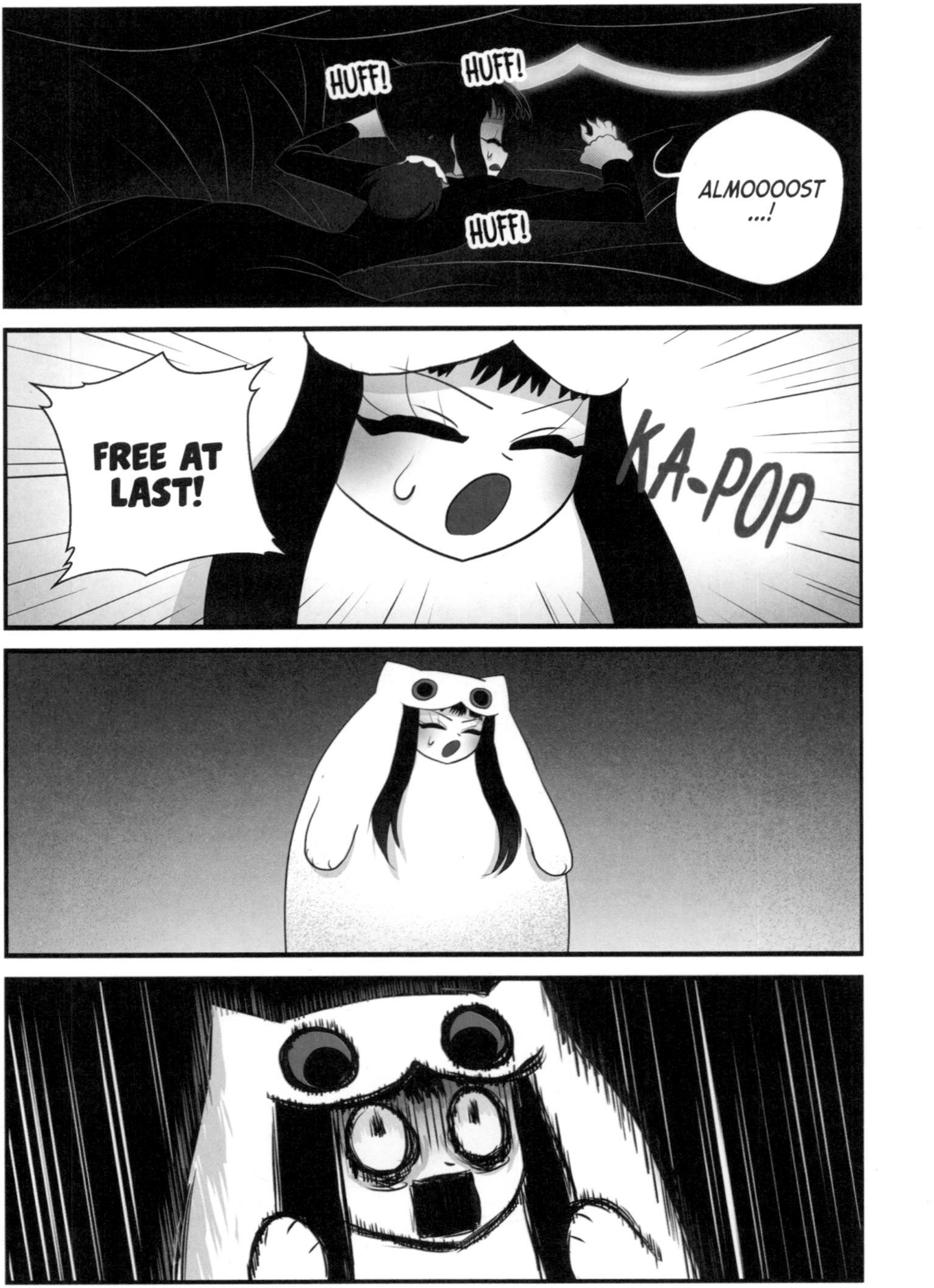
HUFF!
HUFF!
HUFF!
ALMOOOOST ...!
FREE AT LAST!
KA-POP

COSTUME II

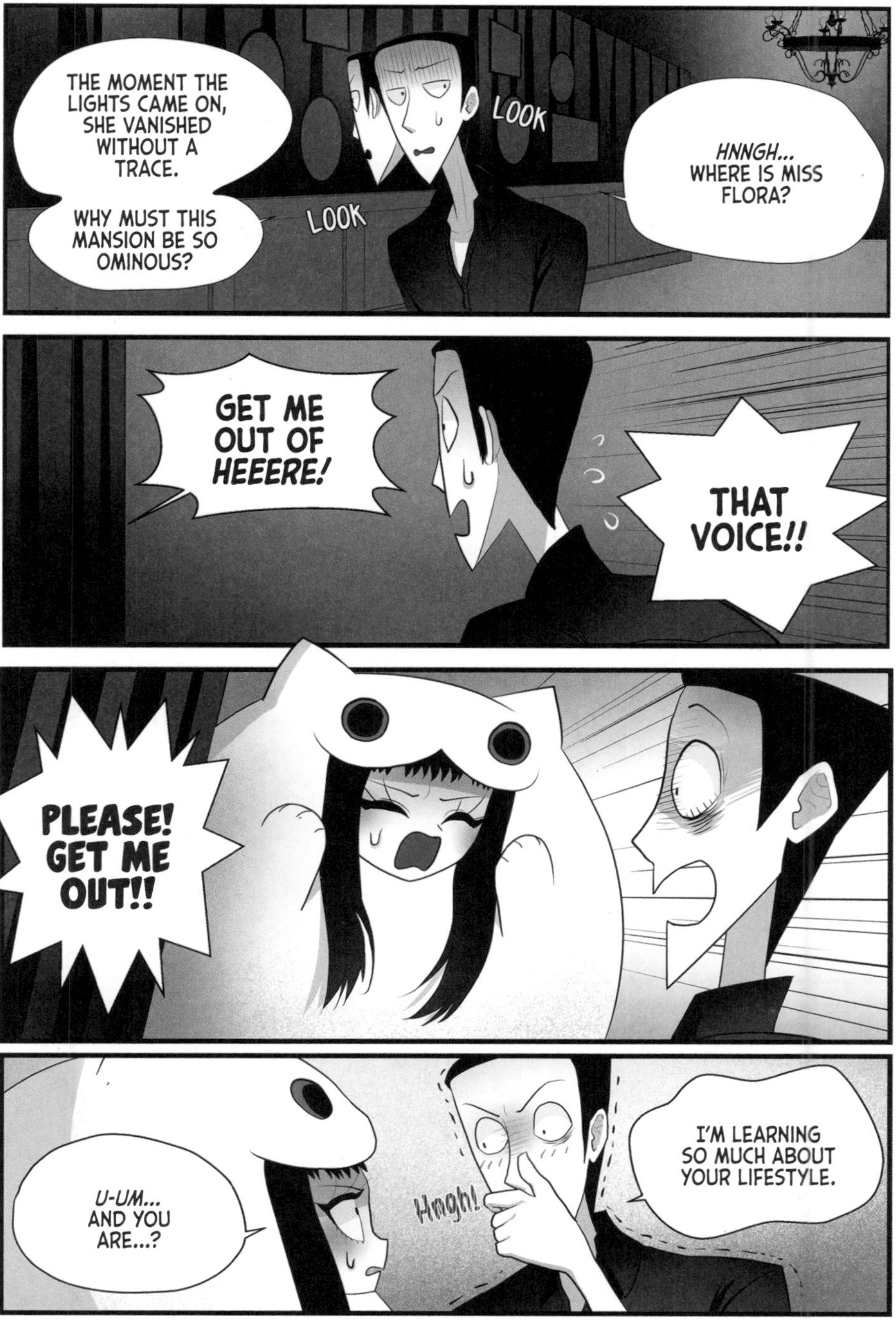

THE MOMENT THE LIGHTS CAME ON, SHE VANISHED WITHOUT A TRACE.
WHY MUST THIS MANSION BE SO OMINOUS?
LOOK
LOOK
HNNGH... WHERE IS MISS FLORA?
GET ME OUT OF HEEERE!
THAT VOICE!!
PLEASE! GET ME OUT!!
I'M LEARNING SO MUCH ABOUT YOUR LIFESTYLE.
Hngh!
U-UM... AND YOU ARE...?

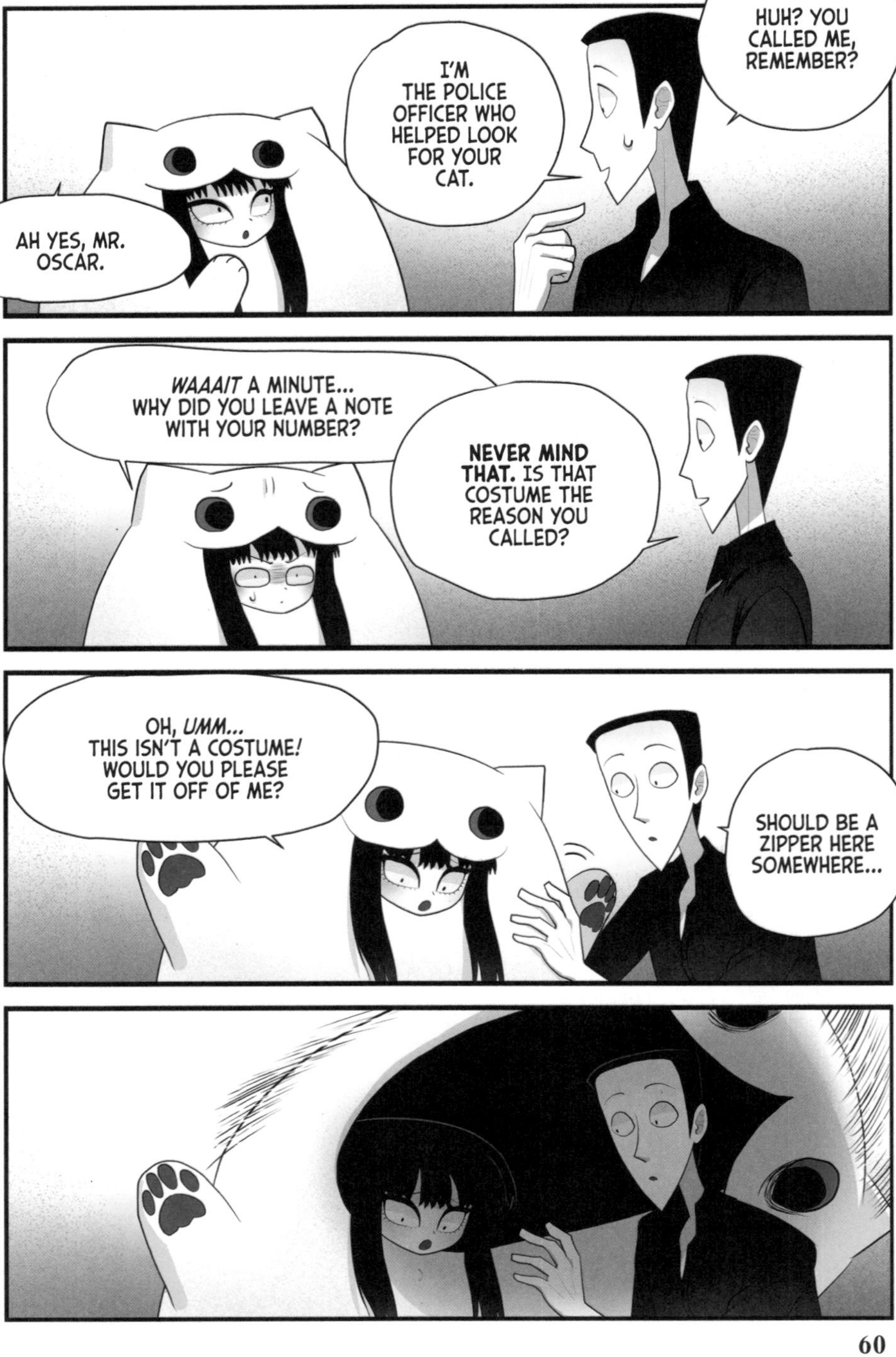
HUH? YOU CALLED ME, REMEMBER?
I'M THE POLICE OFFICER WHO HELPED LOOK FOR YOUR CAT.
AH YES, MR. OSCAR.
WAAAIT A MINUTE... WHY DID YOU LEAVE A NOTE WITH YOUR NUMBER?
NEVER MIND THAT. IS THAT COSTUME THE REASON YOU CALLED?
OH, *UMM*... THIS ISN'T A COSTUME! WOULD YOU PLEASE GET IT OFF OF ME?
SHOULD BE A ZIPPER HERE SOMEWHERE...

NOM NOM

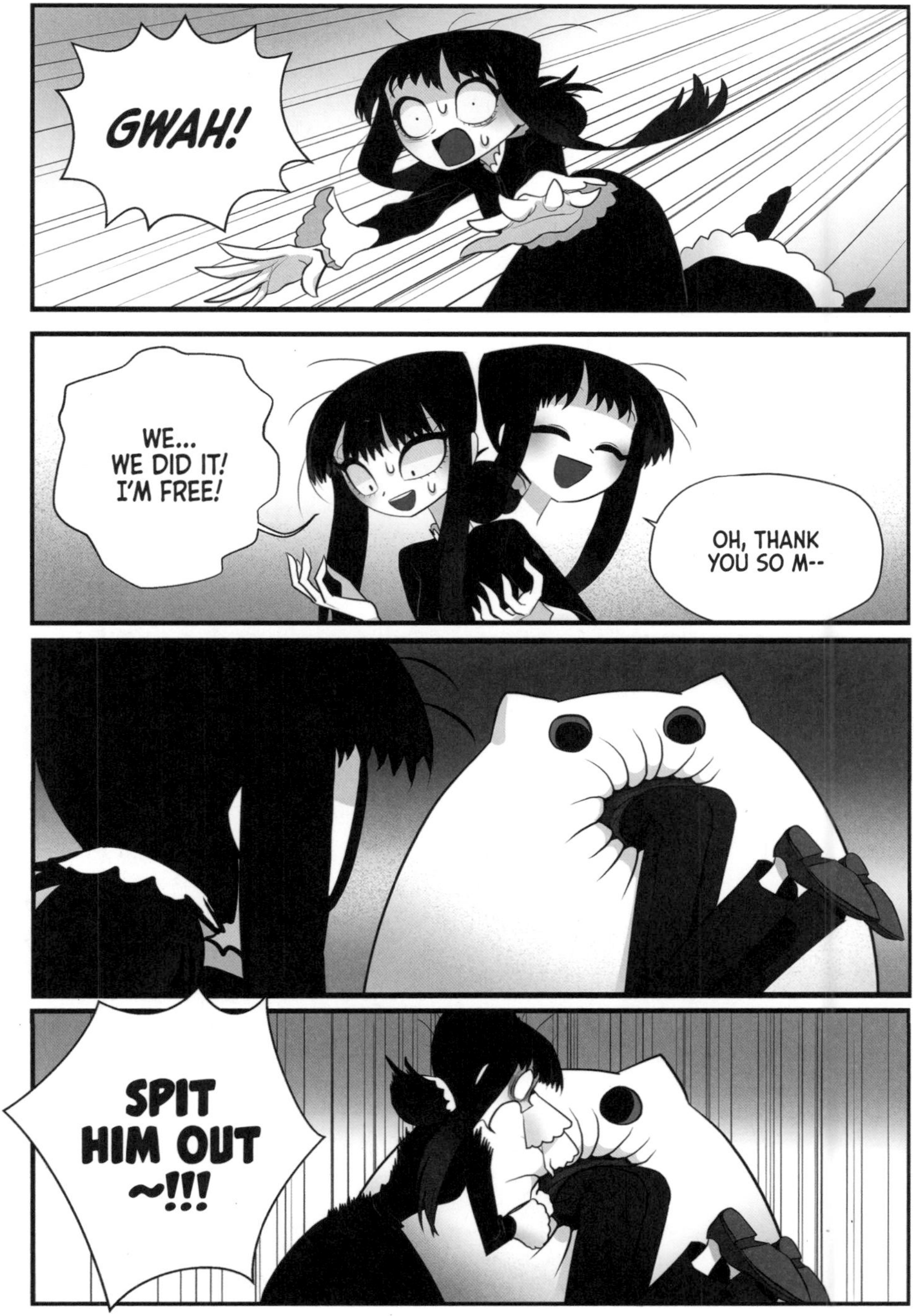

GWAH!
WE... WE DID IT! I'M FREE!
OH, THANK YOU SO M--
SPIT HIM OUT ~!!!

NOT NORMAL

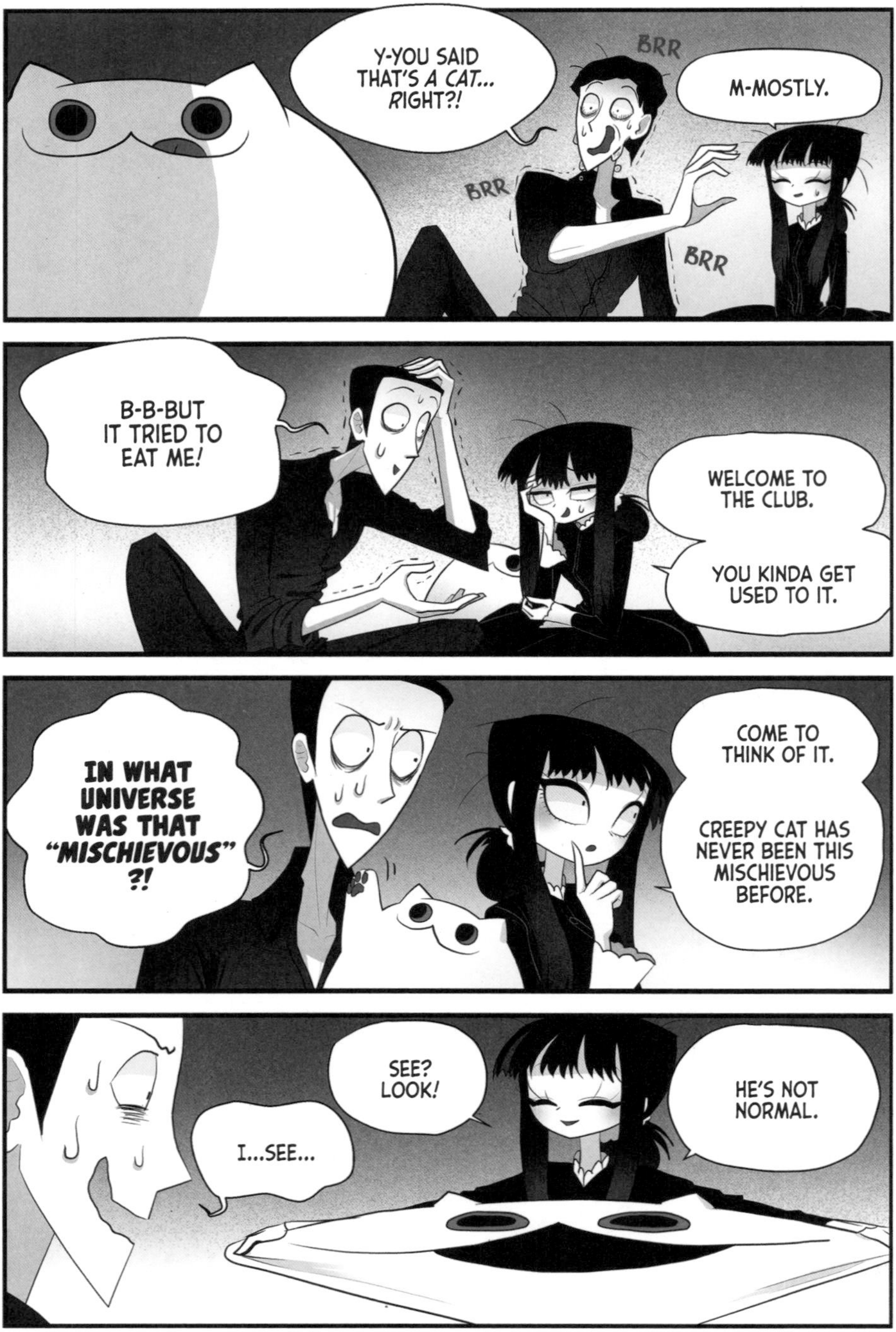

Y-YOU SAID THAT'S A CAT... RIGHT?!
BRR
BRR
BRR
M-MOSTLY.
B-B-BUT IT TRIED TO EAT ME!
WELCOME TO THE CLUB.
YOU KINDA GET USED TO IT.
COME TO THINK OF IT.
CREEPY CAT HAS NEVER BEEN THIS MISCHIEVOUS BEFORE.
IN WHAT UNIVERSE WAS THAT "MISCHIEVOUS" ?!
SEE? LOOK!
HE'S NOT NORMAL.
I...SEE...

I FORGOT

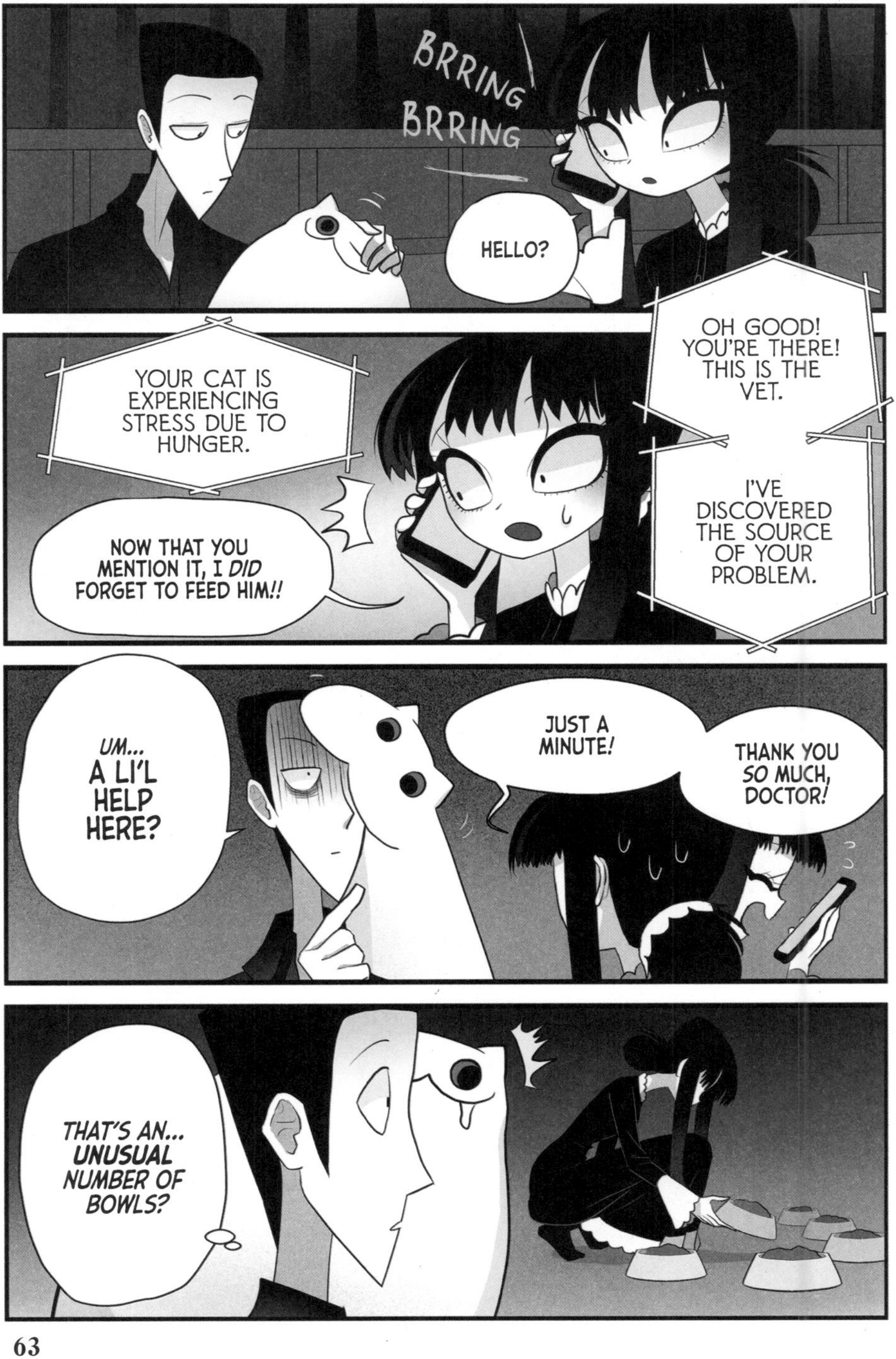
BRRING
BRRING
HELLO?
OH GOOD! YOU'RE THERE! THIS IS THE VET.
I'VE DISCOVERED THE SOURCE OF YOUR PROBLEM.
YOUR CAT IS EXPERIENCING STRESS DUE TO HUNGER.
NOW THAT YOU MENTION IT, I DID FORGET TO FEED HIM!!
JUST A MINUTE!
THANK YOU SO MUCH, DOCTOR!
UM... A LI'L HELP HERE?
THAT'S AN... UNUSUAL NUMBER OF BOWLS?

CENTIPAWD

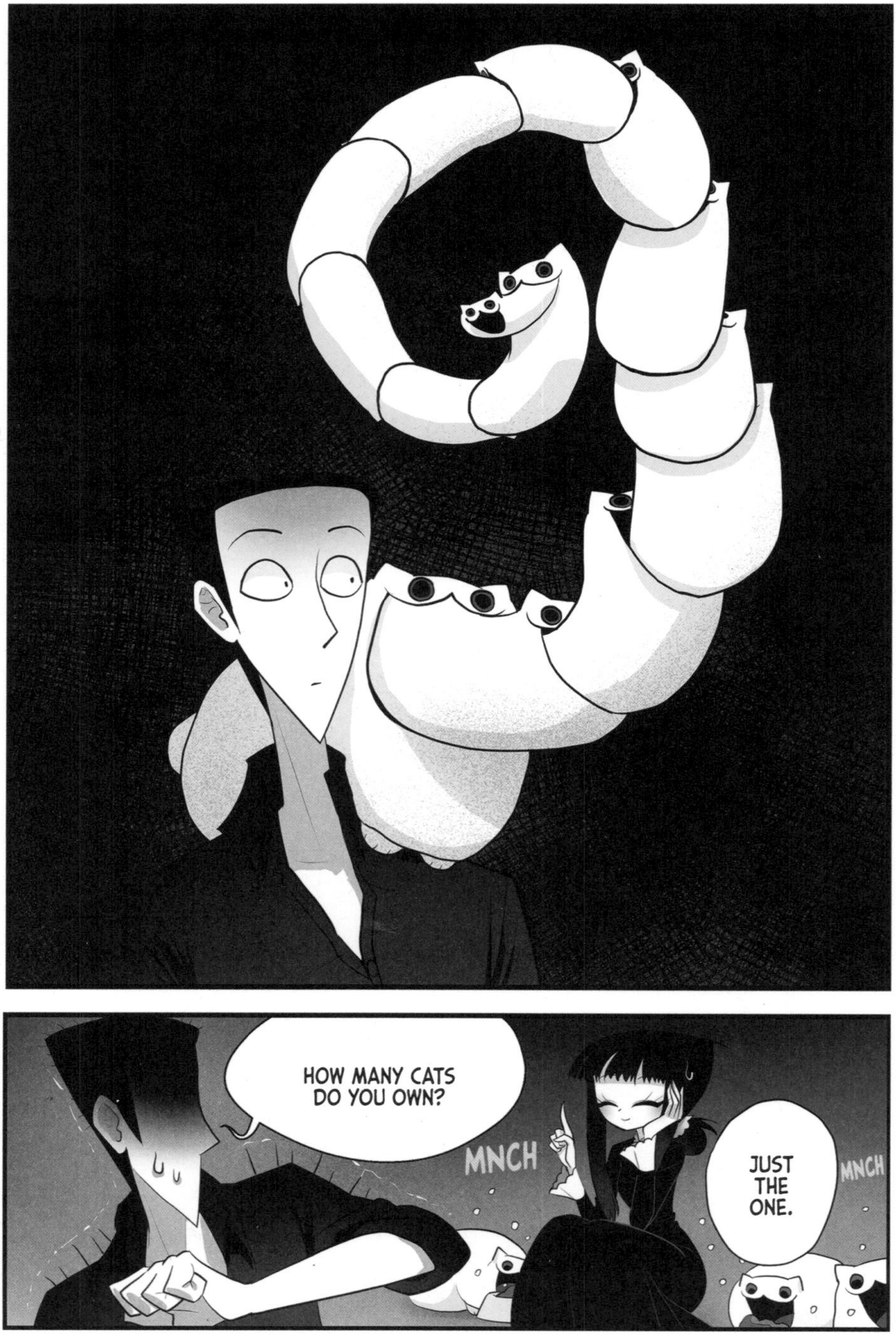

HOW MANY CATS DO YOU OWN?
MNCH
JUST THE ONE.
MNCH

Creepy Cat

SHOOTING STARS

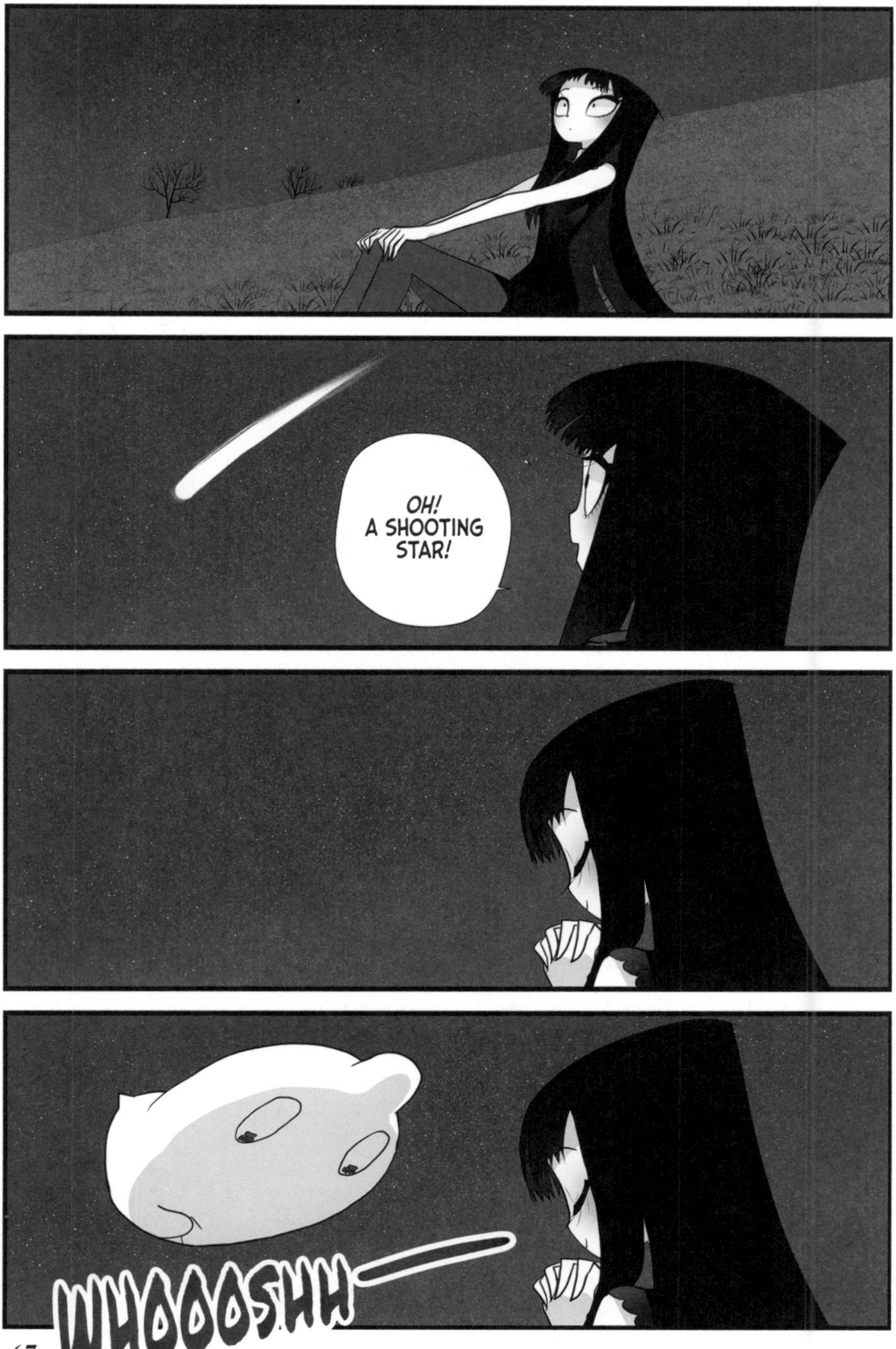
OH!
A SHOOTING
STAR!
WHOOOSHH

UNIDENTIFIED FURRY OBJECTS

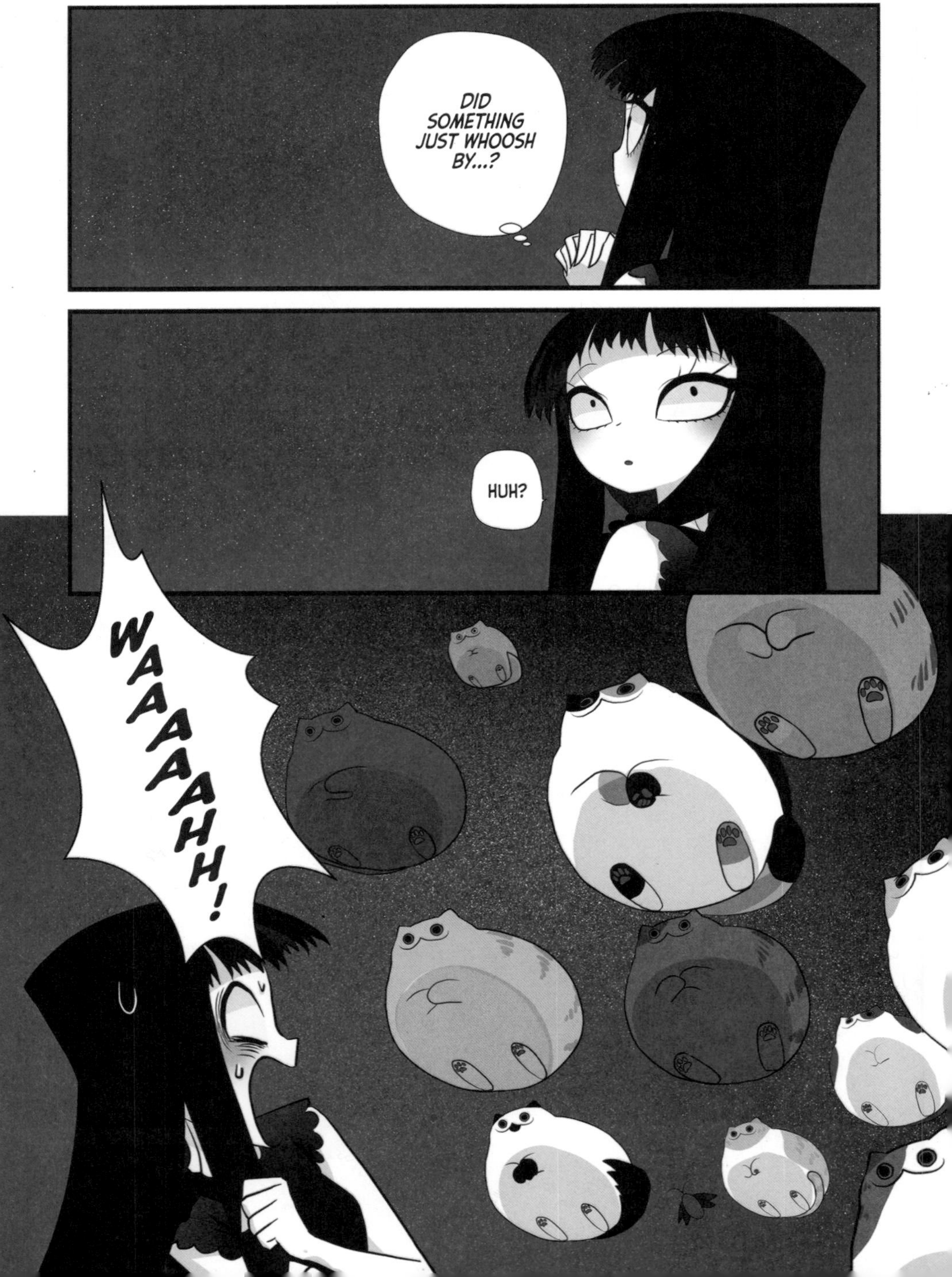
DID SOMETHING JUST WHOOSH BY...?
HUH?
WAAAAAHH!

APPLYING PRESSURE

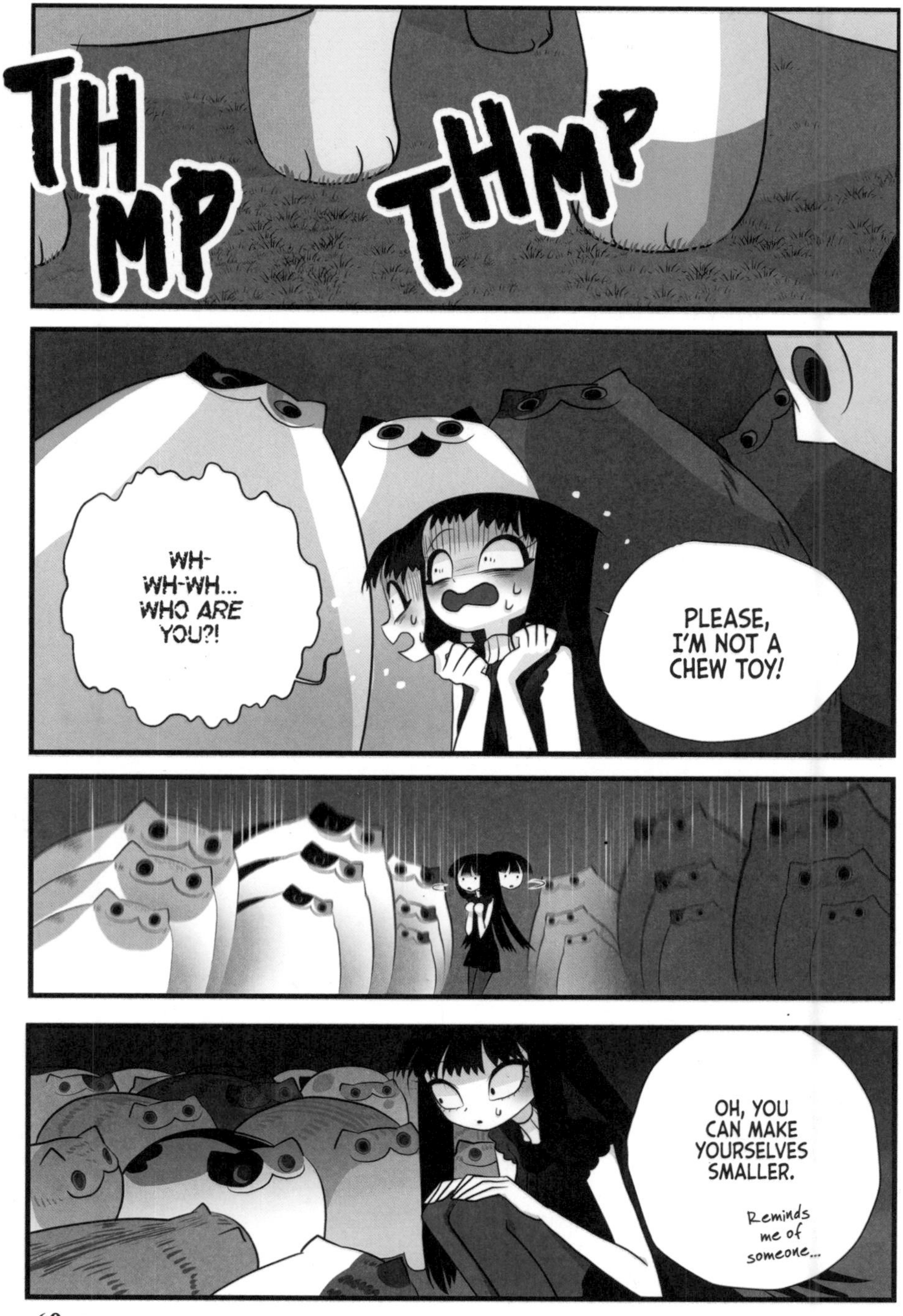
THMP
THMP
WH-WH-WH... WHO ARE YOU?!
PLEASE, I'M NOT A CHEW TOY!
OH, YOU CAN MAKE YOURSELVES SMALLER.
Reminds me of someone...

INTERPRETER

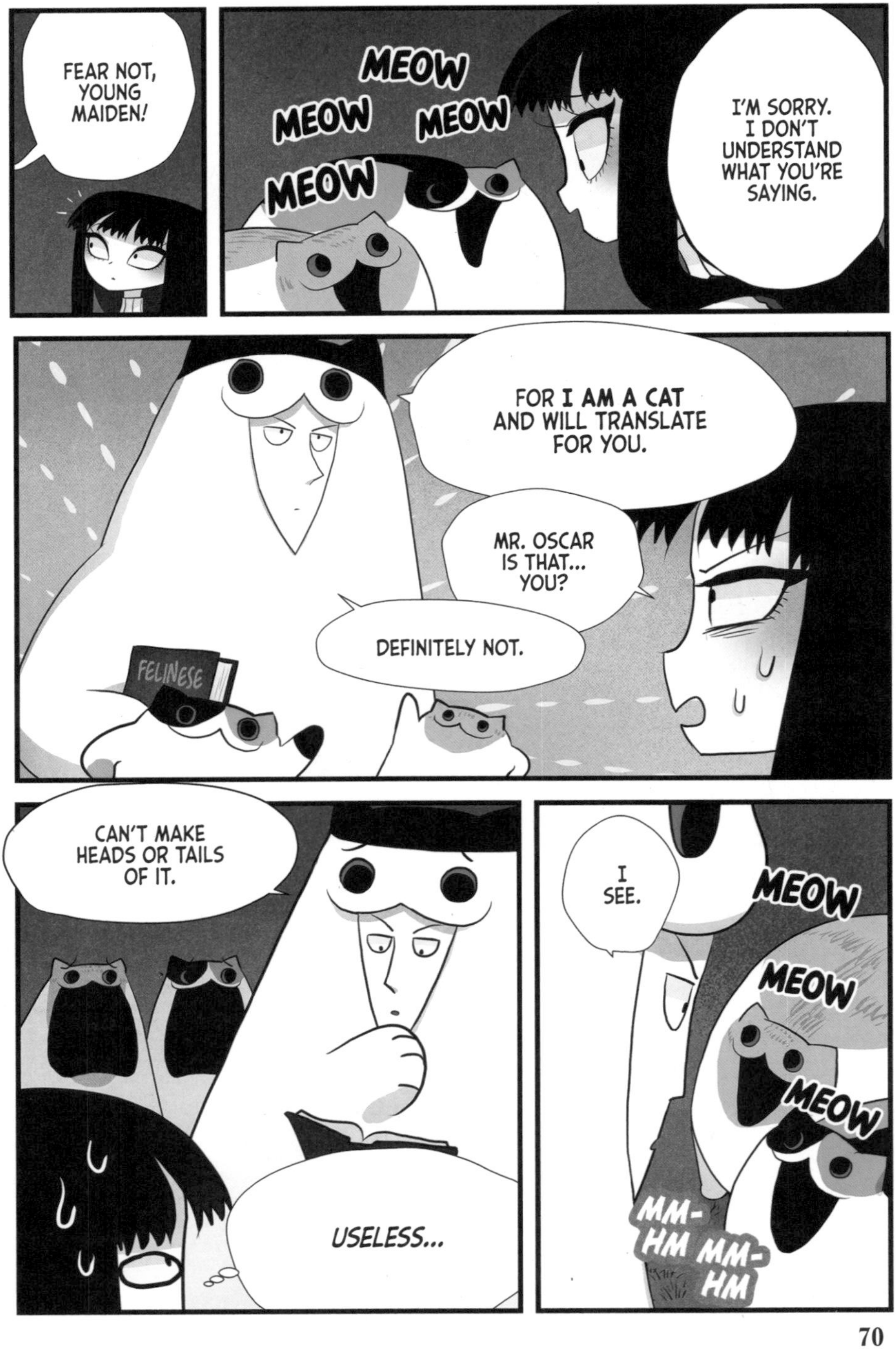
FEAR NOT, YOUNG MAIDEN!
MEOW
MEOW
MEOW
MEOW
I'M SORRY. I DON'T UNDERSTAND WHAT YOU'RE SAYING.
FOR **I AM A CAT** AND WILL TRANSLATE FOR YOU.
MR. OSCAR IS THAT... YOU?
DEFINITELY NOT.
FELINESE
CAN'T MAKE HEADS OR TAILS OF IT.
USELESS...
I SEE.
MEOW
MEOW
MEOW
MM-HM MM-HM

SCRITCH SCRITCH

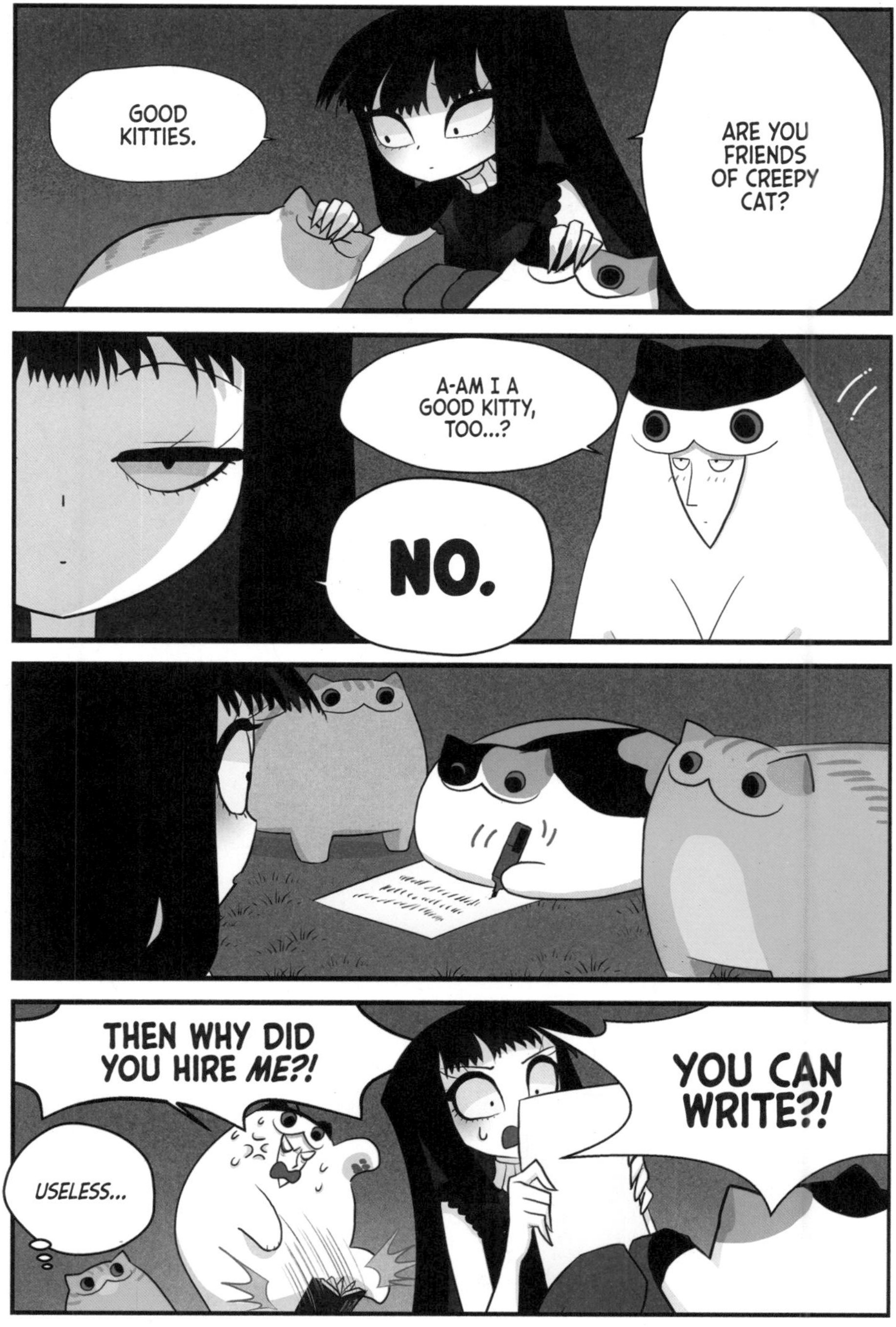
GOOD KITTIES.
ARE YOU FRIENDS OF CREEPY CAT?
A-AM I A GOOD KITTY, TOO...?
NO.
THEN WHY DID YOU HIRE *ME?!*
YOU CAN WRITE?!
USELESS...

REBELLION

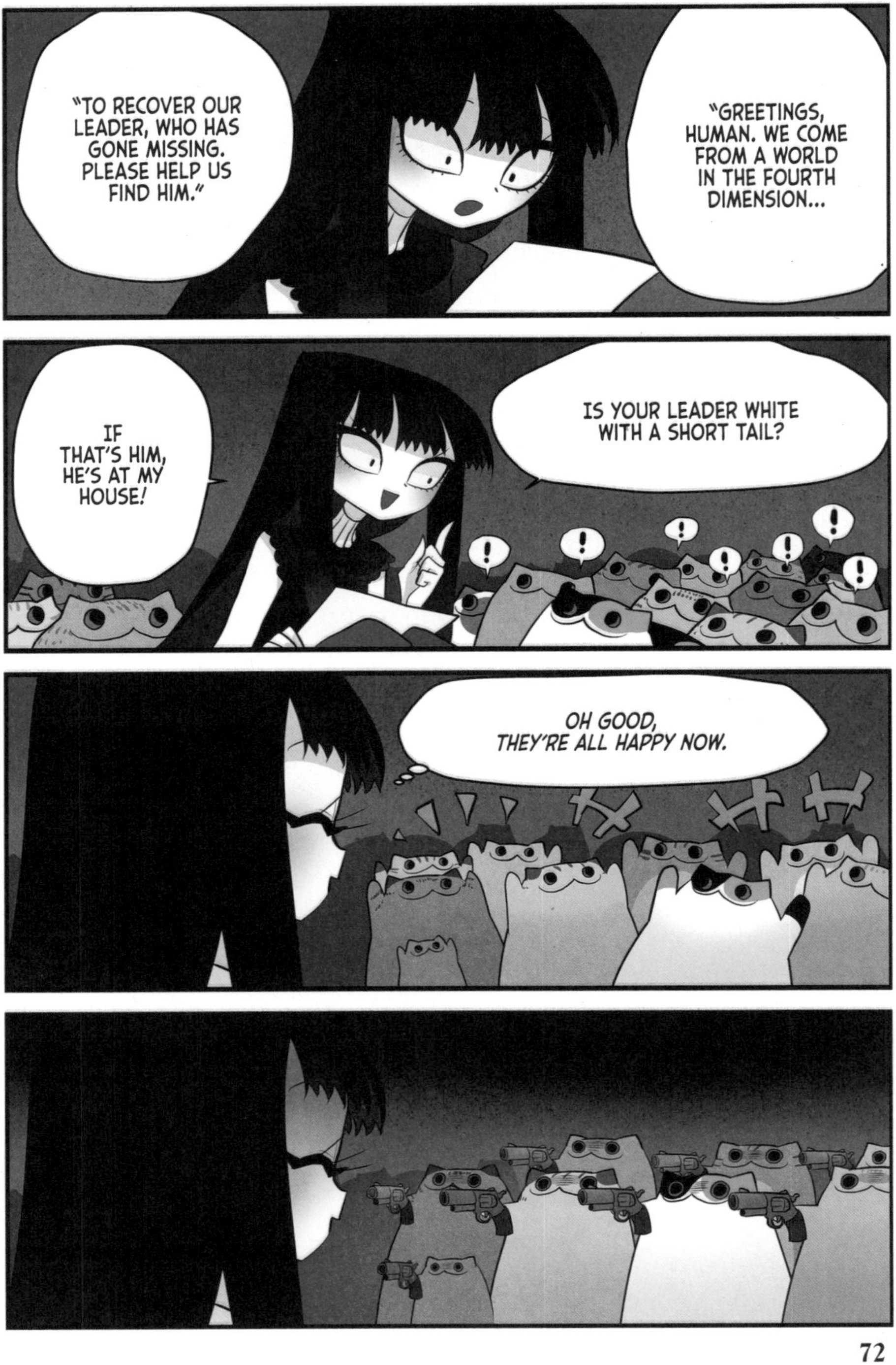
"GREETINGS, HUMAN. WE COME FROM A WORLD IN THE FOURTH DIMENSION...
"TO RECOVER OUR LEADER, WHO HAS GONE MISSING. PLEASE HELP US FIND HIM."
IS YOUR LEADER WHITE WITH A SHORT TAIL?
IF THAT'S HIM, HE'S AT MY HOUSE!
OH GOOD, THEY'RE ALL HAPPY NOW.

ACCOMPLICE

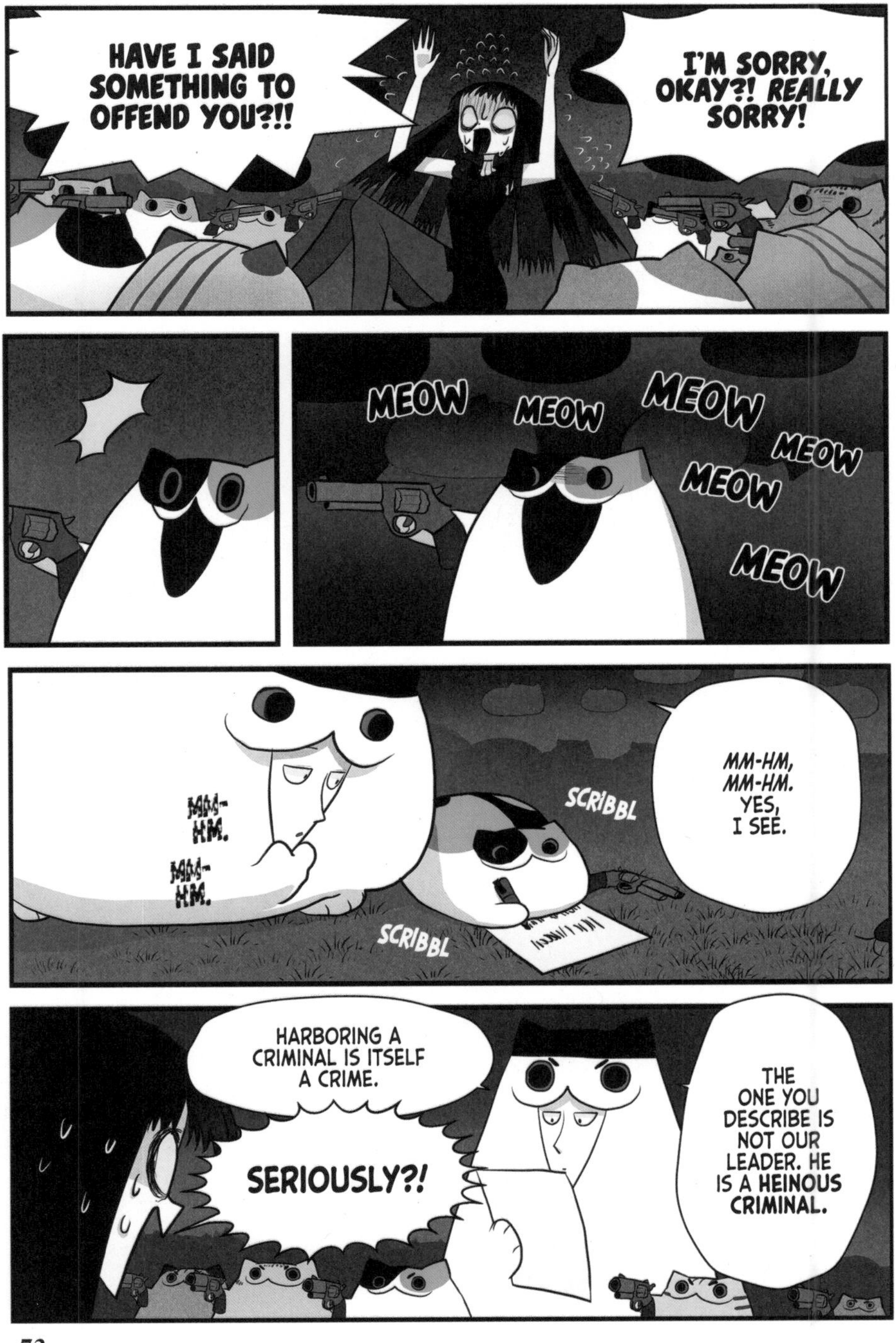

HAVE I SAID SOMETHING TO OFFEND YOU?!!
I'M SORRY, OKAY?! REALLY SORRY!
MEOW
MEOW
MEOW
MEOW
MEOW
MEOW
MM-HM, MM-HM. YES, I SEE.
SCRIBBL
MM-HM.
MM-HM.
SCRIBBL
THE ONE YOU DESCRIBE IS NOT OUR LEADER. HE IS A HEINOUS CRIMINAL.
HARBORING A CRIMINAL IS ITSELF A CRIME.
SERIOUSLY?!

TERROR

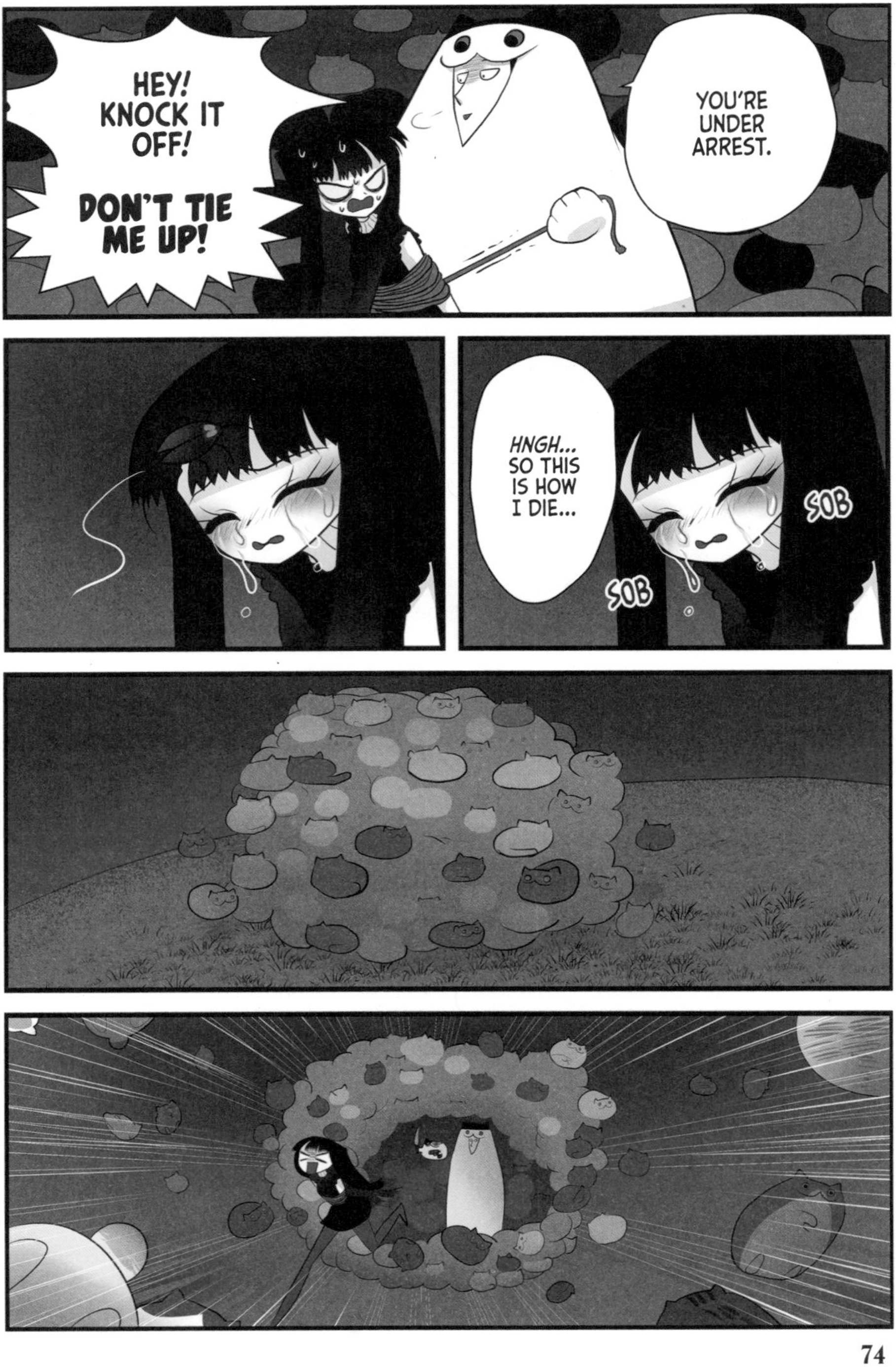
HEY! KNOCK IT OFF!
DON'T TIE ME UP!
YOU'RE UNDER ARREST.
HNGH... SO THIS IS HOW I DIE...
SOB
SOB

DREAM

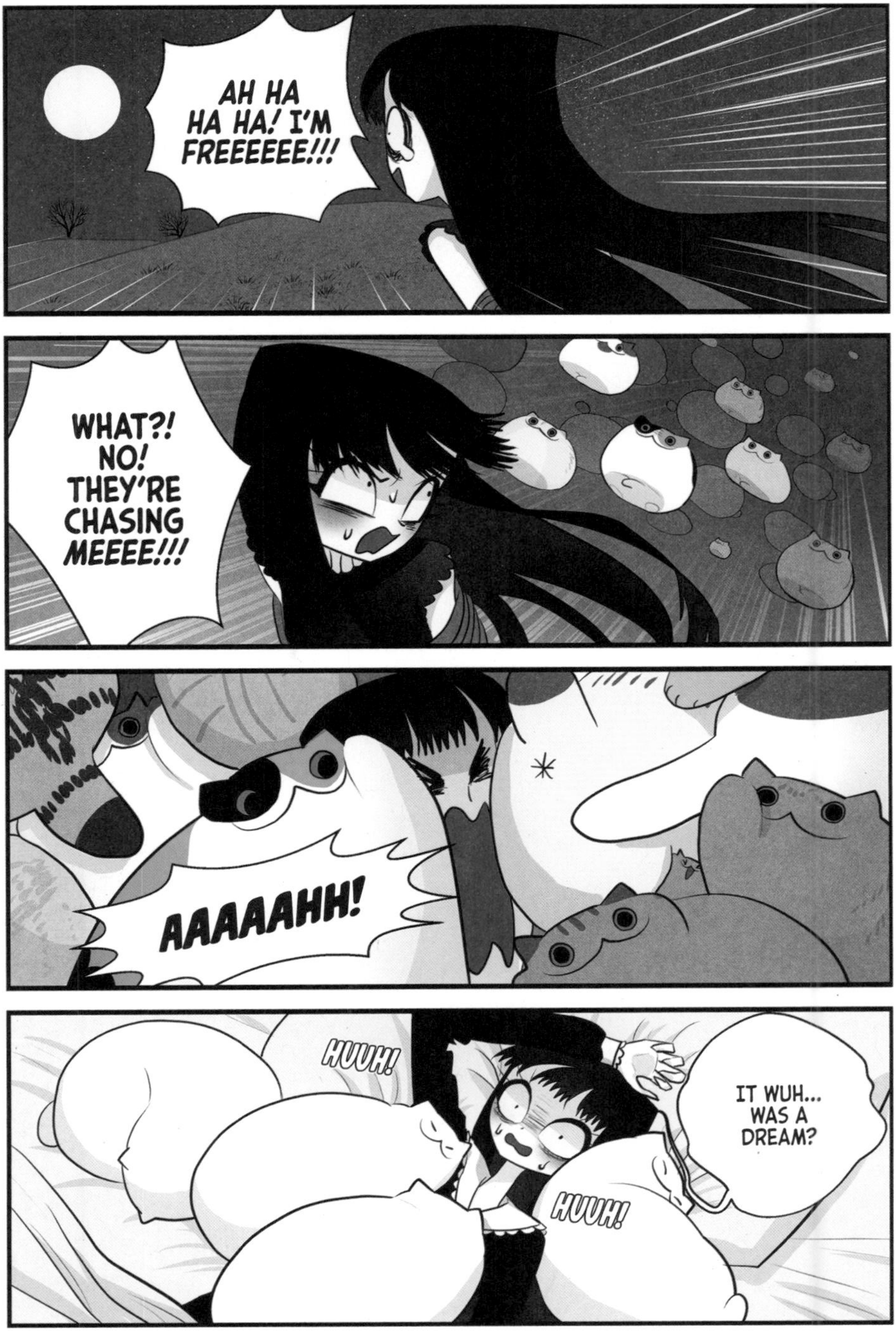

AH HA HA HA! I'M FREEEEEE!!!
WHAT?! NO! THEY'RE CHASING MEEEE!!!
AAAAAHH!
HUUH!
IT WUH... WAS A DREAM?
HUUH!

CREEPIER CAT

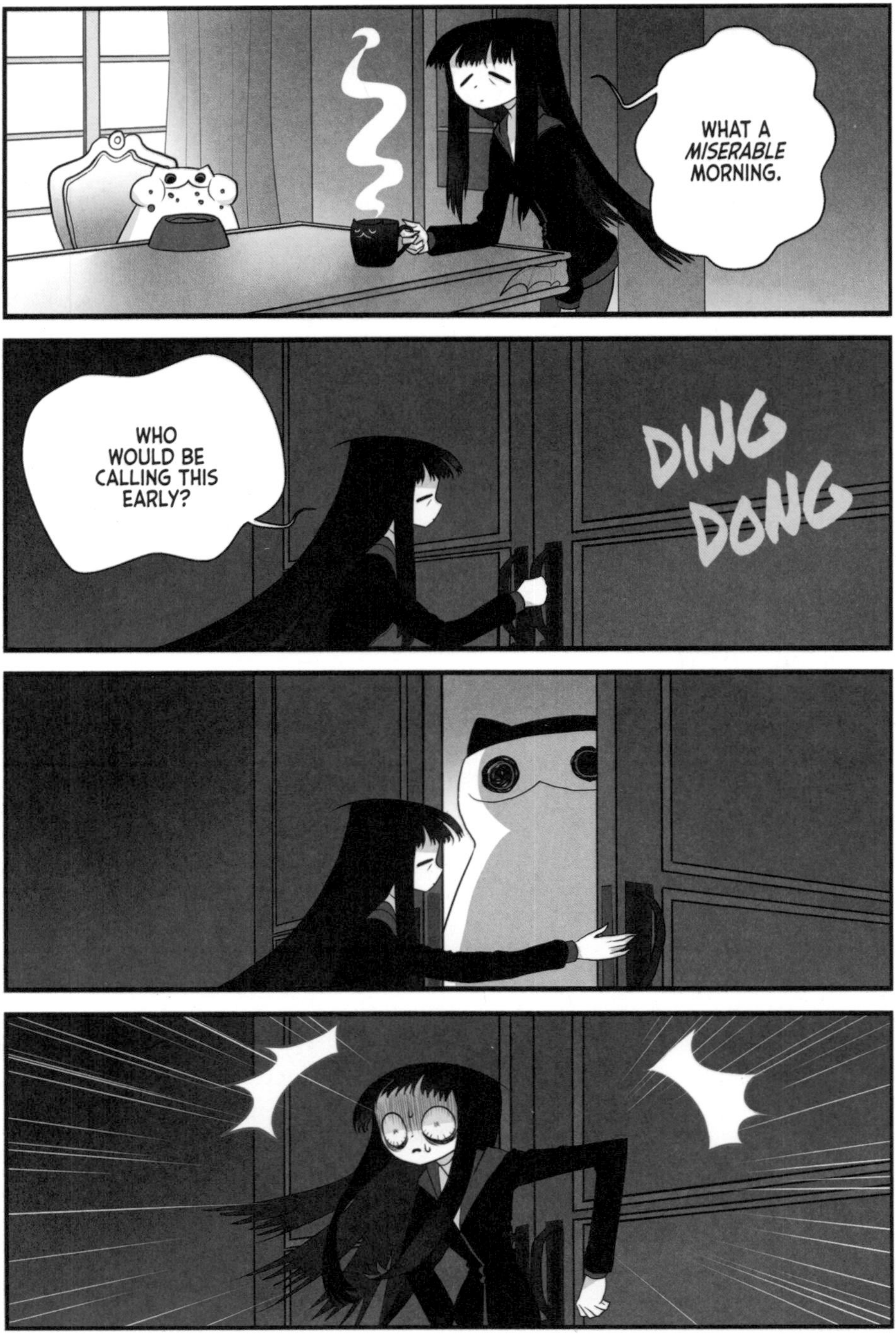

WHAT A *MISERABLE* MORNING.
WHO WOULD BE CALLING THIS EARLY?
DING DONG

MEETING

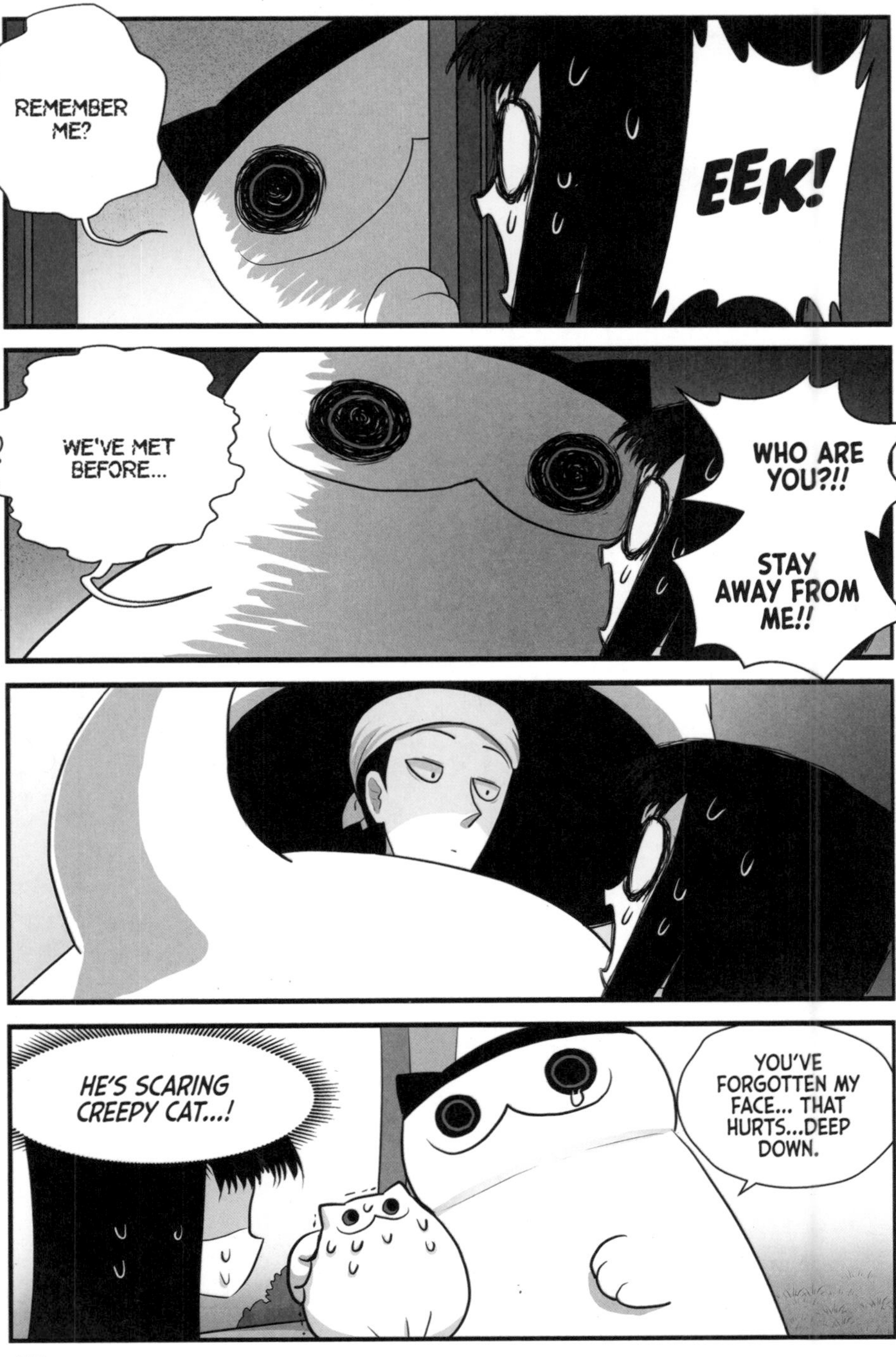
REMEMBER ME?
EEK!
WE'VE MET BEFORE...
WHO ARE YOU?!!
STAY AWAY FROM ME!!
HE'S SCARING CREEPY CAT...!
YOU'VE FORGOTTEN MY FACE... THAT HURTS...DEEP DOWN.

ANIMAL COSTUMES

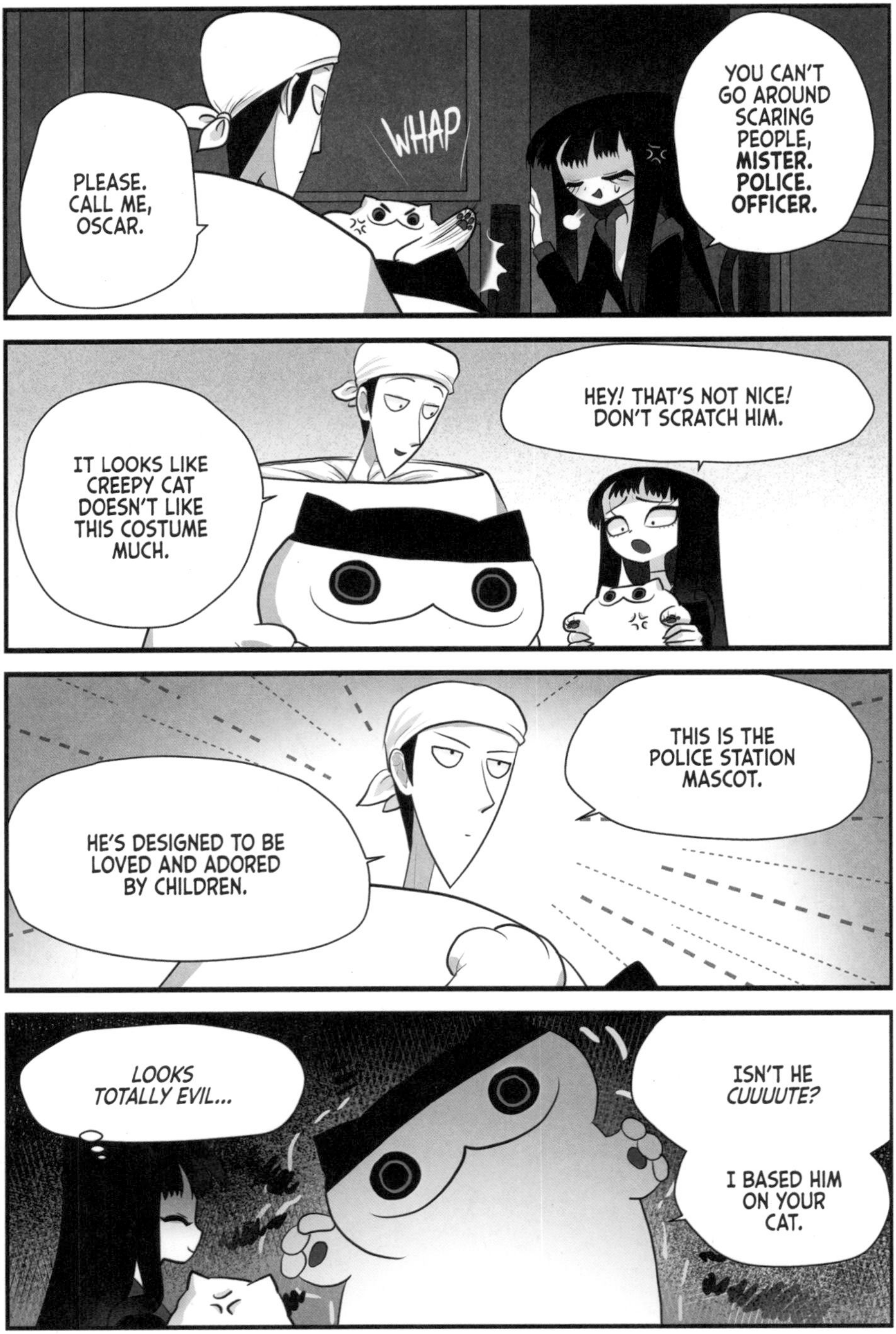

YOU CAN'T GO AROUND SCARING PEOPLE, **MISTER. POLICE. OFFICER.**
WHAP
PLEASE. CALL ME, OSCAR.
HEY! THAT'S NOT NICE! DON'T SCRATCH HIM.
IT LOOKS LIKE CREEPY CAT DOESN'T LIKE THIS COSTUME MUCH.
THIS IS THE POLICE STATION MASCOT.
HE'S DESIGNED TO BE LOVED AND ADORED BY CHILDREN.
ISN'T HE *CUUUUTE?*
I BASED HIM ON YOUR CAT.
LOOKS TOTALLY EVIL...

JUST A DREAM

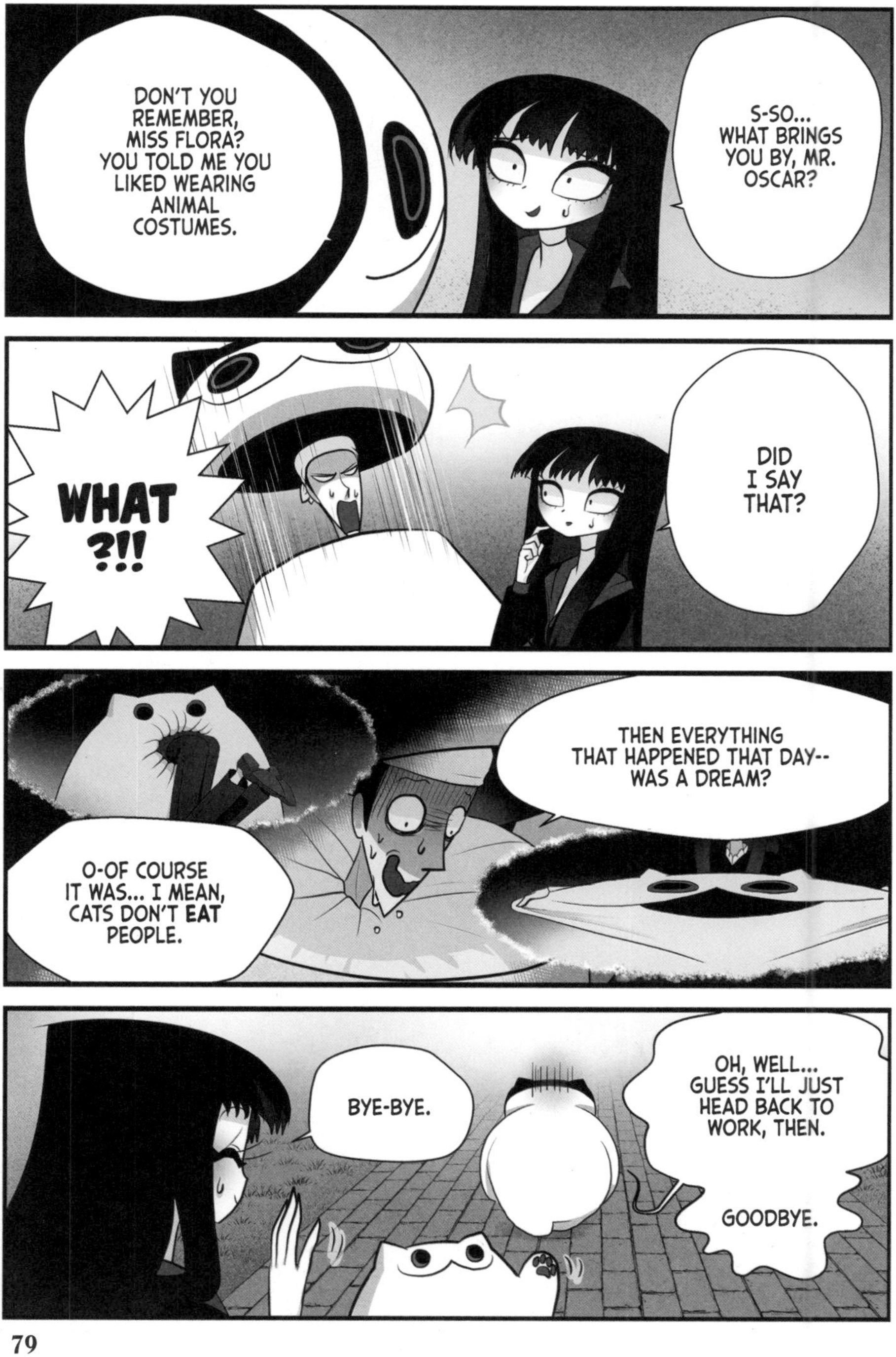
DON'T YOU REMEMBER, MISS FLORA? YOU TOLD ME YOU LIKED WEARING ANIMAL COSTUMES.
S-SO... WHAT BRINGS YOU BY, MR. OSCAR?
WHAT ?!!
DID I SAY THAT?
THEN EVERYTHING THAT HAPPENED THAT DAY-- WAS A DREAM?
O-OF COURSE IT WAS... I MEAN, CATS DON'T EAT PEOPLE.
OH, WELL... GUESS I'LL JUST HEAD BACK TO WORK, THEN.
GOODBYE.
BYE-BYE.

CREEPY KITTY

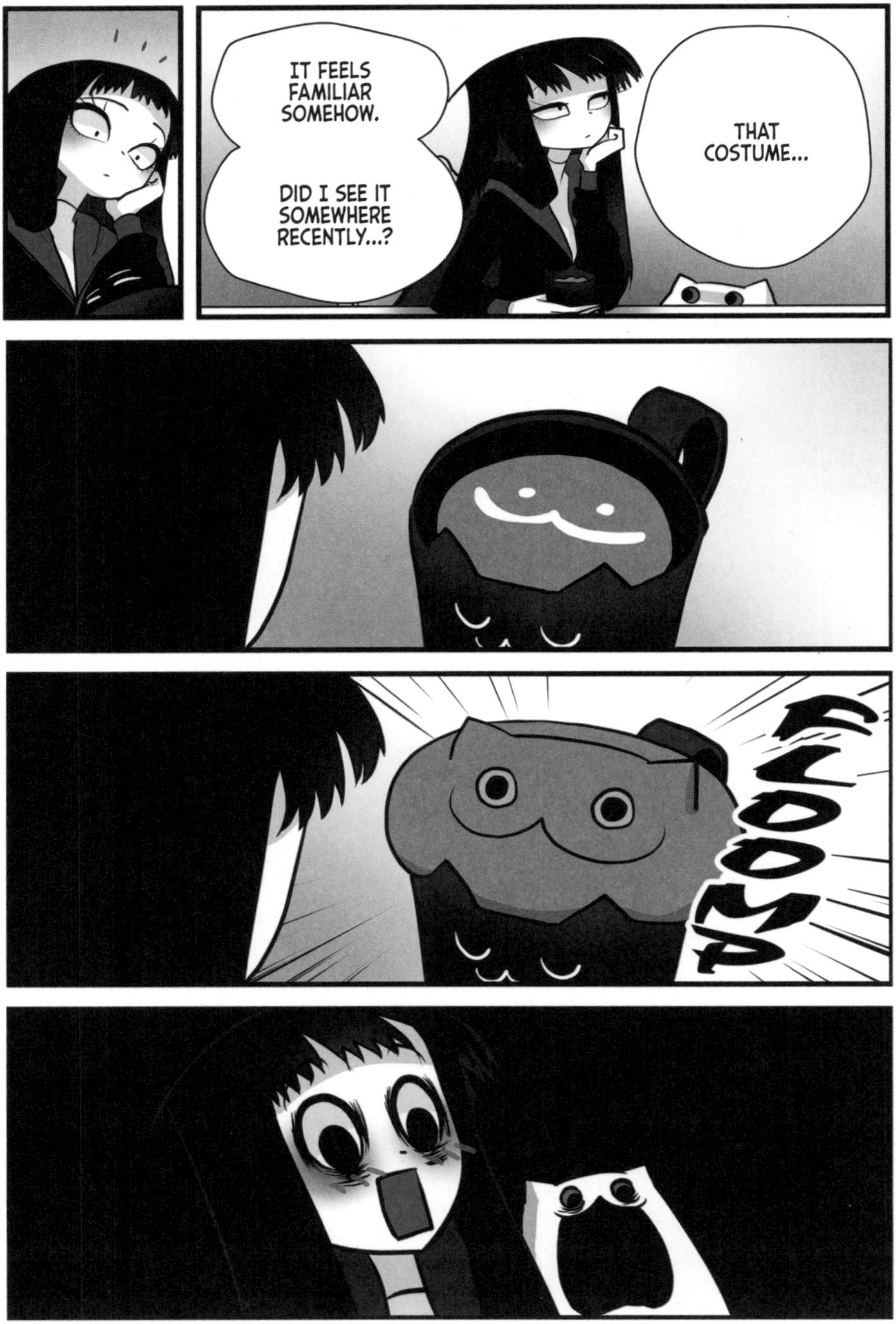
THAT COSTUME...
IT FEELS FAMILIAR SOMEHOW.
DID I SEE IT SOMEWHERE RECENTLY...?
FLOOMP

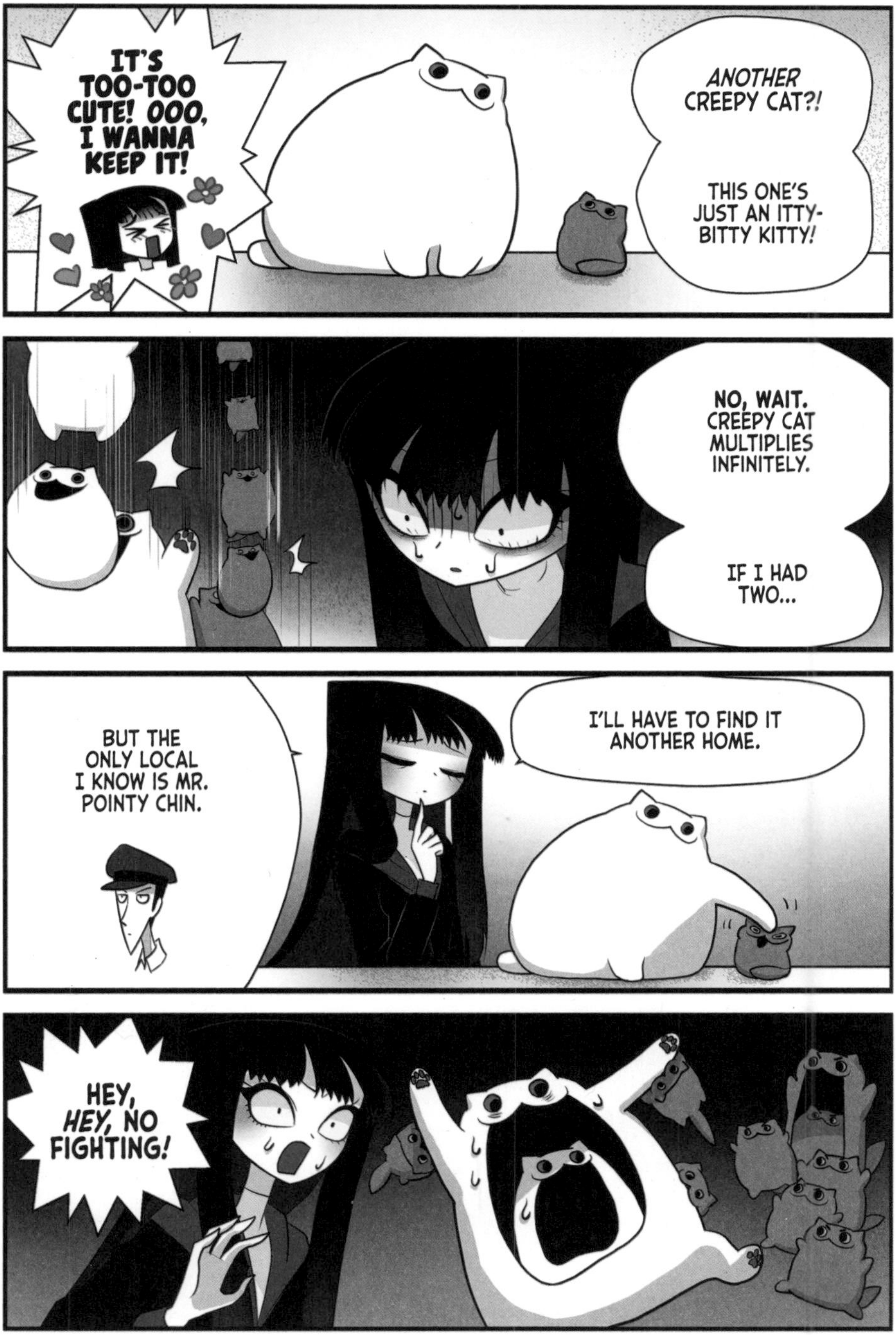
IT'S TOO-TOO CUTE! OOO, I WANNA KEEP IT!
ANOTHER CREEPY CAT?!
THIS ONE'S JUST AN ITTY-BITTY KITTY!
NO, WAIT. CREEPY CAT MULTIPLIES INFINITELY.
IF I HAD TWO...
I'LL HAVE TO FIND IT ANOTHER HOME.
BUT THE ONLY LOCAL I KNOW IS MR. POINTY CHIN.
HEY, HEY, NO FIGHTING!

AT THE POLICE STATION

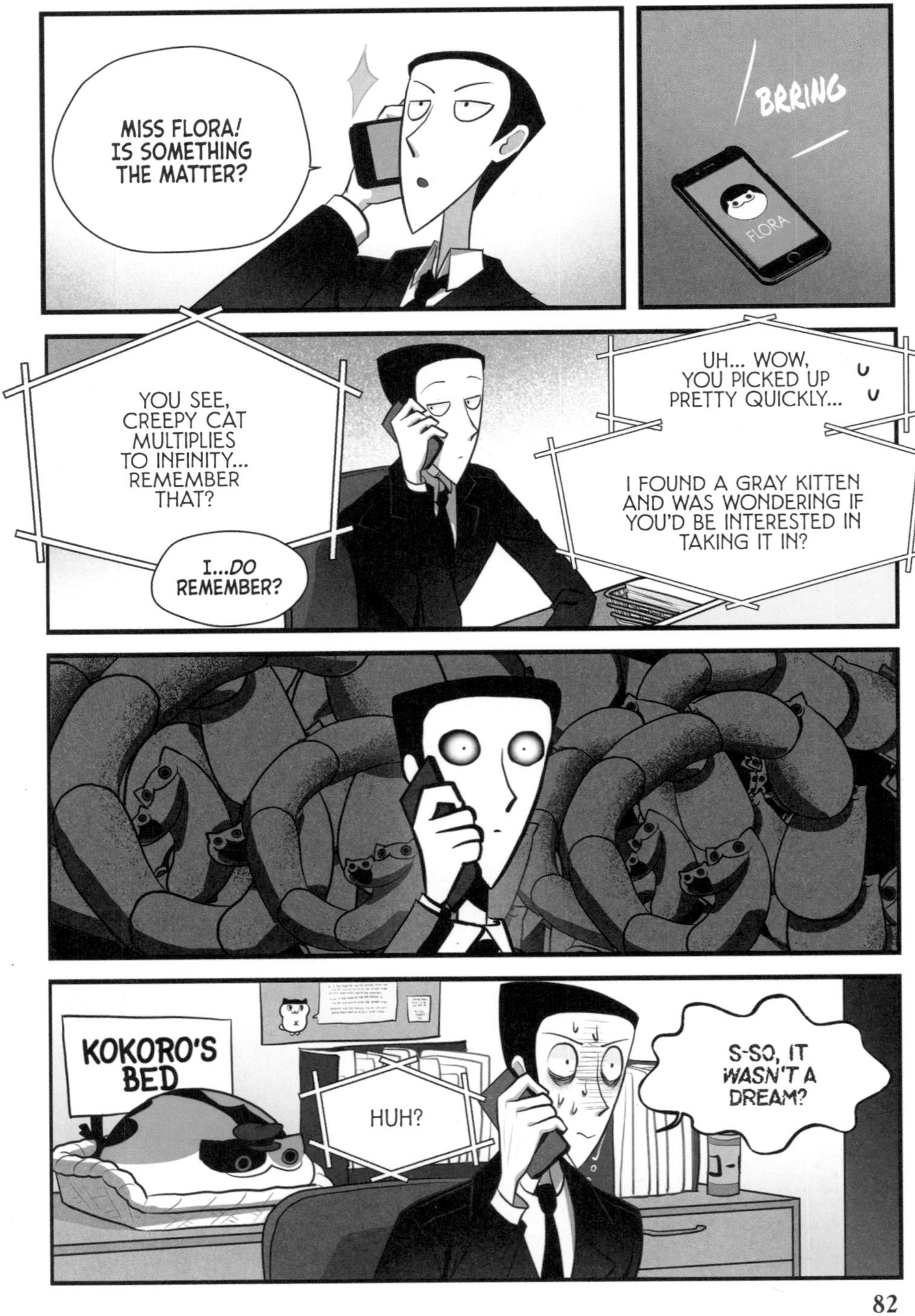
BRRING
FLORA
MISS FLORA! IS SOMETHING THE MATTER?
YOU SEE, CREEPY CAT MULTIPLIES TO INFINITY... REMEMBER THAT?
I...DO REMEMBER?
UH... WOW, YOU PICKED UP PRETTY QUICKLY...
I FOUND A GRAY KITTEN AND WAS WONDERING IF YOU'D BE INTERESTED IN TAKING IT IN?
KOKORO'S BED
HUH?
S-SO, IT WASN'T A DREAM?

TOO BAD

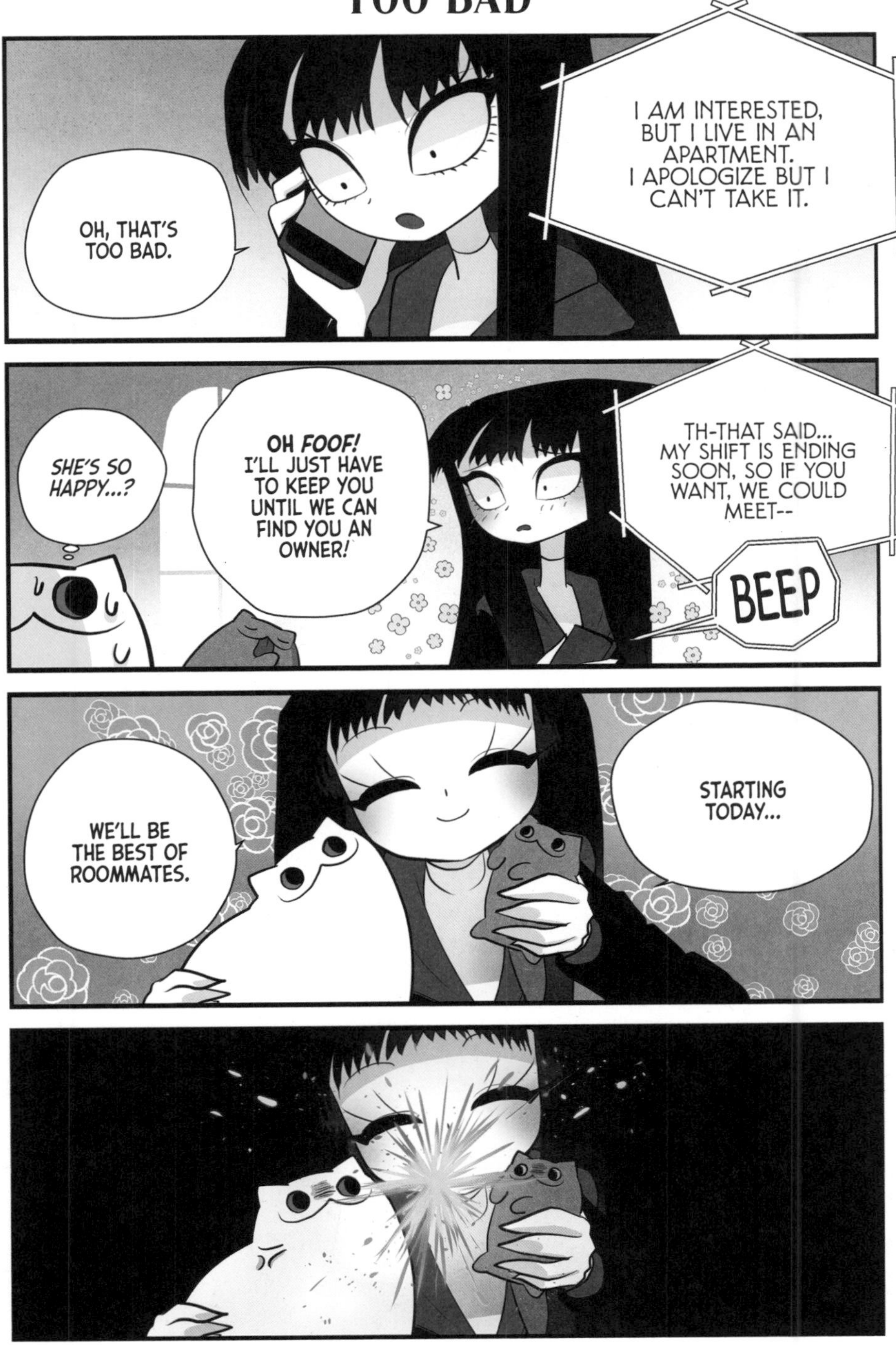

I *AM* INTERESTED, BUT I LIVE IN AN APARTMENT. I APOLOGIZE BUT I CAN'T TAKE IT.
OH, THAT'S TOO BAD.
TH-THAT SAID... MY SHIFT IS ENDING SOON, SO IF YOU WANT, WE COULD MEET--
BEEP
OH *FOOF!* I'LL JUST HAVE TO KEEP YOU UNTIL WE CAN FIND YOU AN OWNER!
SHE'S SO HAPPY...?
STARTING TODAY...
WE'LL BE THE BEST OF ROOMMATES.

OOPS! MY BED

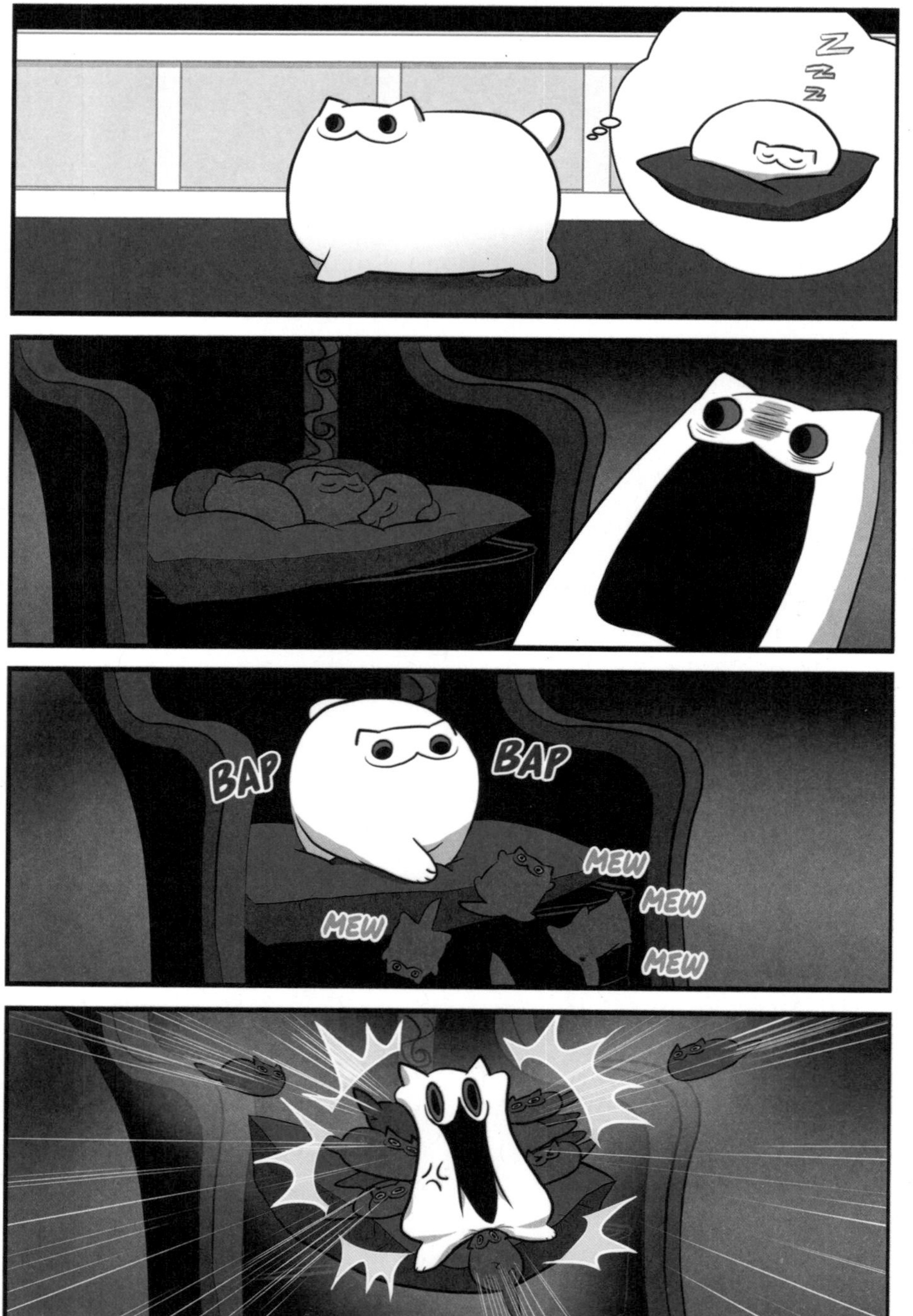
Z
Z
Z
BAP
BAP
MEW
MEW
MEW
MEW

MY SLAVE

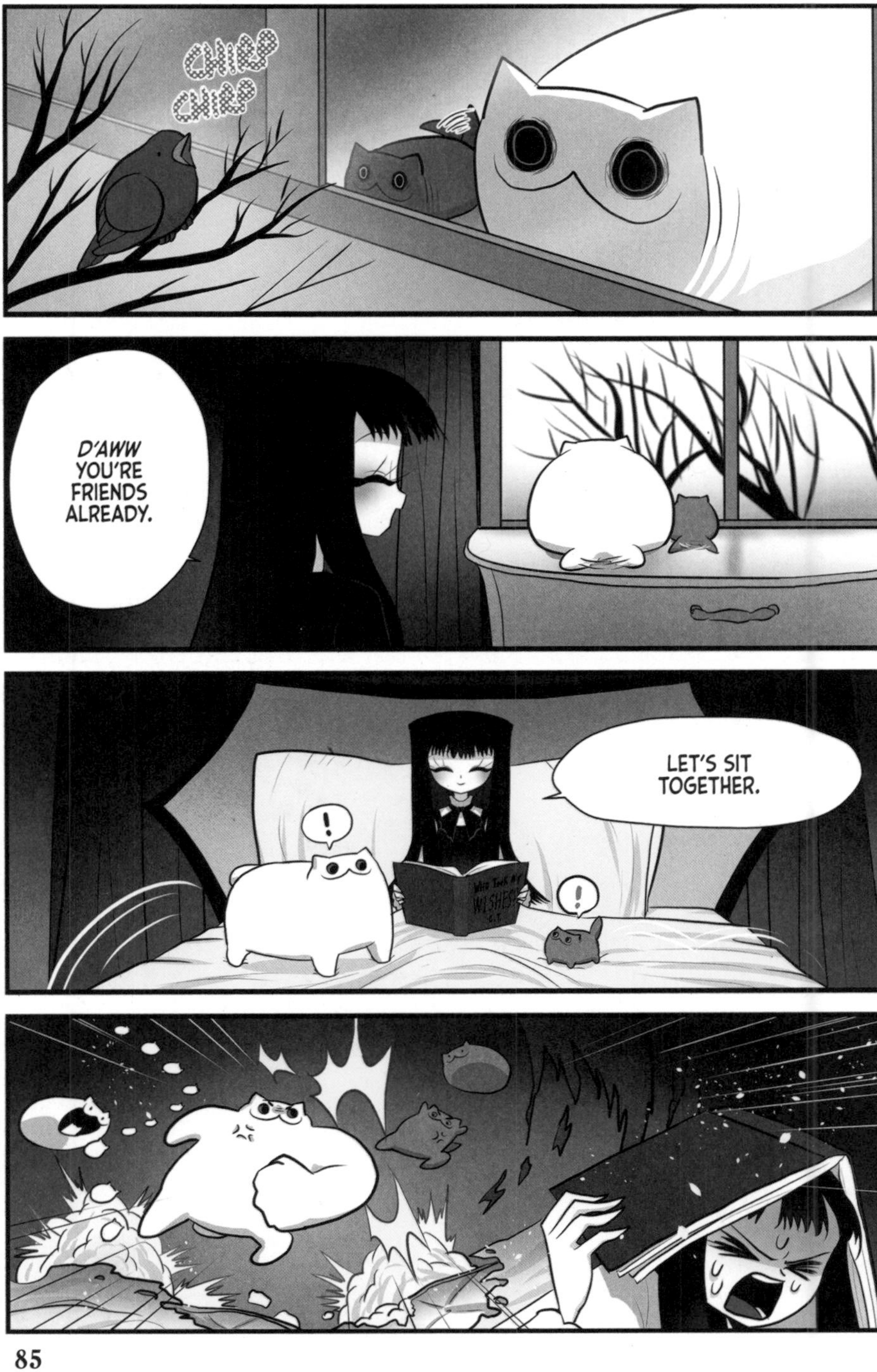
CHIRP
CHIRP
D'AWW YOU'RE FRIENDS ALREADY.
LET'S SIT TOGETHER.
!
!

THIEF I

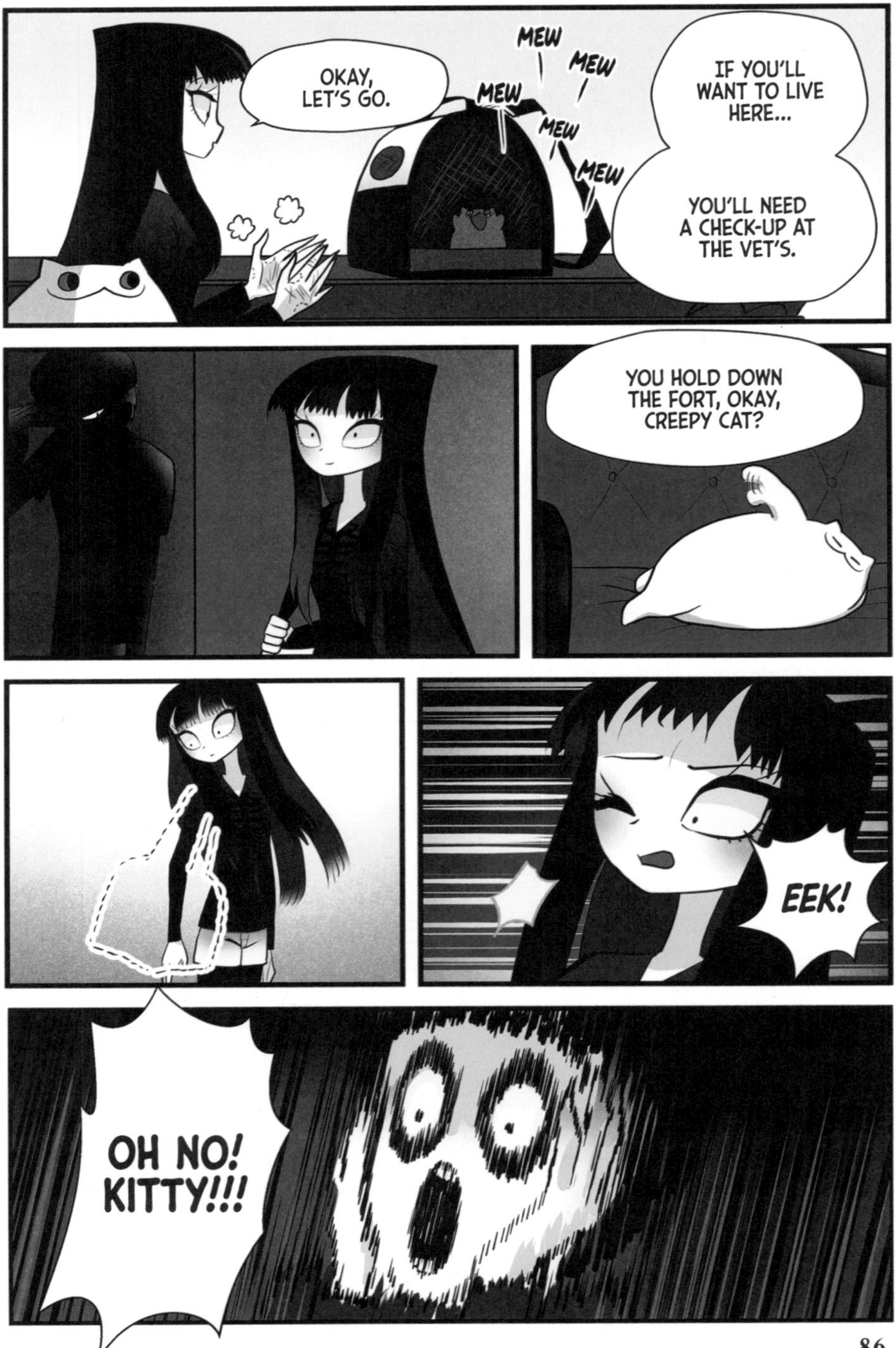

OKAY, LET'S GO.
MEW
MEW
MEW
MEW
MEW
IF YOU'LL WANT TO LIVE HERE...
YOU'LL NEED A CHECK-UP AT THE VET'S.
YOU HOLD DOWN THE FORT, OKAY, CREEPY CAT?
EEK!
OH NO! KITTY!!!

THIEF II

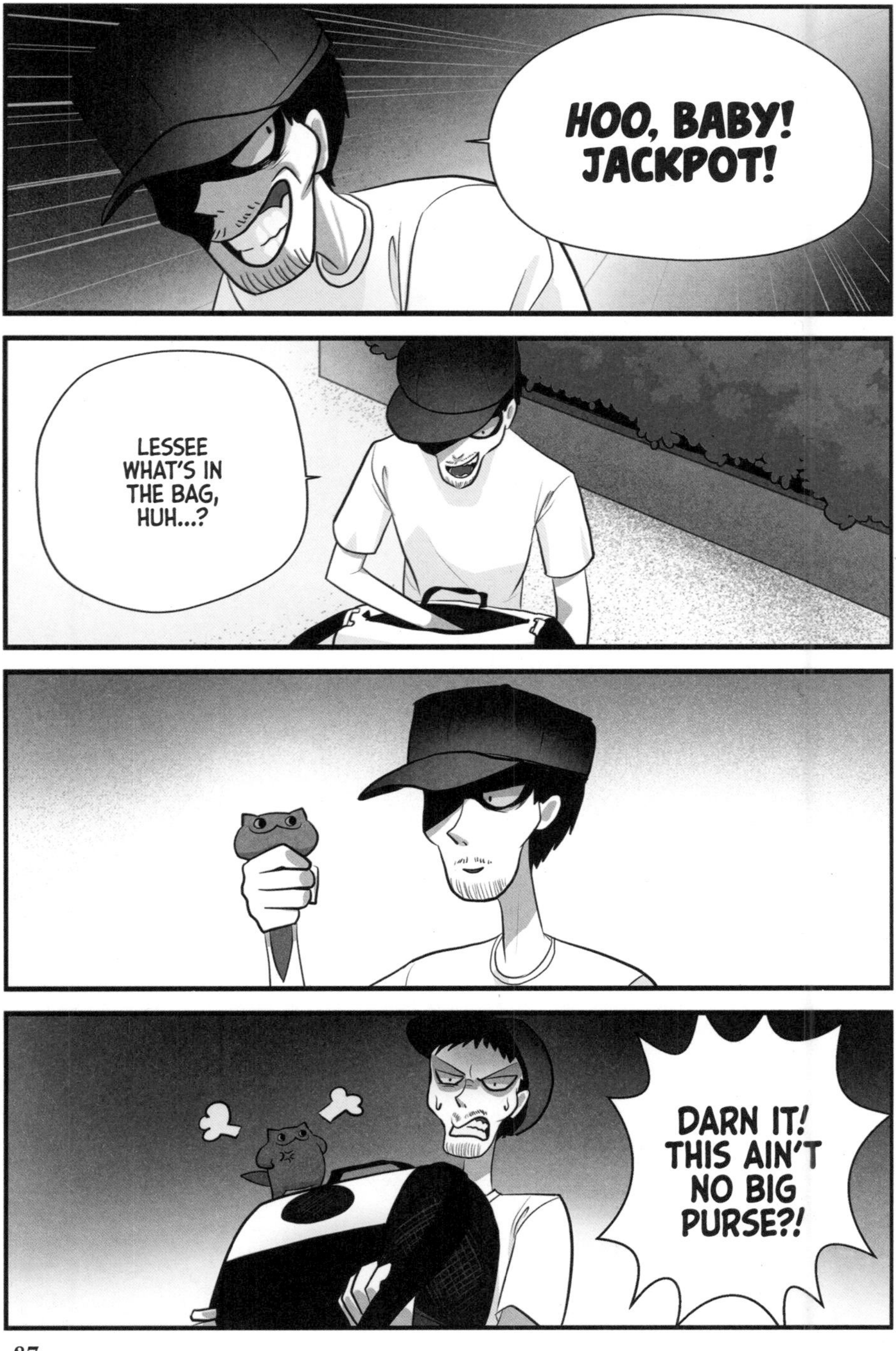
HOO, BABY! JACKPOT!
LESSEE WHAT'S IN THE BAG, HUH...?
DARN IT! THIS AIN'T NO BIG PURSE?!

THIEF III

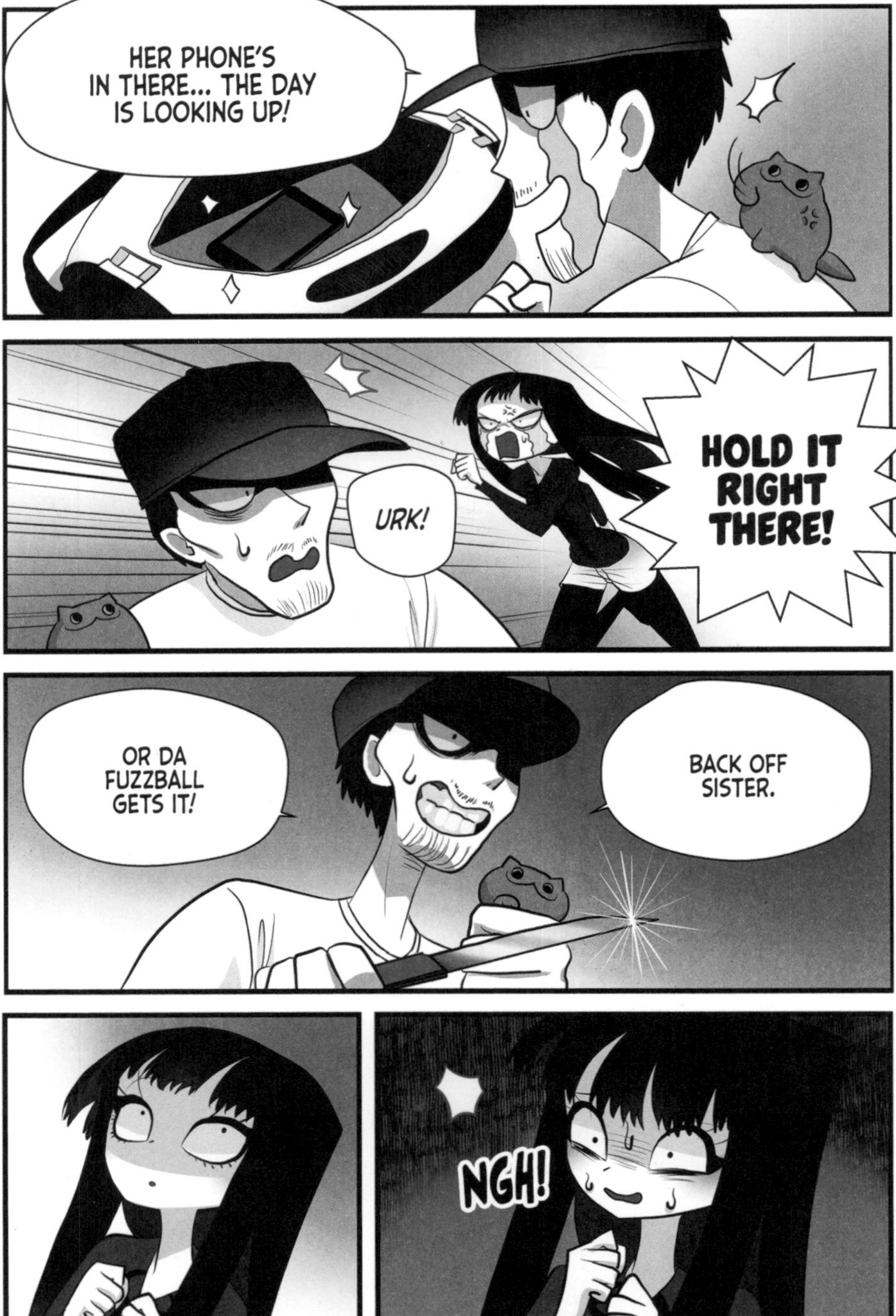
HER PHONE'S IN THERE... THE DAY IS LOOKING UP!
HOLD IT RIGHT THERE!
URK!
BACK OFF SISTER.
OR DA FUZZBALL GETS IT!
NGH!

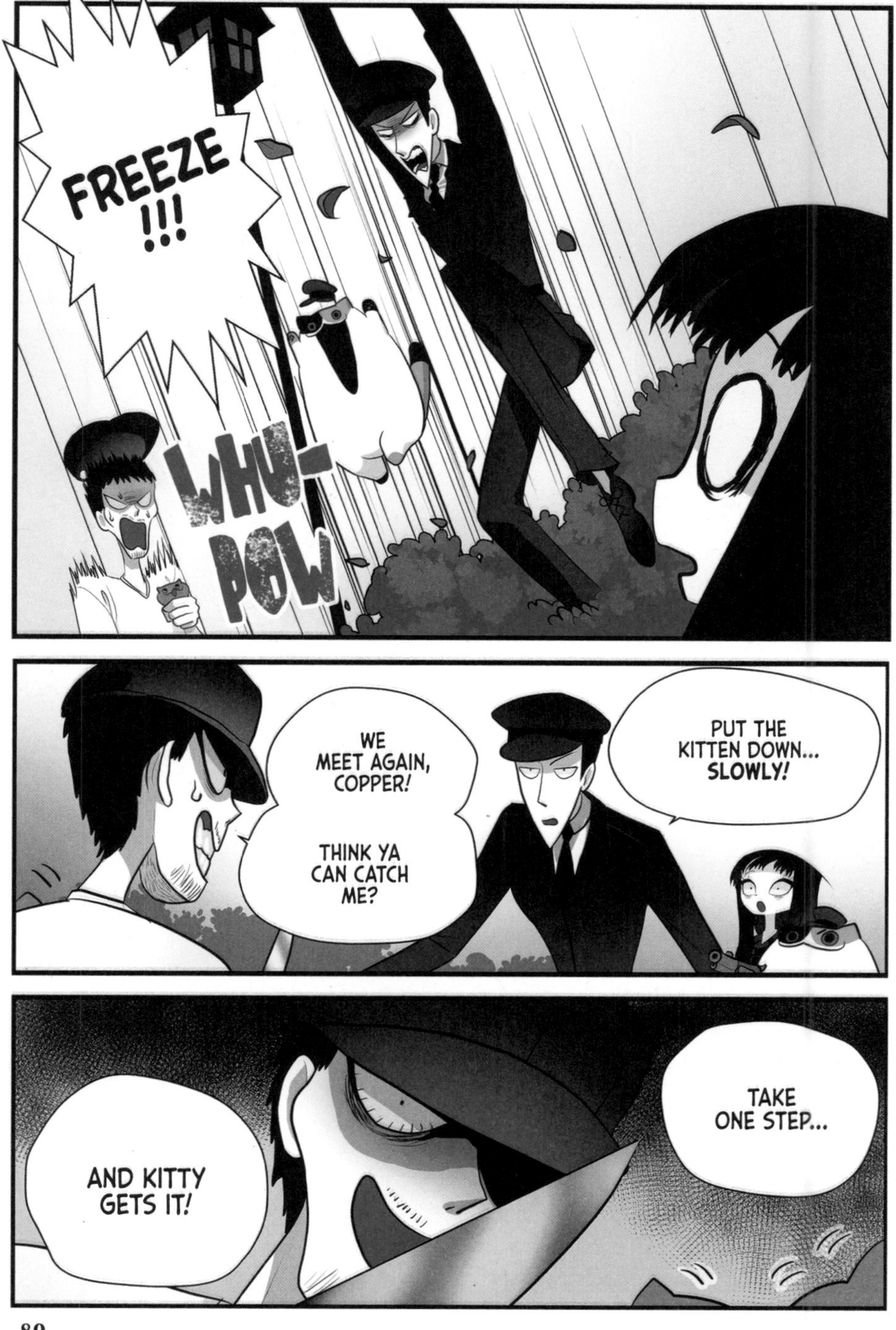
FREEZE !!!
WHU-POW
WE MEET AGAIN, COPPER!
THINK YA CAN CATCH ME?
PUT THE KITTEN DOWN... SLOWLY!
TAKE ONE STEP...
AND KITTY GETS IT!

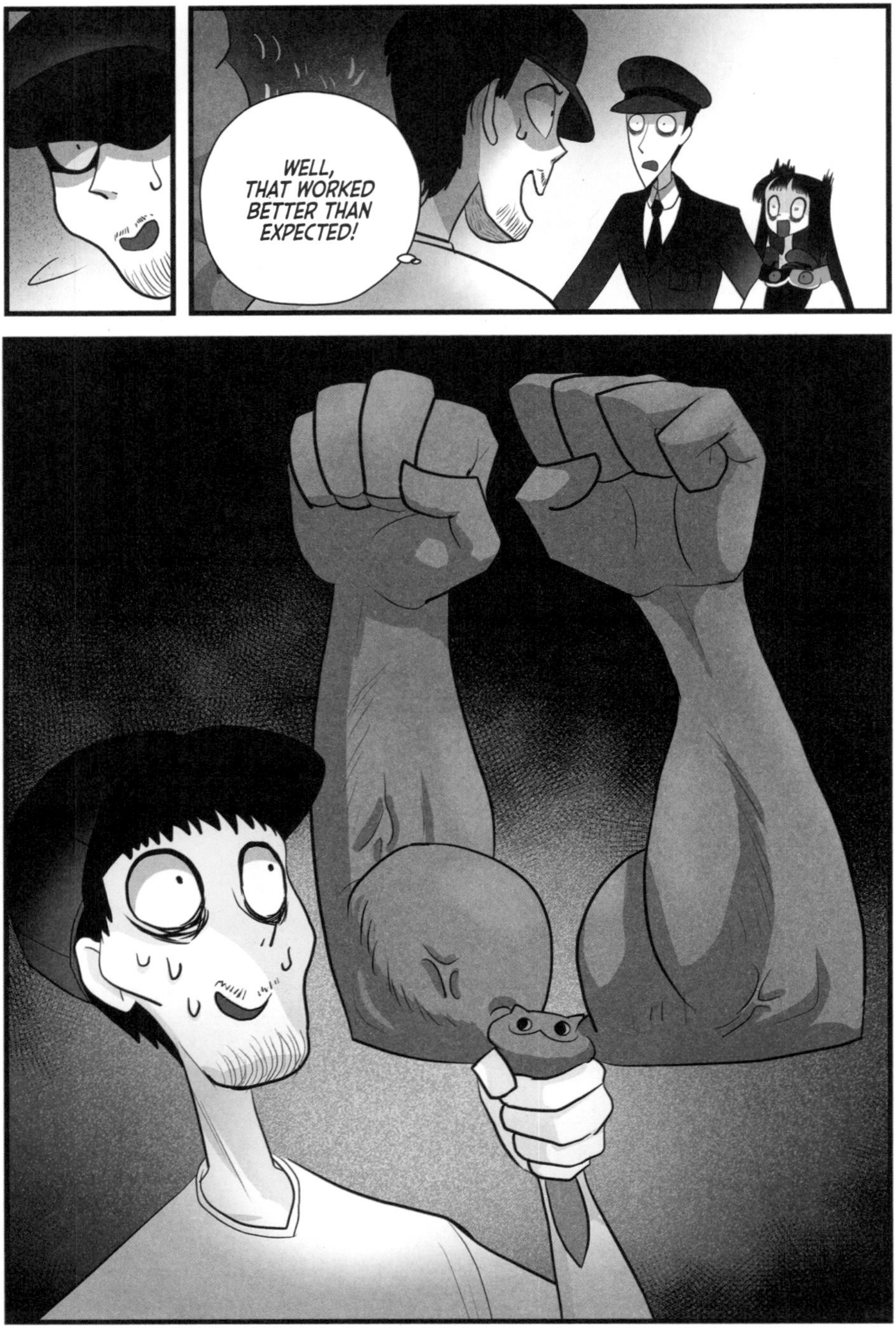
WELL, THAT WORKED BETTER THAN EXPECTED!

STRONG KITTY II

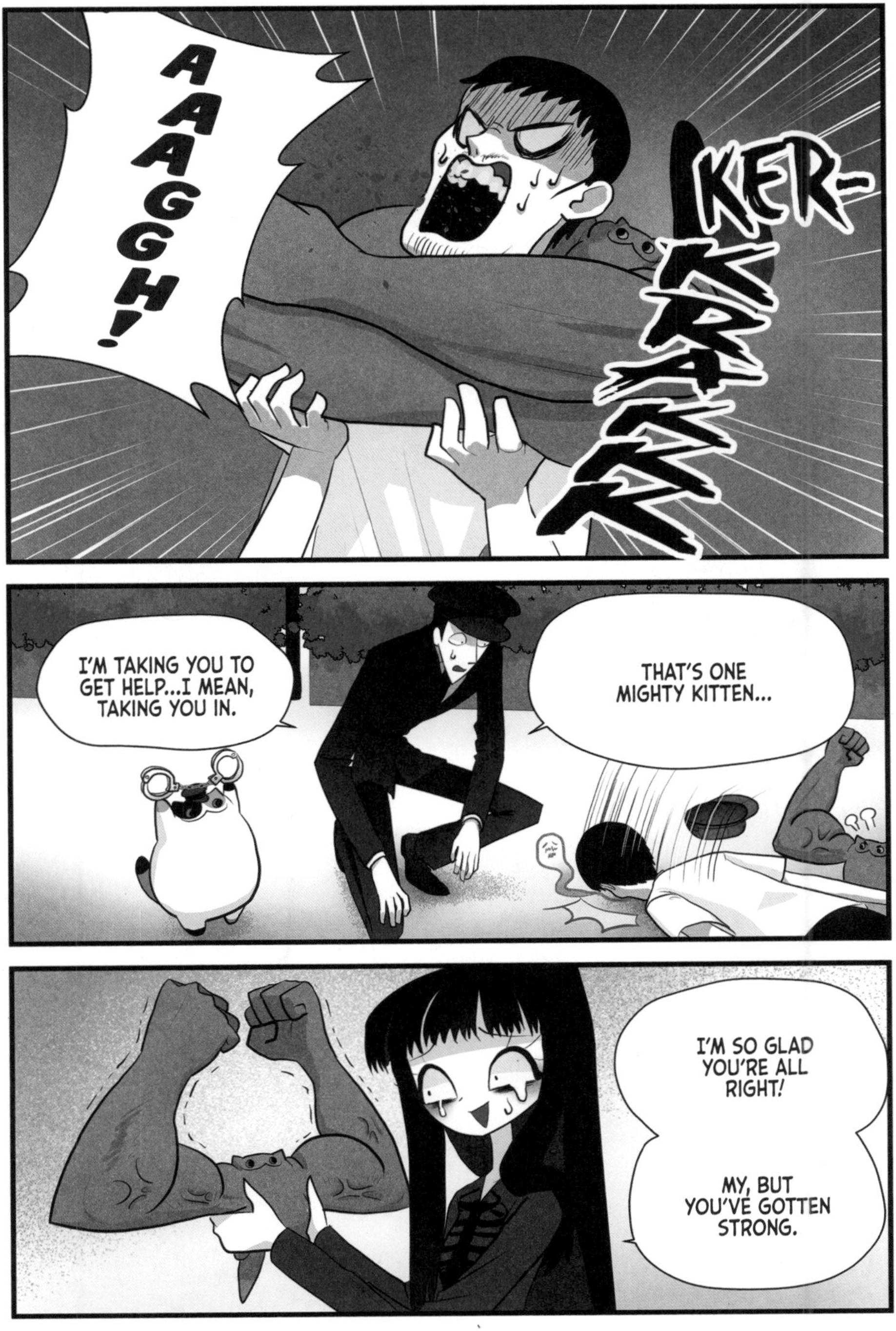
AAAGGH!
KER-KRAKK
I'M TAKING YOU TO GET HELP...I MEAN, TAKING YOU IN.
THAT'S ONE MIGHTY KITTEN...
I'M SO GLAD YOU'RE ALL RIGHT!
MY, BUT YOU'VE GOTTEN STRONG.

A NEW TEAM

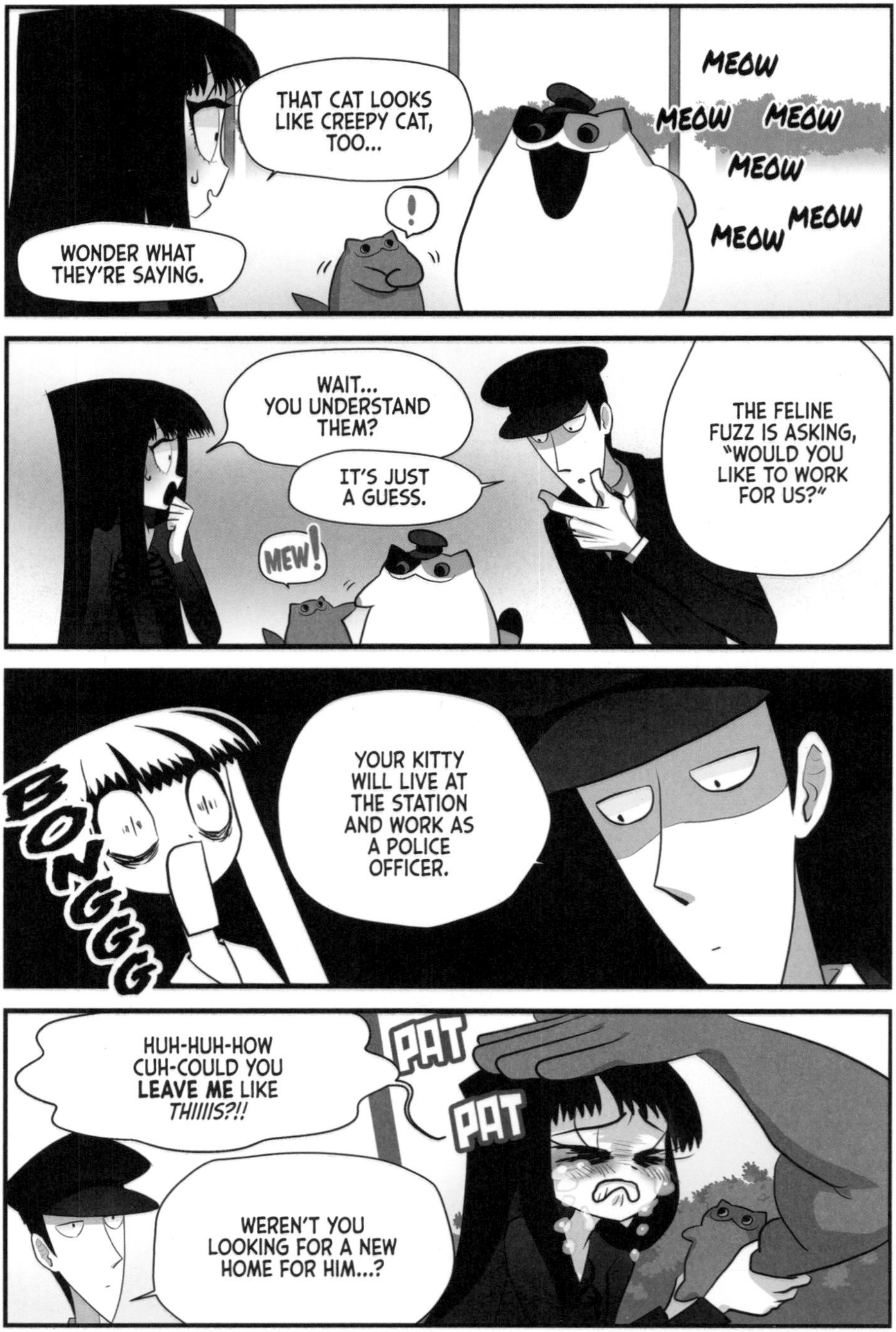
THAT CAT LOOKS LIKE CREEPY CAT, TOO...
WONDER WHAT THEY'RE SAYING.
!
MEOW
MEOW MEOW
MEOW
MEOW MEOW
WAIT... YOU UNDERSTAND THEM?
IT'S JUST A GUESS.
THE FELINE FUZZ IS ASKING, "WOULD YOU LIKE TO WORK FOR US?"
MEW!
BONGGG
YOUR KITTY WILL LIVE AT THE STATION AND WORK AS A POLICE OFFICER.
HUH-HUH-HOW CUH-COULD YOU **LEAVE ME** LIKE *THIIIIS?!!*
PAT
PAT
WEREN'T YOU LOOKING FOR A NEW HOME FOR HIM...?

GOODBYE

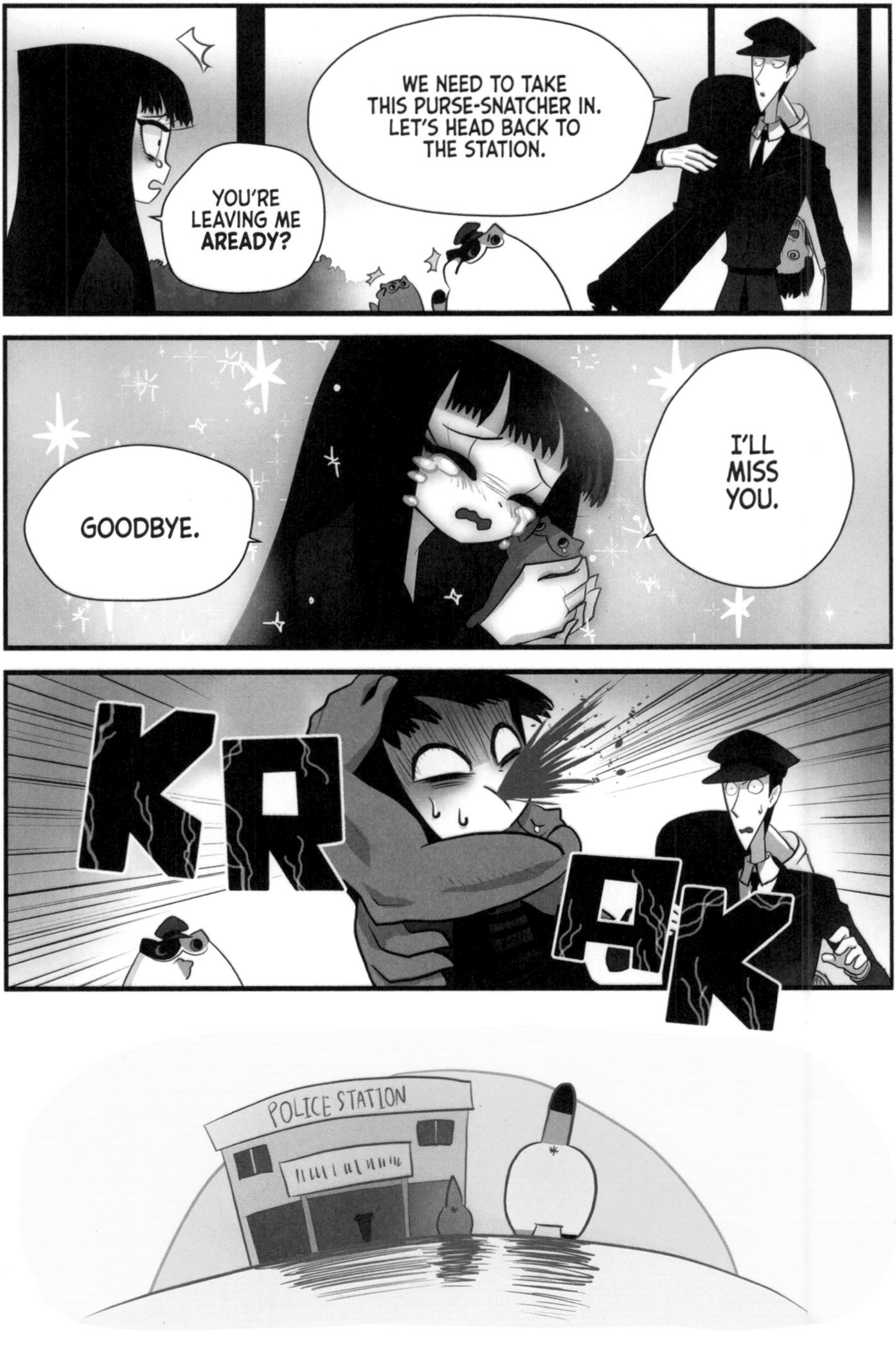
WE NEED TO TAKE THIS PURSE-SNATCHER IN. LET'S HEAD BACK TO THE STATION.
YOU'RE LEAVING ME AREADY?
I'LL MISS YOU.
GOODBYE.
KRAK
POLICE STATION

JUST THE TWO OF US

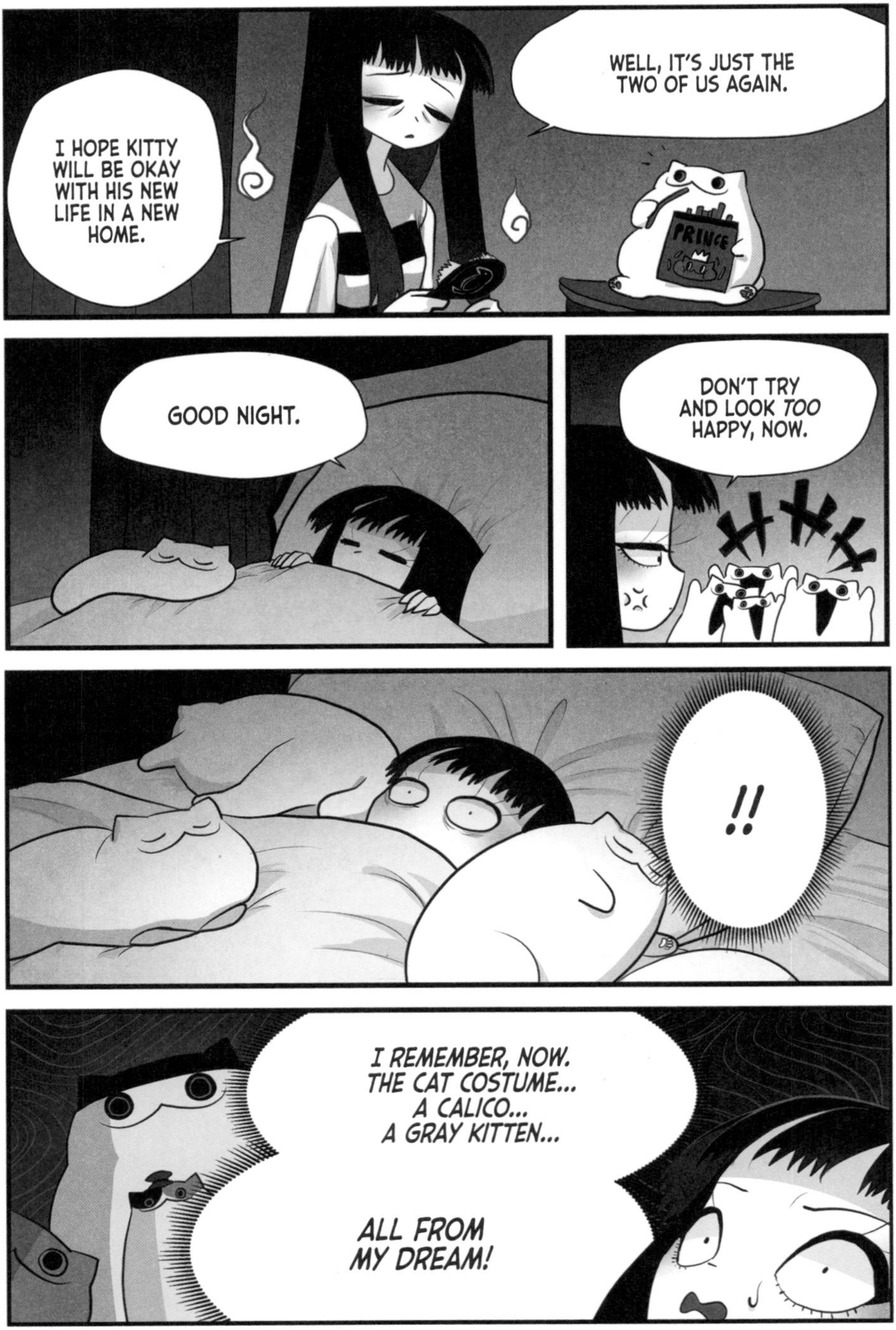

WELL, IT'S JUST THE TWO OF US AGAIN.
I HOPE KITTY WILL BE OKAY WITH HIS NEW LIFE IN A NEW HOME.
PRINCE
GOOD NIGHT.
DON'T TRY AND LOOK *TOO* HAPPY, NOW.
!!
I REMEMBER, NOW. THE CAT COSTUME... A CALICO... A GRAY KITTEN...
ALL FROM MY DREAM!

GOOD NIGHT

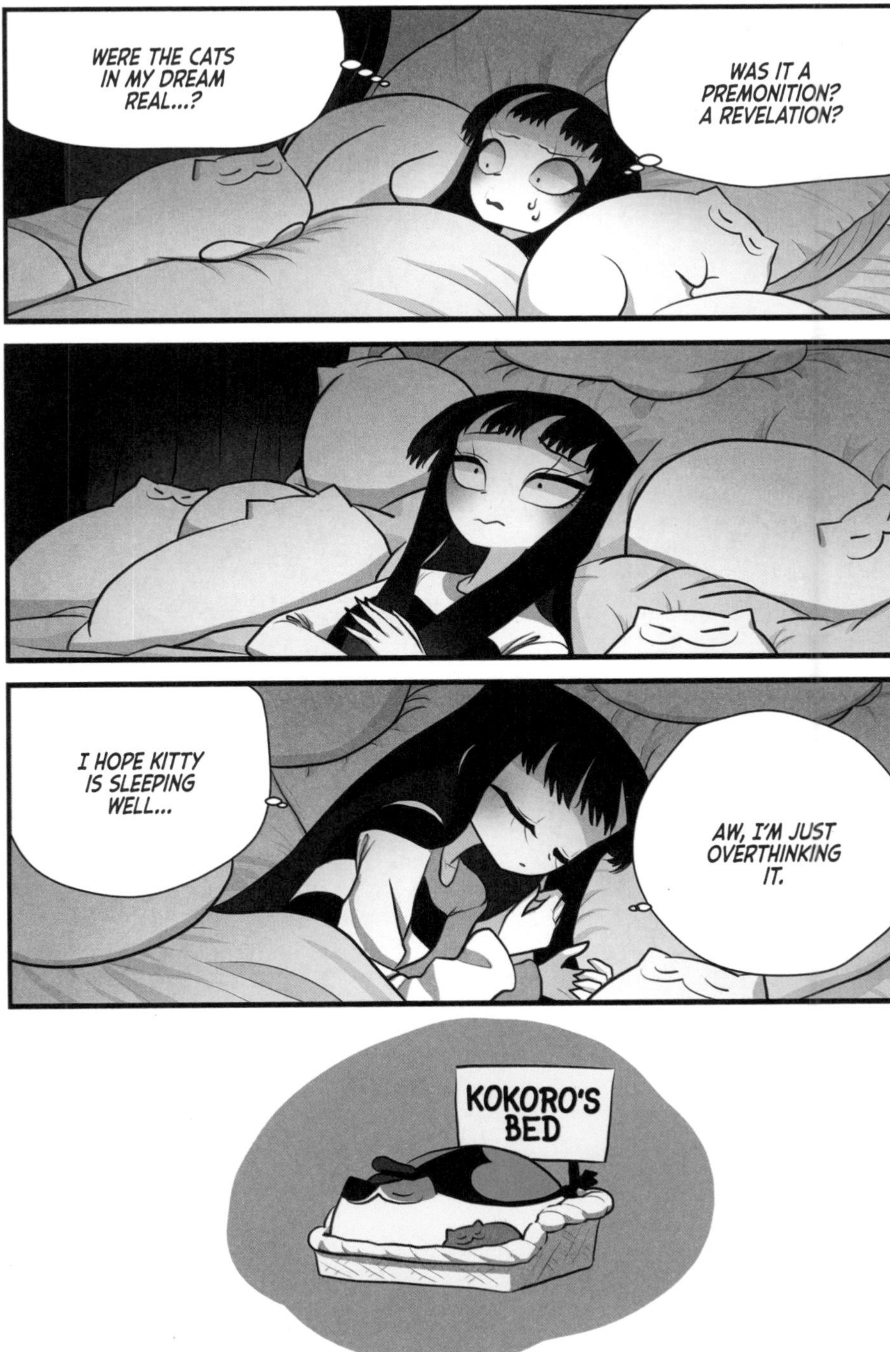

WERE THE CATS IN MY DREAM REAL...?
WAS IT A PREMONITION? A REVELATION?
I HOPE KITTY IS SLEEPING WELL...
AW, I'M JUST OVERTHINKING IT.
KOKORO'S BED

A NORMAL CAT

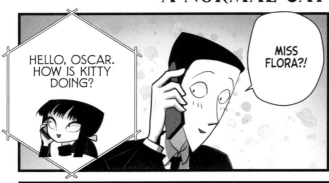

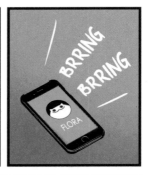

BRRING
BRRING
FLORA
MISS FLORA?!
HELLO, OSCAR. HOW IS KITTY DOING?
OH, YES... YOUR KITTEN IS DOING JUST FINE.
SHE'S WITH KOKORO.
HUH?
KOKORO? IS THAT THE CALICO CAT? PARDON MY ASKING, BUT IS KOKORO A CREEPY CAT AS WELL?
KOKORO'S BED
HIME'S BED
NO, KOKORO IS AS NORMAL AS THEY COME.
SHE AND YOUR KITTEN STICK TO EACH OTHER LIKE GLUE.
MWAH
HIME'S BED
WHAT A RELIEF!

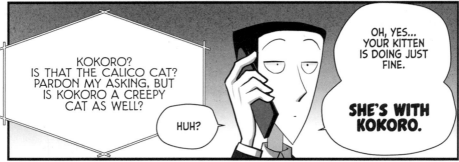

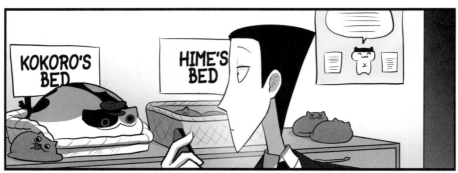

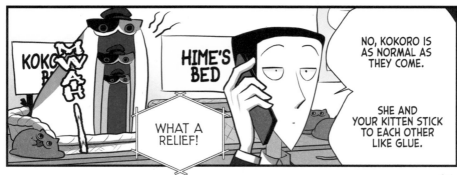

WINTER

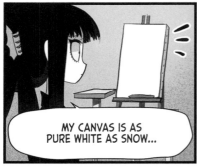

MY CANVAS IS AS PURE WHITE AS SNOW...

IT'S SNOWING!

MUMBLE...

REMINDS ME OF WHEN I WAS A LITTLE GIRL.

BACK THEN I HAD NO WORRIES ABOUT THE FUTURE, AND ALL THE LITTLE SURPRISES OF LIFE MADE ME HAPPY, LIKE I WAS RECEIVING GIFTS.

GIVE ME *THAT* GIFT AND YOU'RE **CAT PATÉ!!**

STRAY CATS I

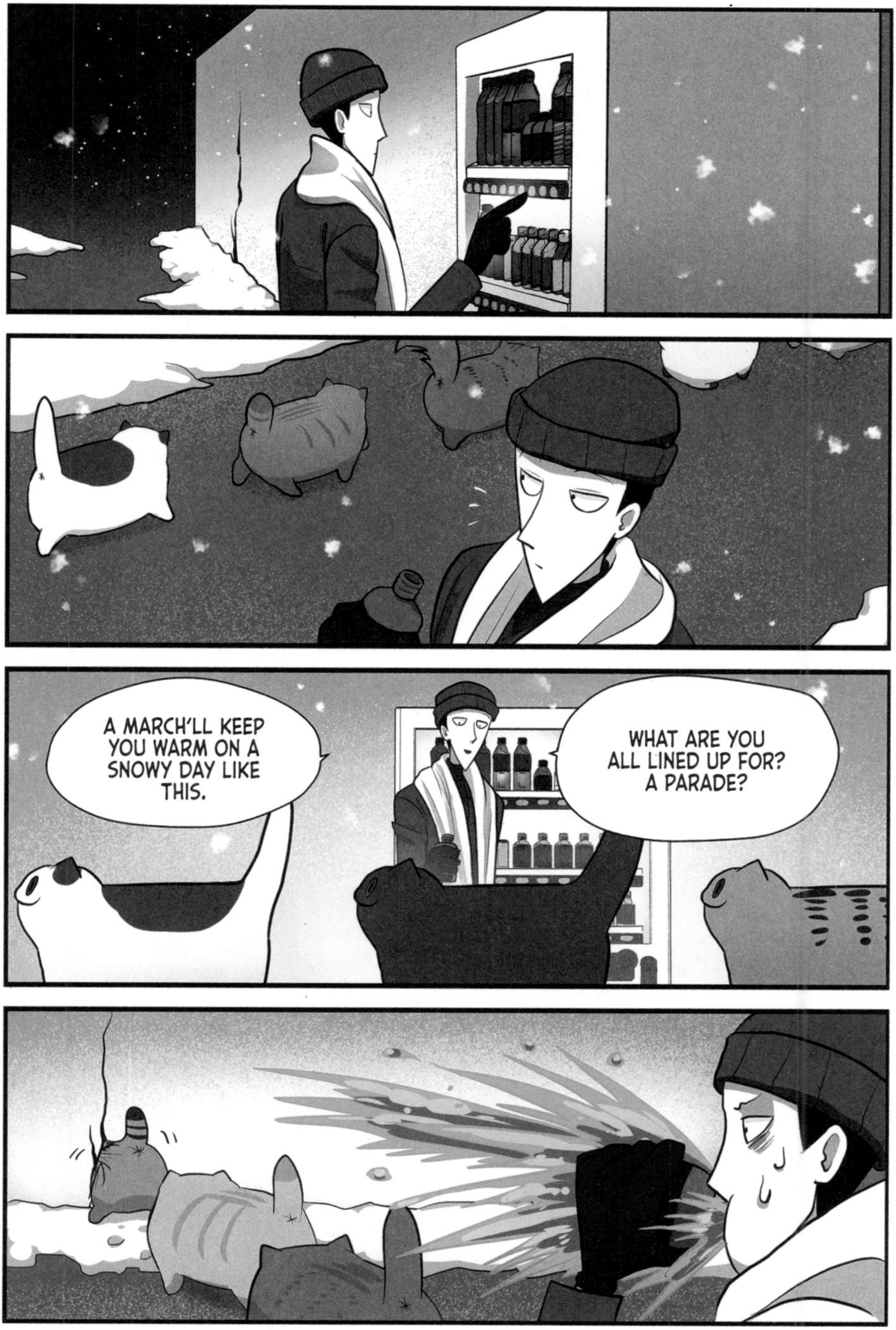
A MARCH'LL KEEP YOU WARM ON A SNOWY DAY LIKE THIS.
WHAT ARE YOU ALL LINED UP FOR? A PARADE?

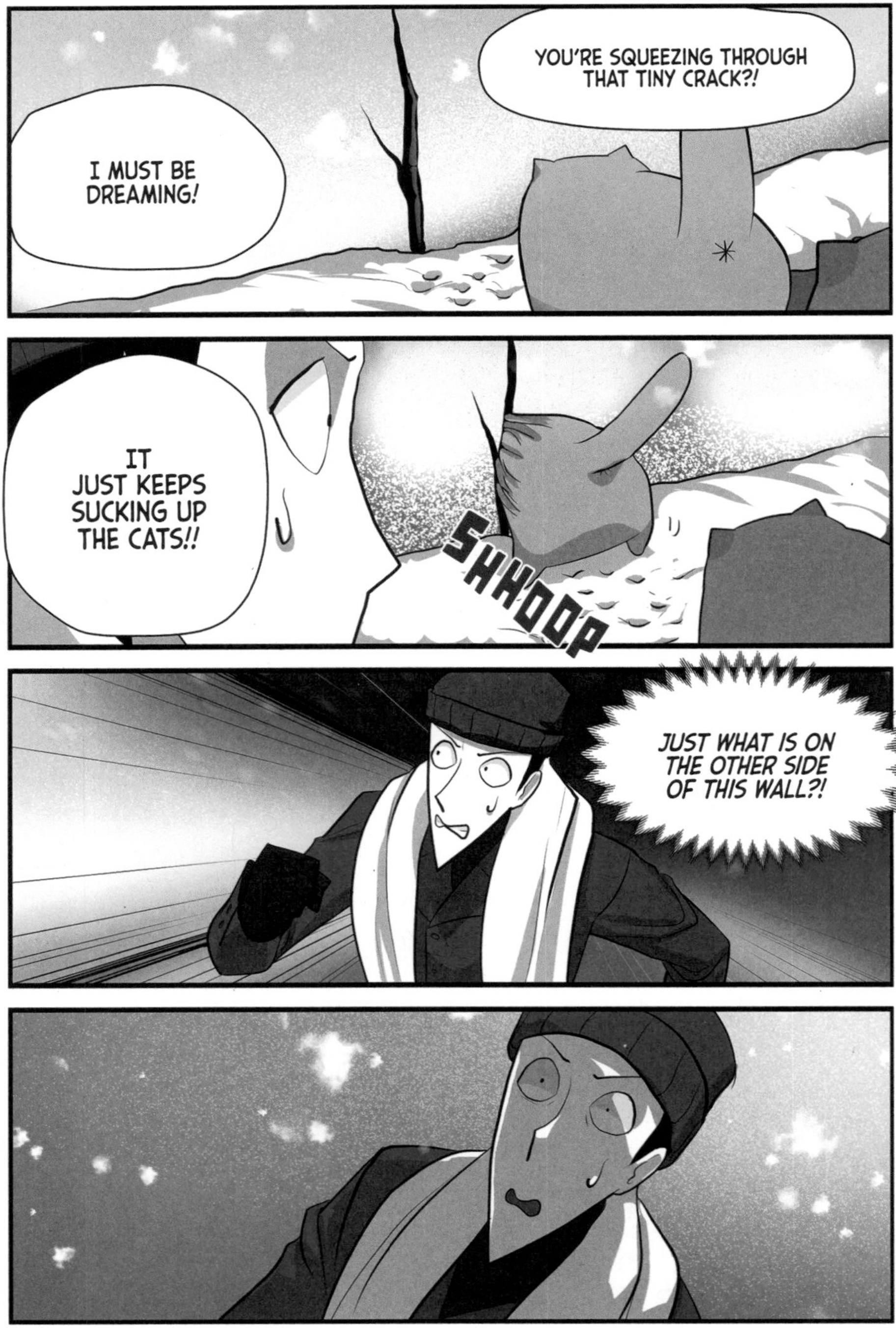
YOU'RE SQUEEZING THROUGH THAT TINY CRACK?!
I MUST BE DREAMING!
IT JUST KEEPS SUCKING UP THE CATS!!
SHHOOP
JUST WHAT IS ON THE OTHER SIDE OF THIS WALL?!

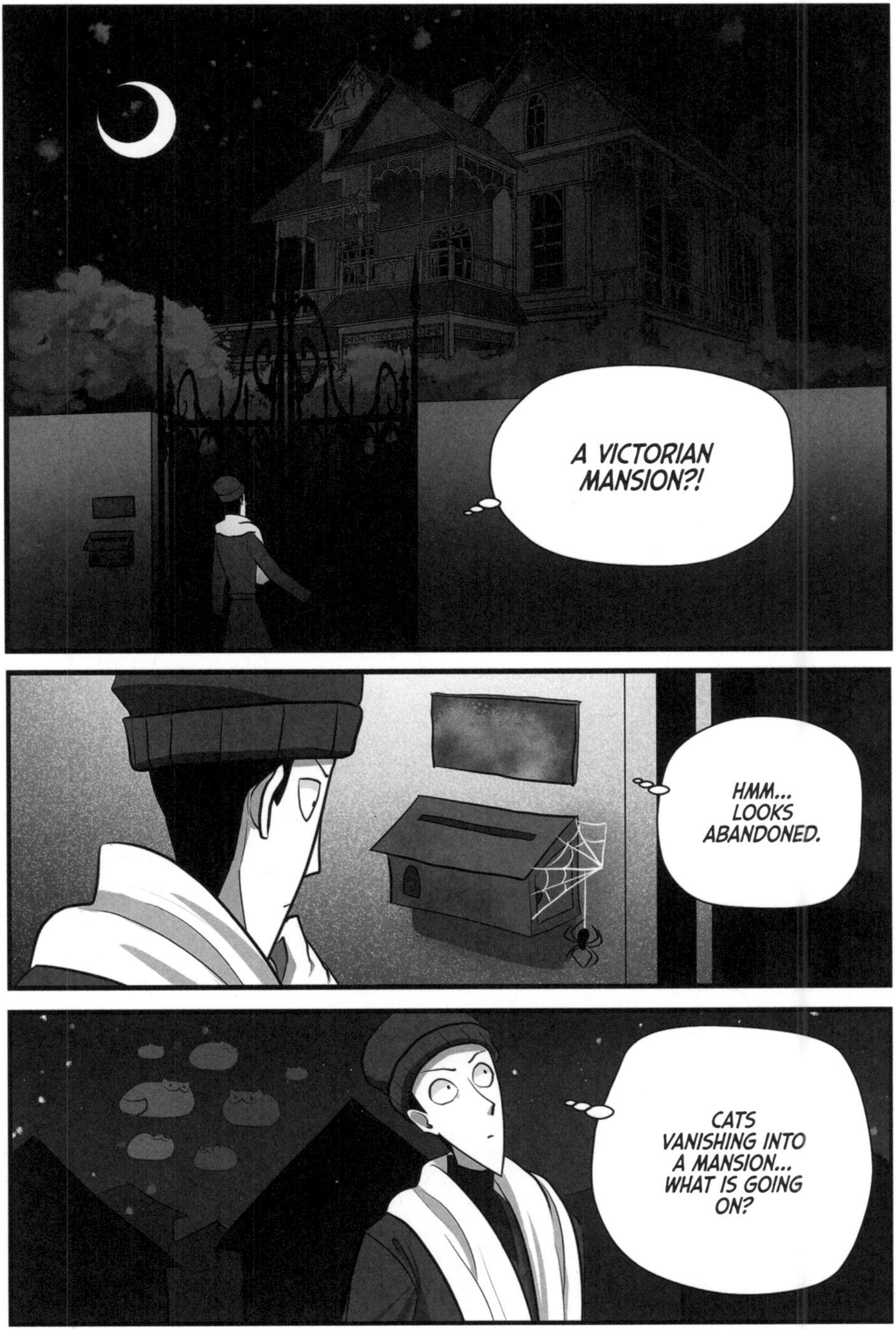
A VICTORIAN MANSION?!
HMM... LOOKS ABANDONED.
CATS VANISHING INTO A MANSION... WHAT IS GOING ON?

SNOWMEN

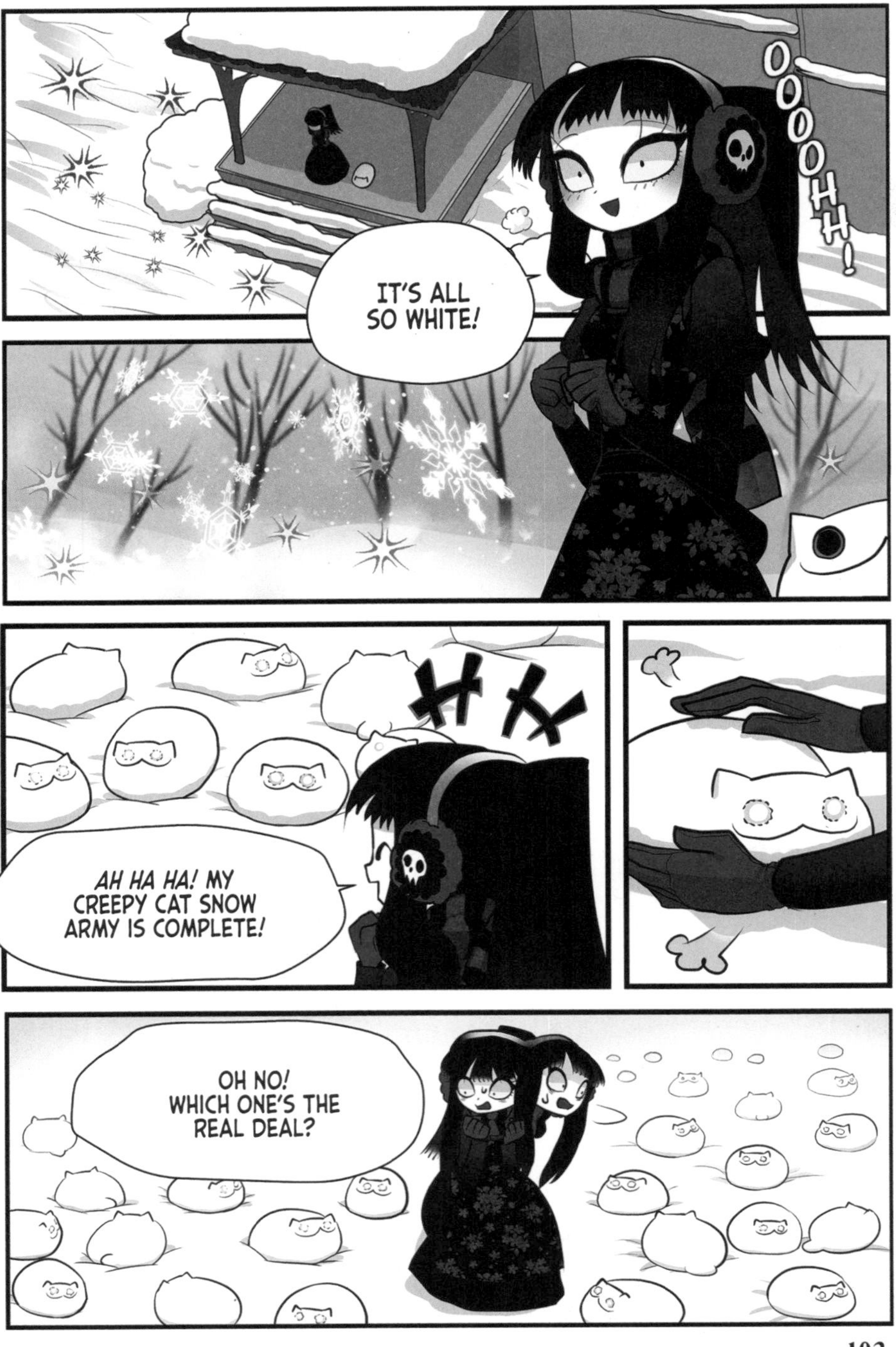
OOOOOHH!
IT'S ALL SO WHITE!
AH HA HA! MY CREEPY CAT SNOW ARMY IS COMPLETE!
OH NO! WHICH ONE'S THE REAL DEAL?

SNOW-MEOWS I

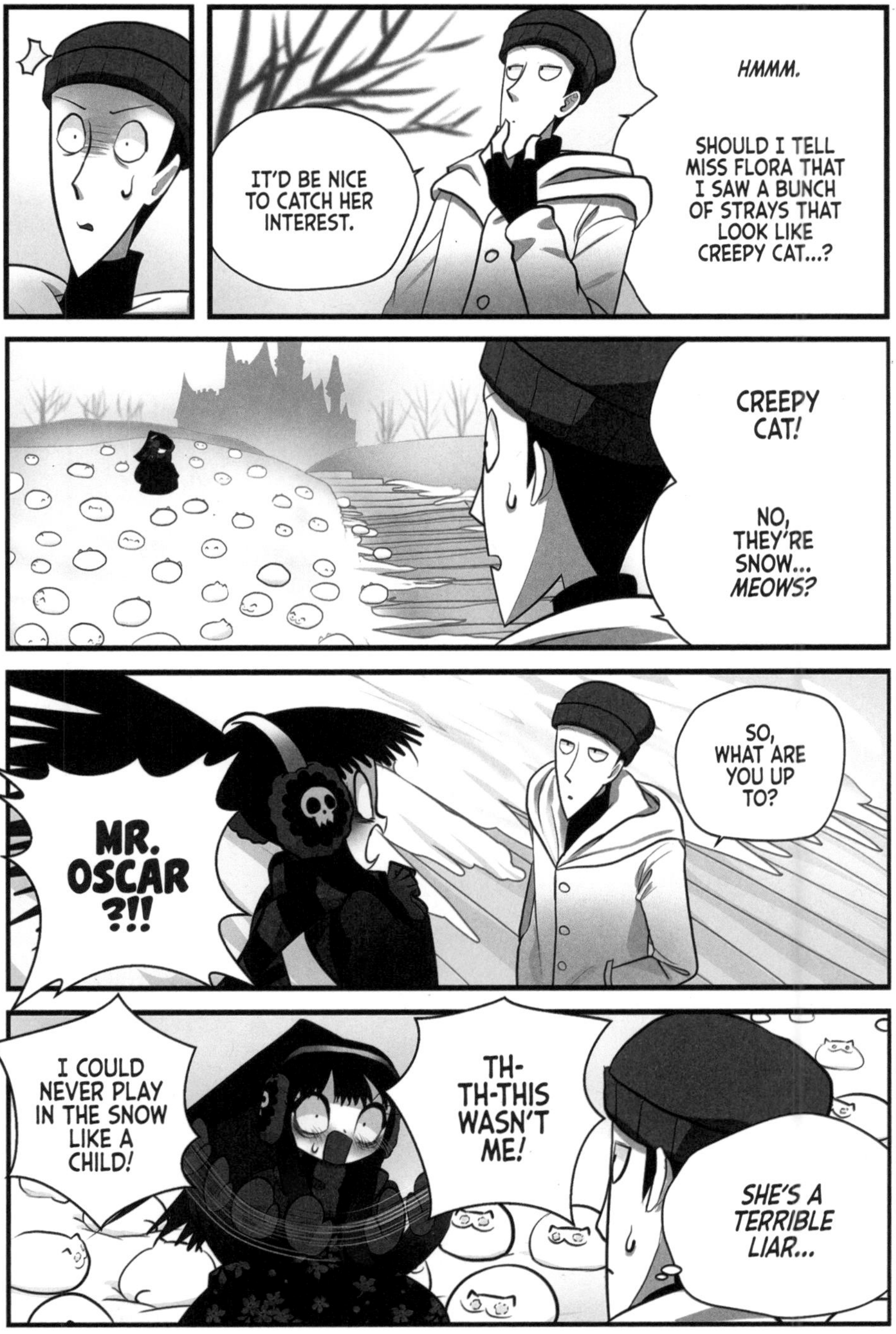

HMMM.
SHOULD I TELL MISS FLORA THAT I SAW A BUNCH OF STRAYS THAT LOOK LIKE CREEPY CAT...?
IT'D BE NICE TO CATCH HER INTEREST.
CREEPY CAT!
NO, THEY'RE SNOW... *MEOWS?*
SO, WHAT ARE YOU UP TO?
MR. OSCAR ?!!
TH-TH-THIS WASN'T ME!
I COULD NEVER PLAY IN THE SNOW LIKE A CHILD!
SHE'S A TERRIBLE LIAR...

SNOW-MEOWS II

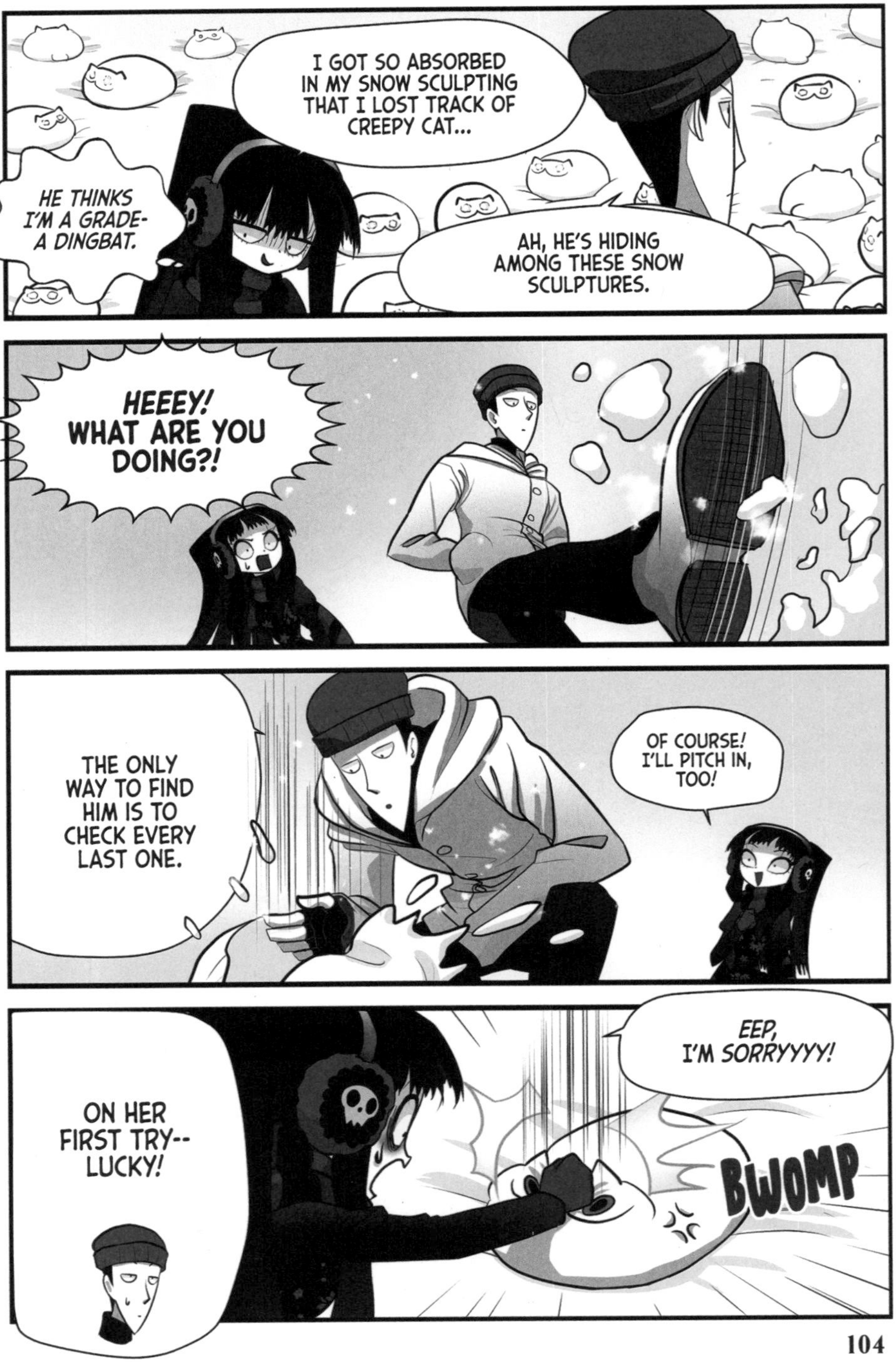

I GOT SO ABSORBED IN MY SNOW SCULPTING THAT I LOST TRACK OF CREEPY CAT...
HE THINKS I'M A GRADE-A DINGBAT.
AH, HE'S HIDING AMONG THESE SNOW SCULPTURES.
HEEEY! WHAT ARE YOU DOING?!
THE ONLY WAY TO FIND HIM IS TO CHECK EVERY LAST ONE.
OF COURSE! I'LL PITCH IN, TOO!
EEP, I'M SORRYYYY!
BWOMP
ON HER FIRST TRY-- LUCKY!

SWING AND MISS

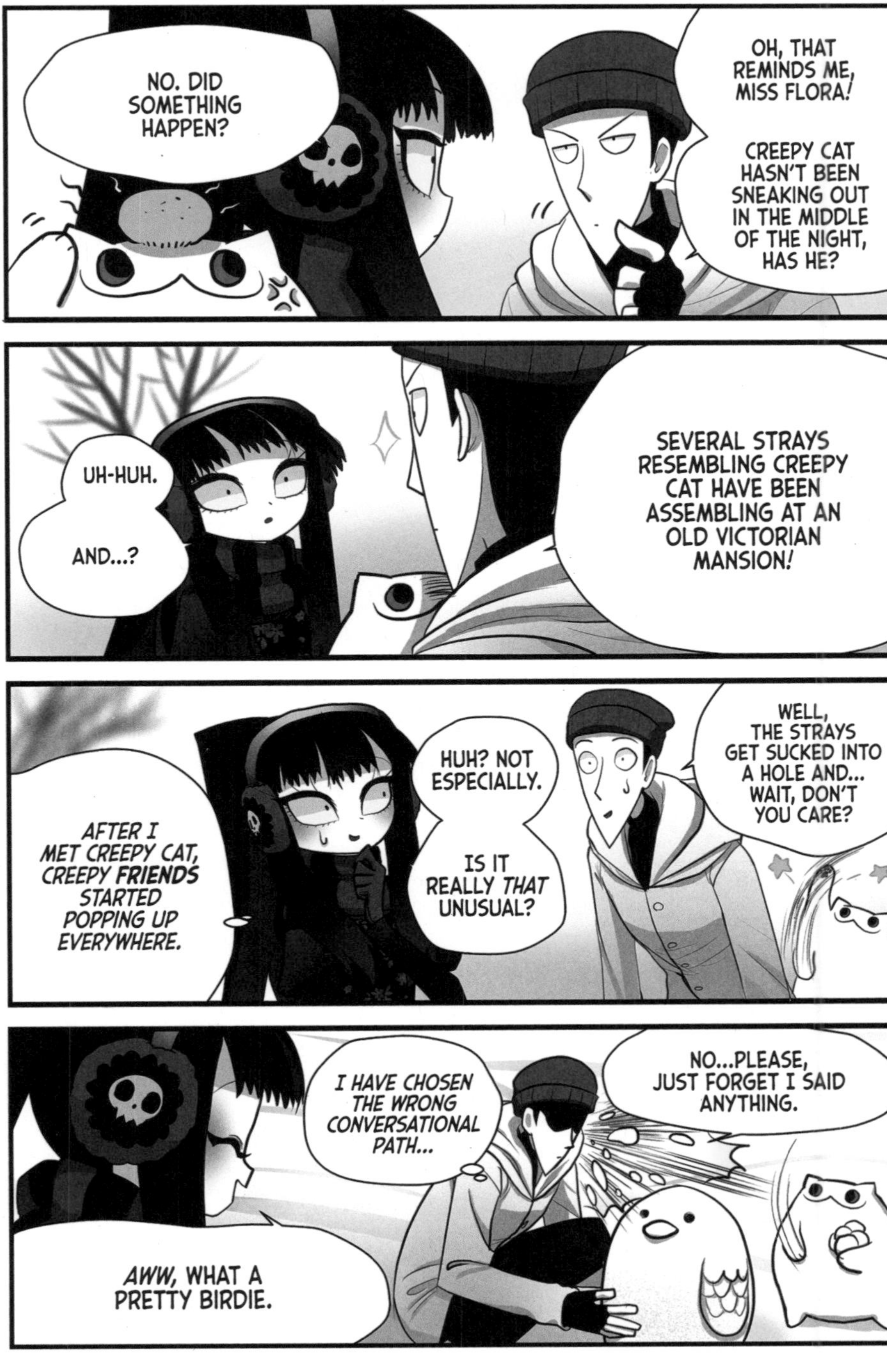
OH, THAT REMINDS ME, MISS FLORA!
CREEPY CAT HASN'T BEEN SNEAKING OUT IN THE MIDDLE OF THE NIGHT, HAS HE?
NO. DID SOMETHING HAPPEN?
SEVERAL STRAYS RESEMBLING CREEPY CAT HAVE BEEN ASSEMBLING AT AN OLD VICTORIAN MANSION!
UH-HUH.
AND...?
WELL, THE STRAYS GET SUCKED INTO A HOLE AND... WAIT, DON'T YOU CARE?
HUH? NOT ESPECIALLY.
IS IT REALLY *THAT* UNUSUAL?
*AFTER I MET CREEPY CAT, CREEPY **FRIENDS** STARTED POPPING UP EVERYWHERE.*
NO...PLEASE, JUST FORGET I SAID ANYTHING.
I HAVE CHOSEN THE WRONG CONVERSATIONAL PATH...
AWW, WHAT A PRETTY BIRDIE.

A NAGGING FEELING

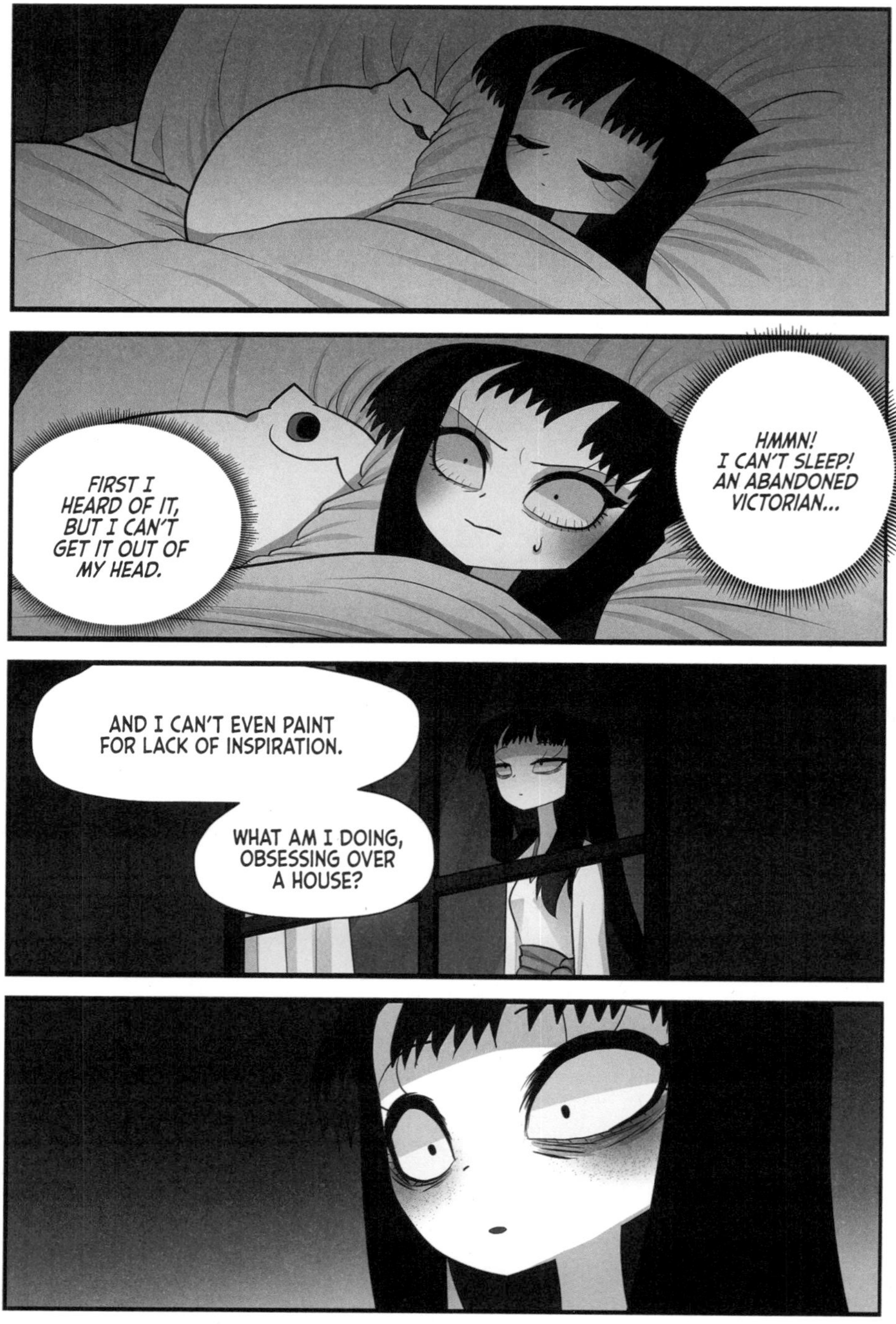
HMMN! I CAN'T SLEEP! AN ABANDONED VICTORIAN...
FIRST I HEARD OF IT, BUT I CAN'T GET IT OUT OF MY HEAD.
AND I CAN'T EVEN PAINT FOR LACK OF INSPIRATION.
WHAT AM I DOING, OBSESSING OVER A HOUSE?

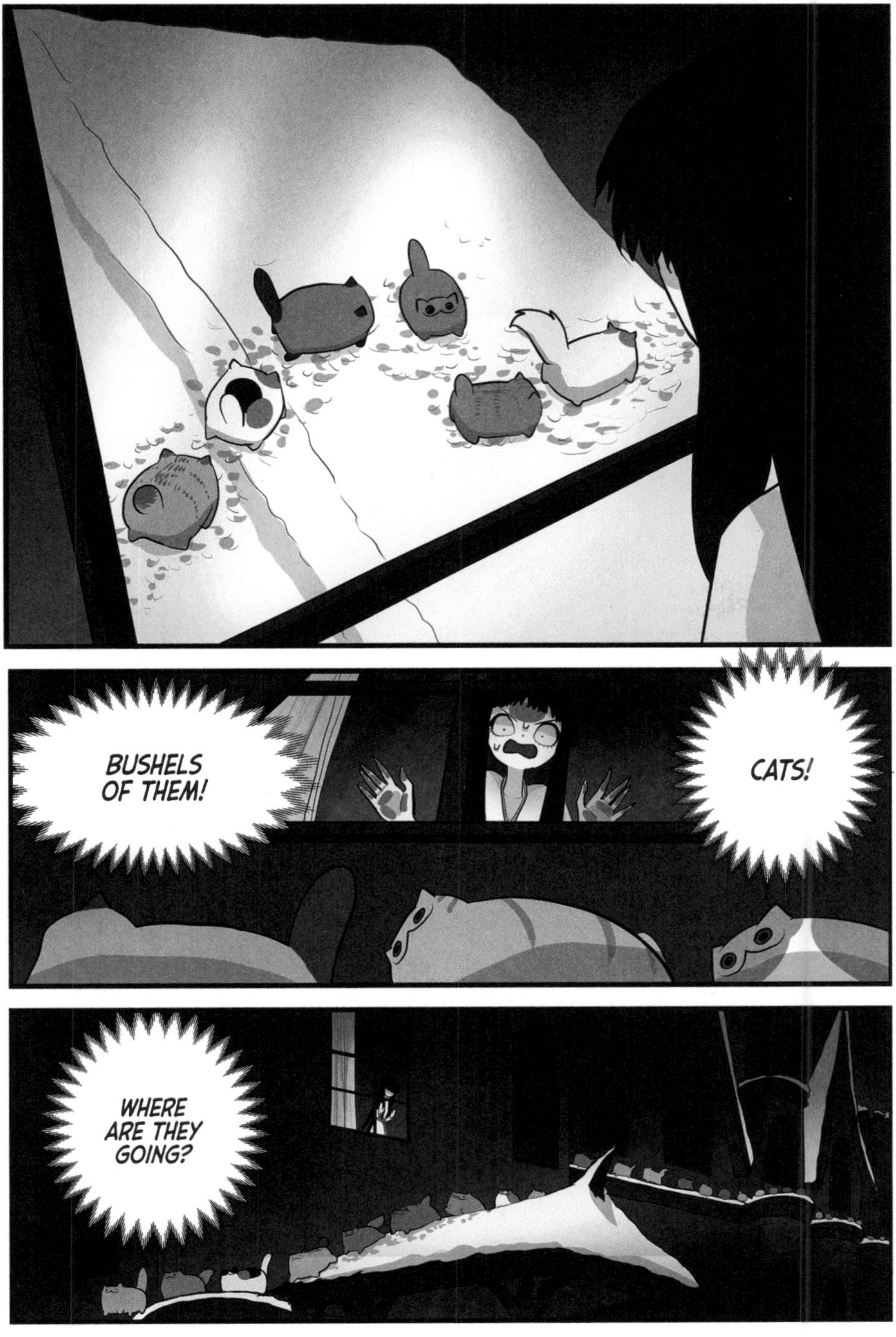
CATS!
BUSHELS OF THEM!
WHERE ARE THEY GOING?

ONE OF YOU

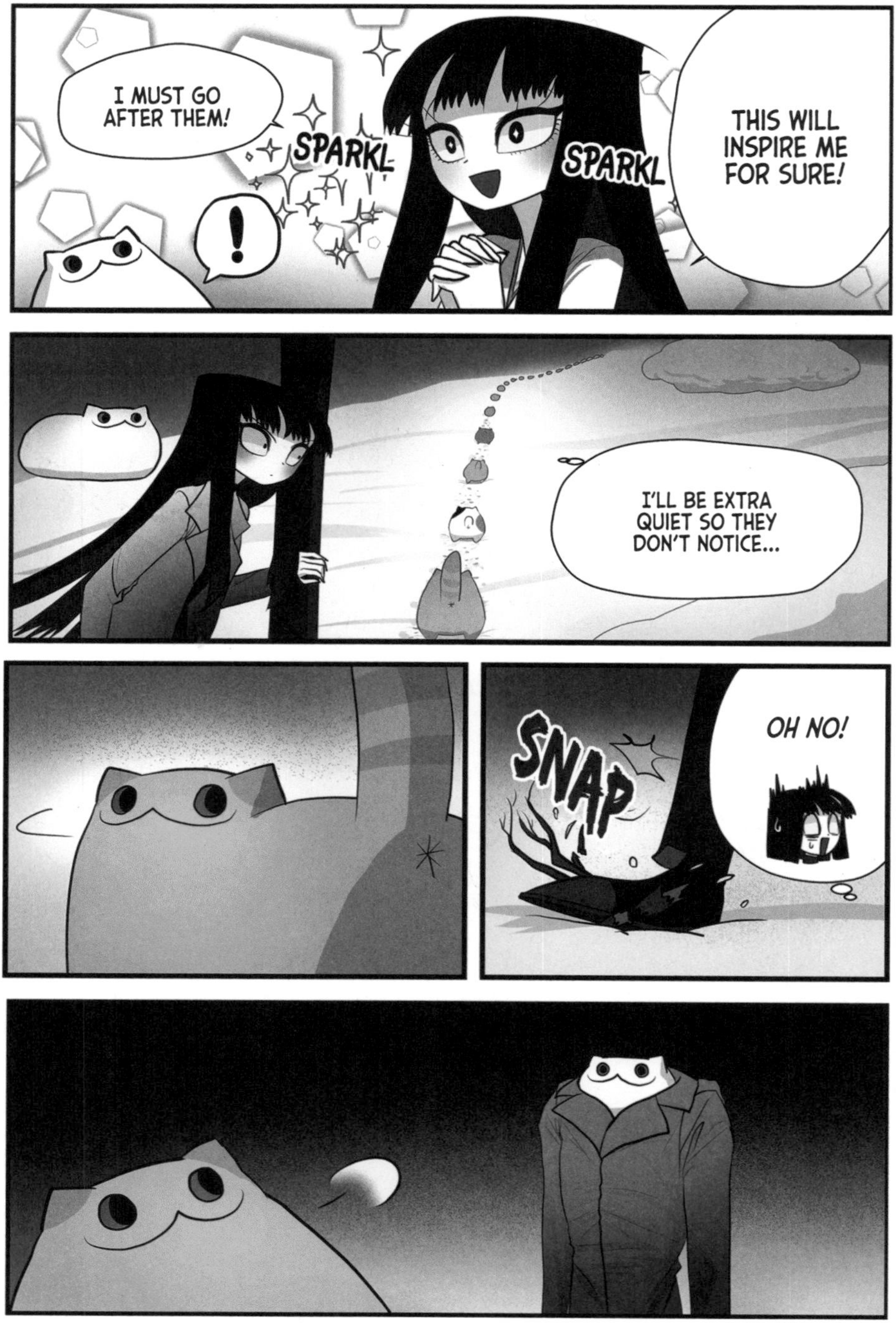
I MUST GO AFTER THEM!
SPARKL
SPARKL
THIS WILL INSPIRE ME FOR SURE!
!
I'LL BE EXTRA QUIET SO THEY DON'T NOTICE...
SNAP
OH NO!

RECONNAISSANCE

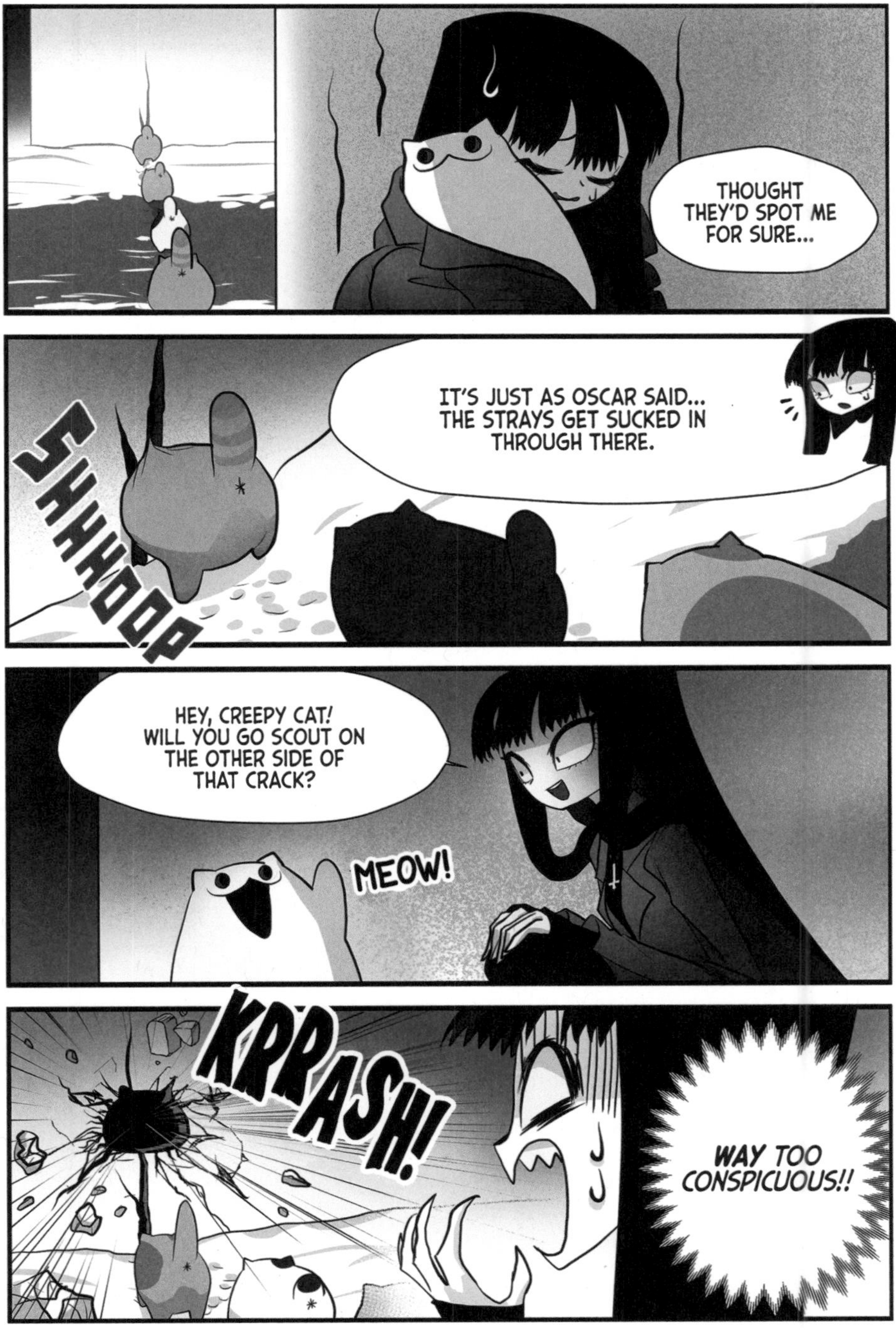

THOUGHT THEY'D SPOT ME FOR SURE...
SHHHOOP
IT'S JUST AS OSCAR SAID... THE STRAYS GET SUCKED IN THROUGH THERE.
HEY, CREEPY CAT! WILL YOU GO SCOUT ON THE OTHER SIDE OF THAT CRACK?
MEOW!
KRRASH!
WAY TOO CONSPICUOUS!!

HOLE

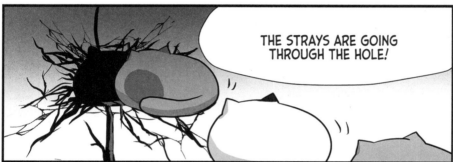

THE STRAYS ARE GOING
THROUGH THE HOLE!

THAT'S
THE LAST
ONE...

THERE SHOULD
BE AN ENTRANCE
AROUND HERE
SOMEWHERE...

GIVE HER A BIG HAND

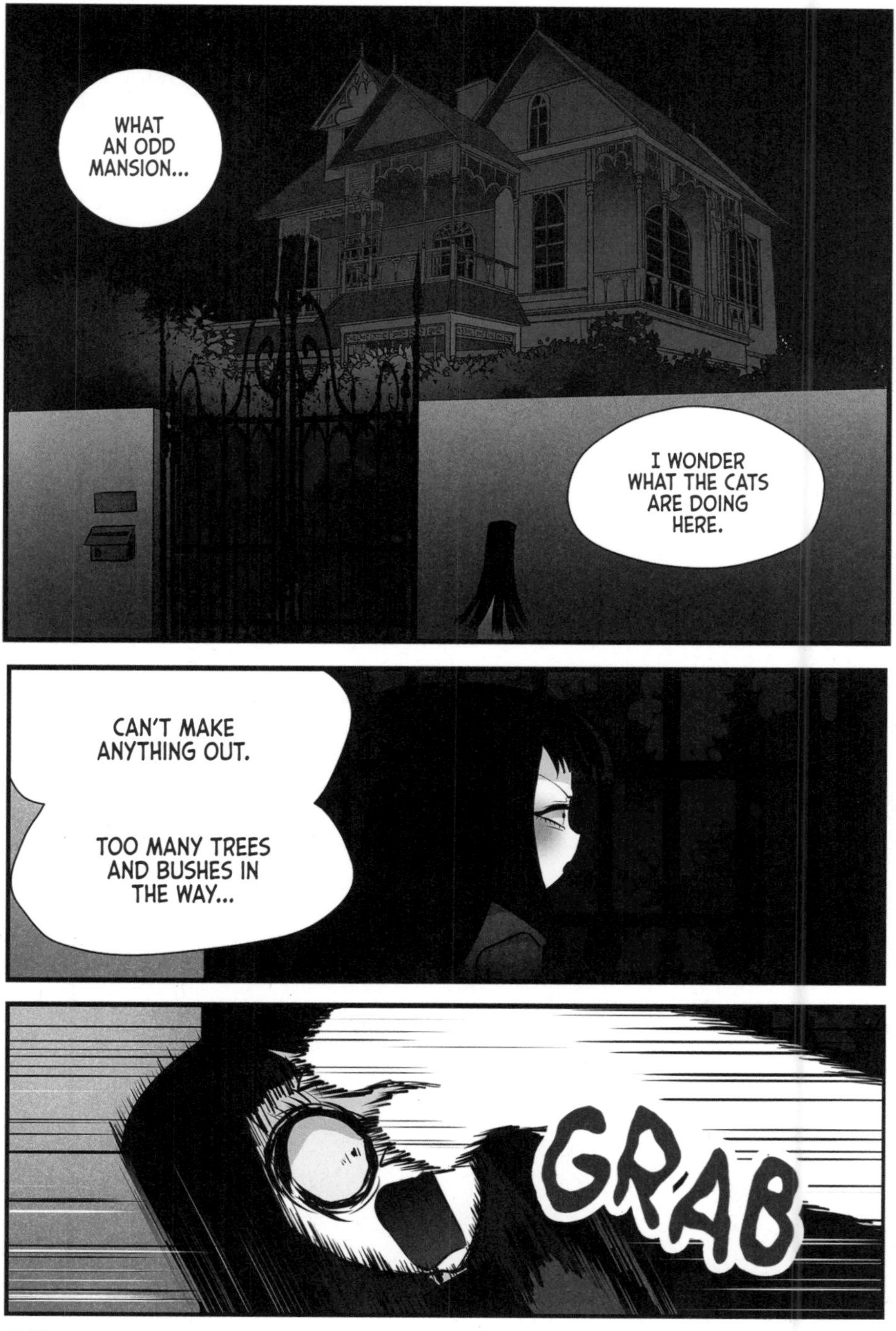

WHAT AN ODD MANSION...
I WONDER WHAT THE CATS ARE DOING HERE.
CAN'T MAKE ANYTHING OUT.
TOO MANY TREES AND BUSHES IN THE WAY...
GRAB

STARING

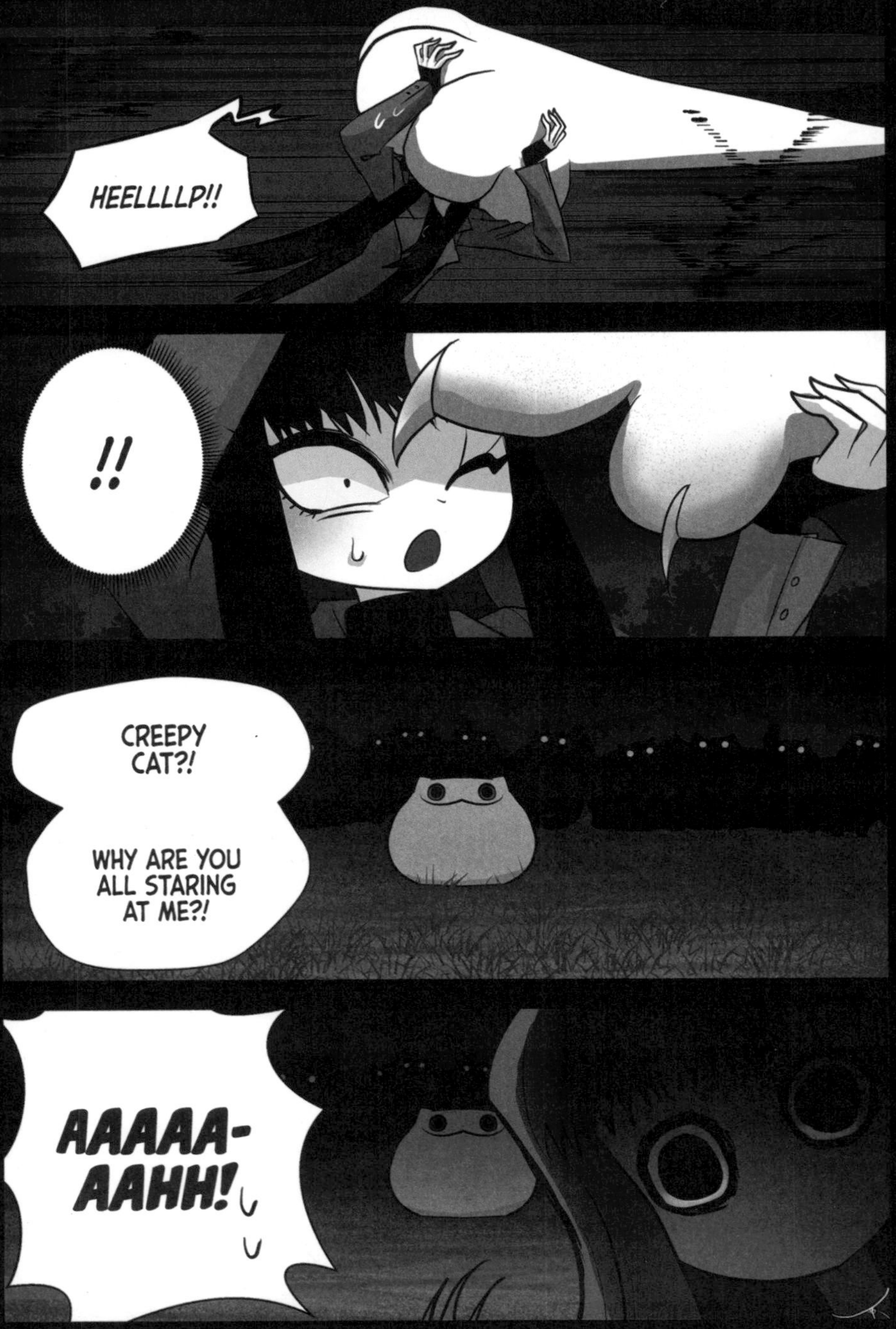
HEELLLLP!!
!!
CREEPY CAT?!
WHY ARE YOU ALL STARING AT ME?!
AAAAA-AAHH!

FOOD

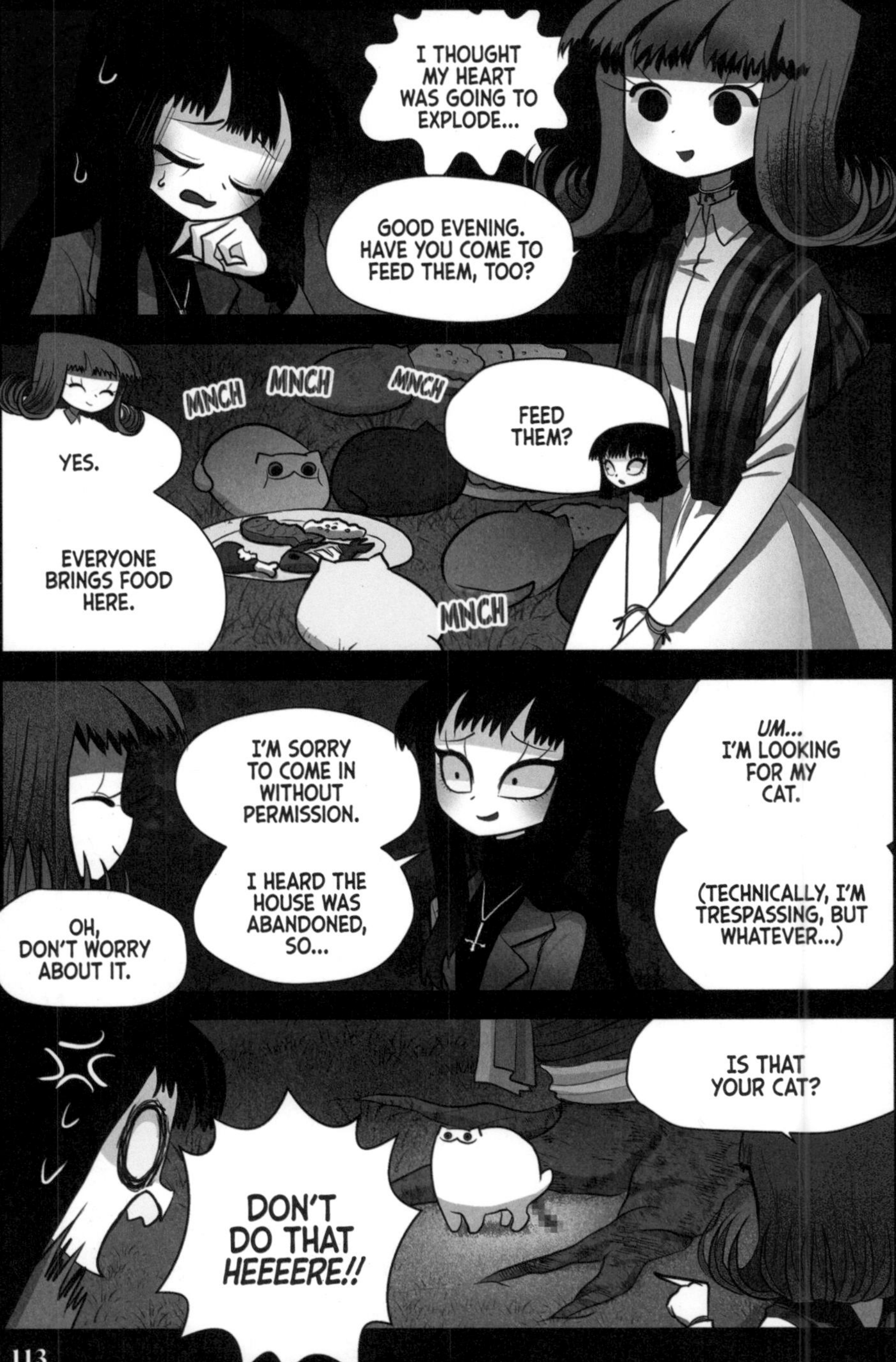
I THOUGHT MY HEART WAS GOING TO EXPLODE...
GOOD EVENING. HAVE YOU COME TO FEED THEM, TOO?
MNCH
MNCH
MNCH
FEED THEM?
YES.
EVERYONE BRINGS FOOD HERE.
MNCH
UM... I'M LOOKING FOR MY CAT.
(TECHNICALLY, I'M TRESPASSING, BUT WHATEVER...)
I'M SORRY TO COME IN WITHOUT PERMISSION.
I HEARD THE HOUSE WAS ABANDONED, SO...
OH, DON'T WORRY ABOUT IT.
IS THAT YOUR CAT?
DON'T DO THAT HEEEERE!!

DÉJÀ VU

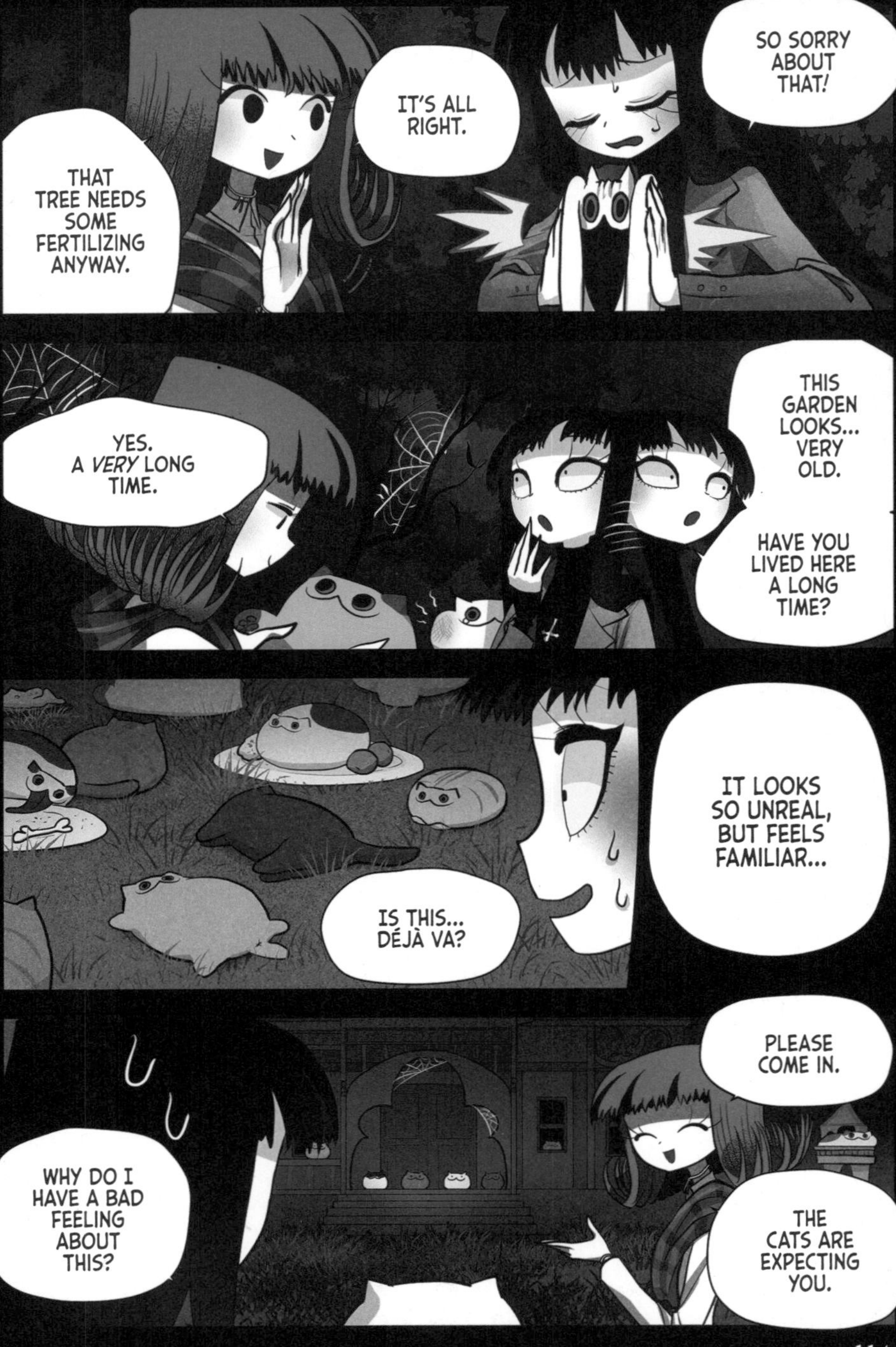
SO SORRY ABOUT THAT!
IT'S ALL RIGHT.
THAT TREE NEEDS SOME FERTILIZING ANYWAY.
THIS GARDEN LOOKS... VERY OLD.
HAVE YOU LIVED HERE A LONG TIME?
YES. A *VERY* LONG TIME.
IT LOOKS SO UNREAL, BUT FEELS FAMILIAR...
IS THIS... DÉJÀ VA?
PLEASE COME IN.
THE CATS ARE EXPECTING YOU.
WHY DO I HAVE A BAD FEELING ABOUT THIS?

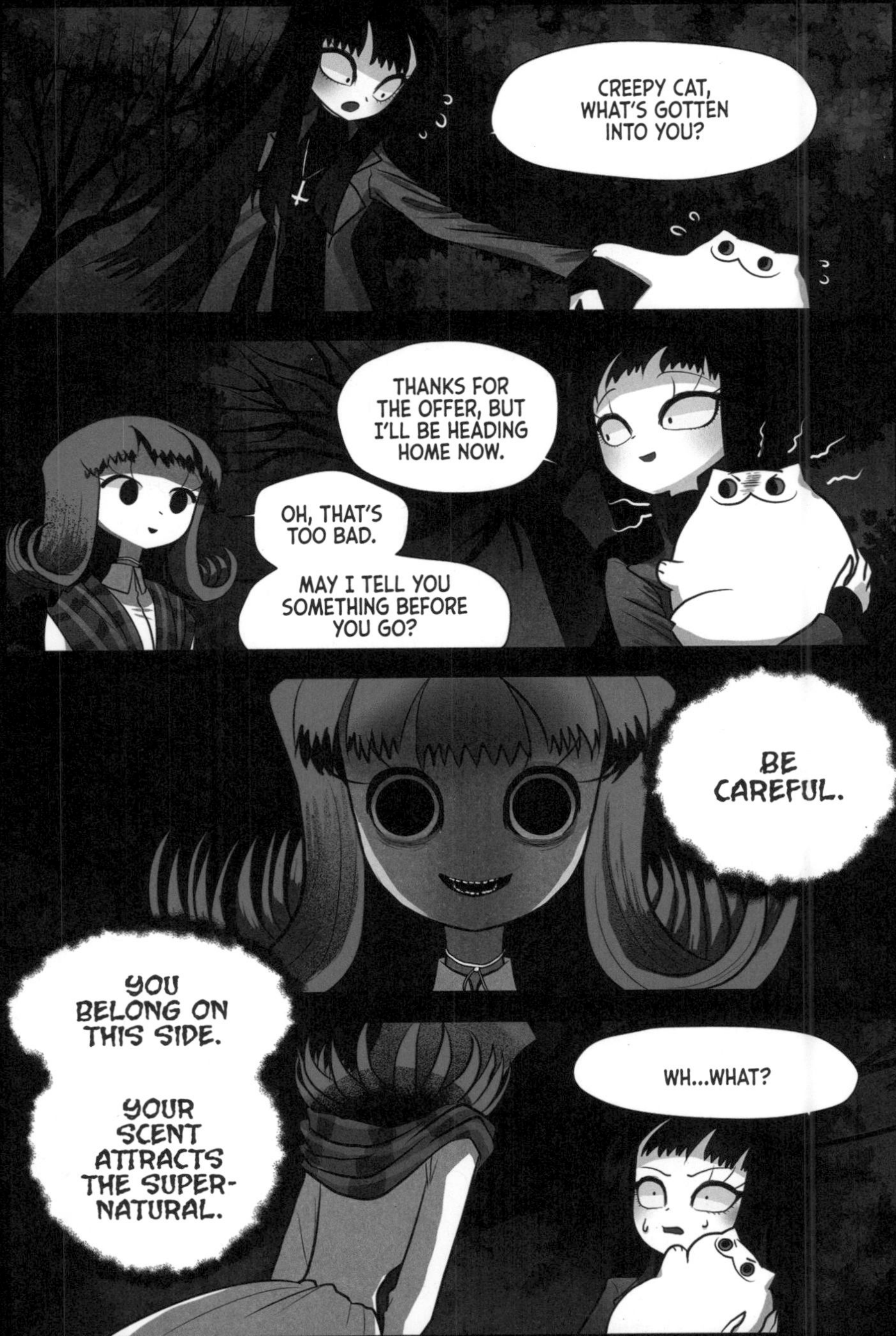
CREEPY CAT, WHAT'S GOTTEN INTO YOU?
THANKS FOR THE OFFER, BUT I'LL BE HEADING HOME NOW.
OH, THAT'S TOO BAD.
MAY I TELL YOU SOMETHING BEFORE YOU GO?
BE CAREFUL.
YOU BELONG ON THIS SIDE.
YOUR SCENT ATTRACTS THE SUPER-NATURAL.
WH...WHAT?

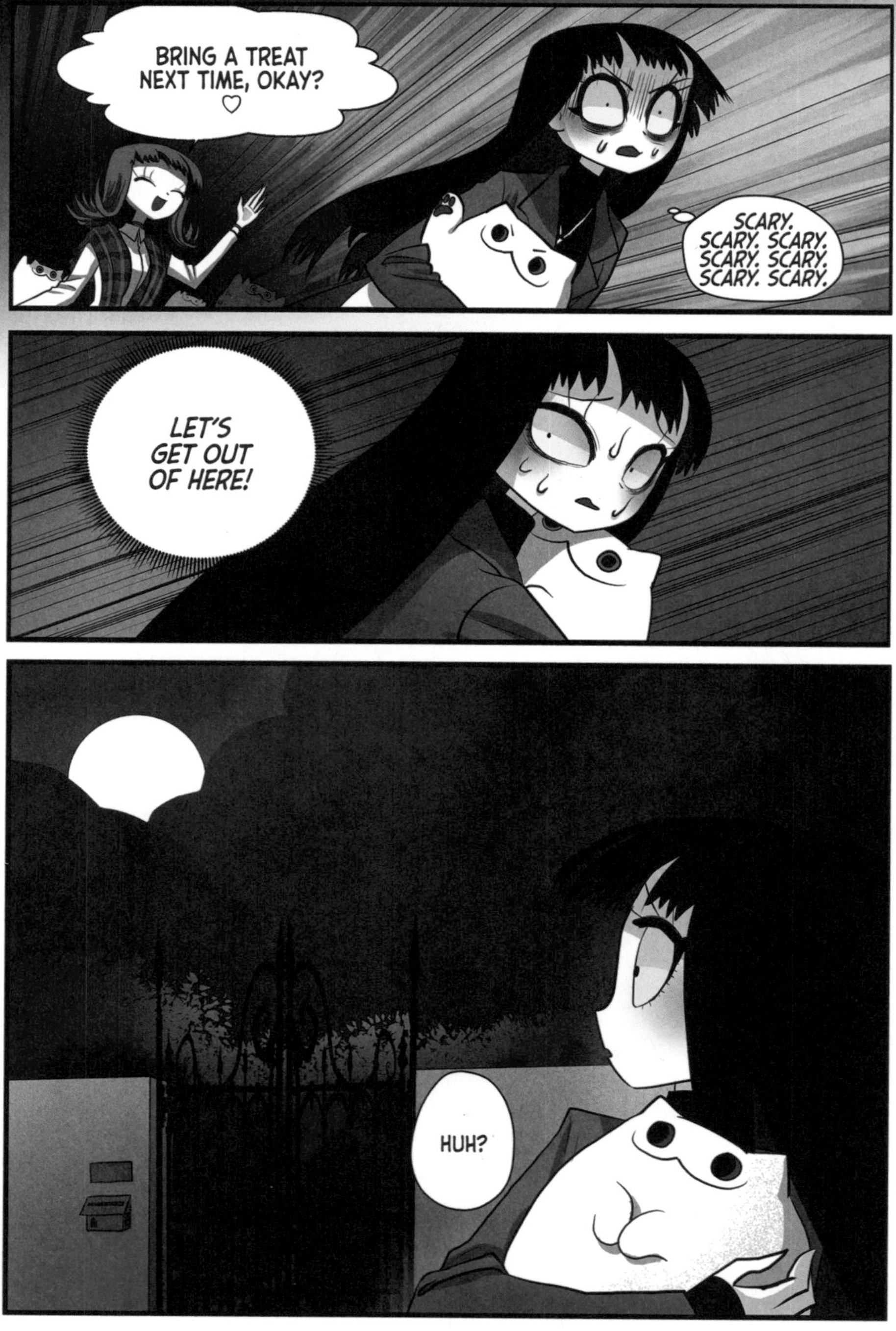
BRING A TREAT NEXT TIME, OKAY? ♡
SCARY. SCARY. SCARY. SCARY. SCARY. SCARY. SCARY. SCARY. SCARY.
LET'S GET OUT OF HERE!
HUH?

SEE YOU LATER

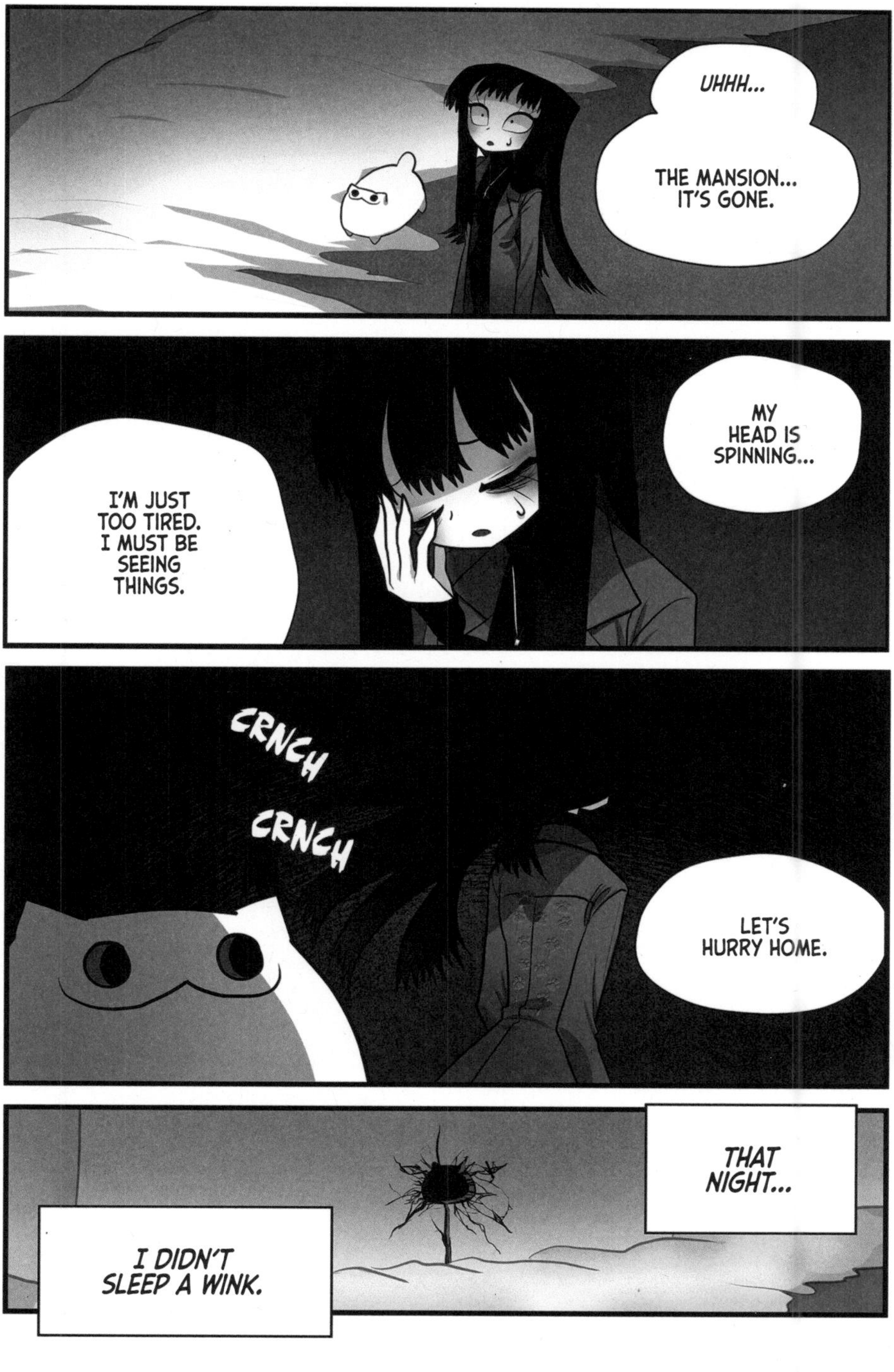
UHHH...
THE MANSION... IT'S GONE.
MY HEAD IS SPINNING...
I'M JUST TOO TIRED. I MUST BE SEEING THINGS.
CRNCH
CRNCH
LET'S HURRY HOME.
THAT NIGHT...
I DIDN'T SLEEP A WINK.

extra story
HALLOWEEN NIGHT

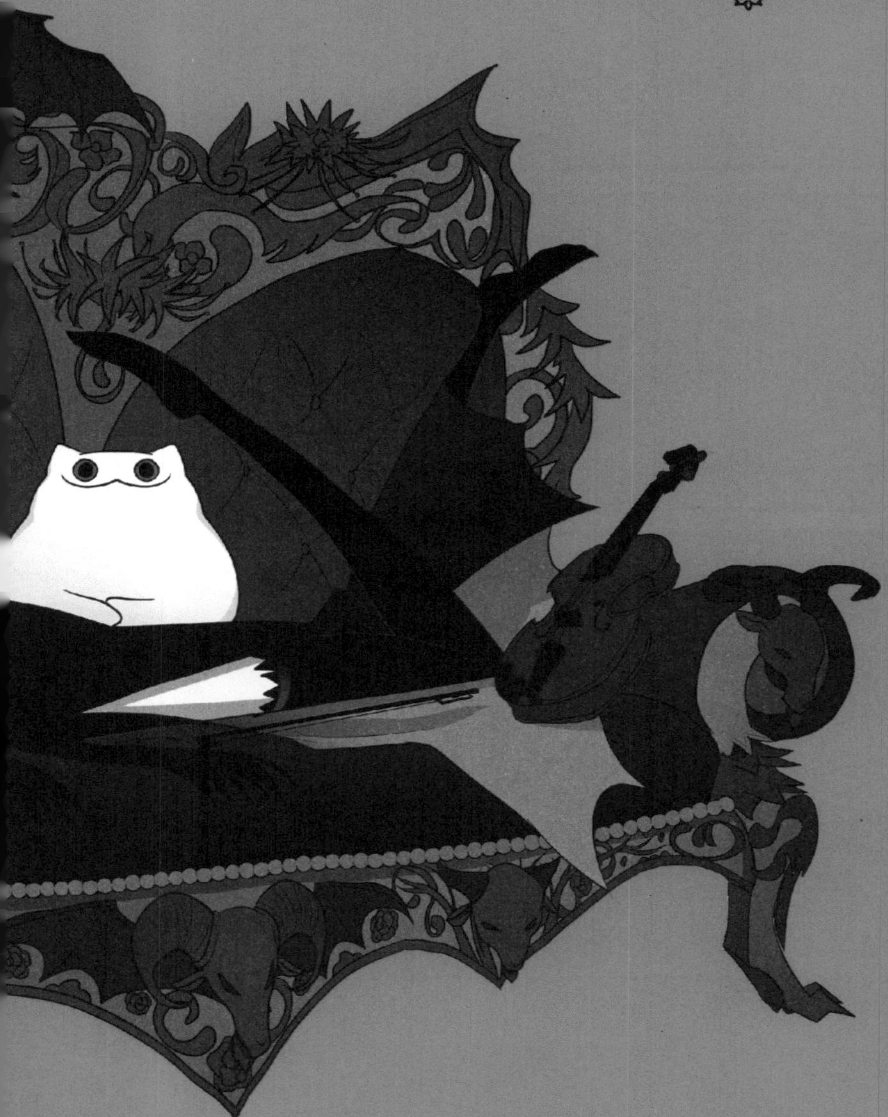

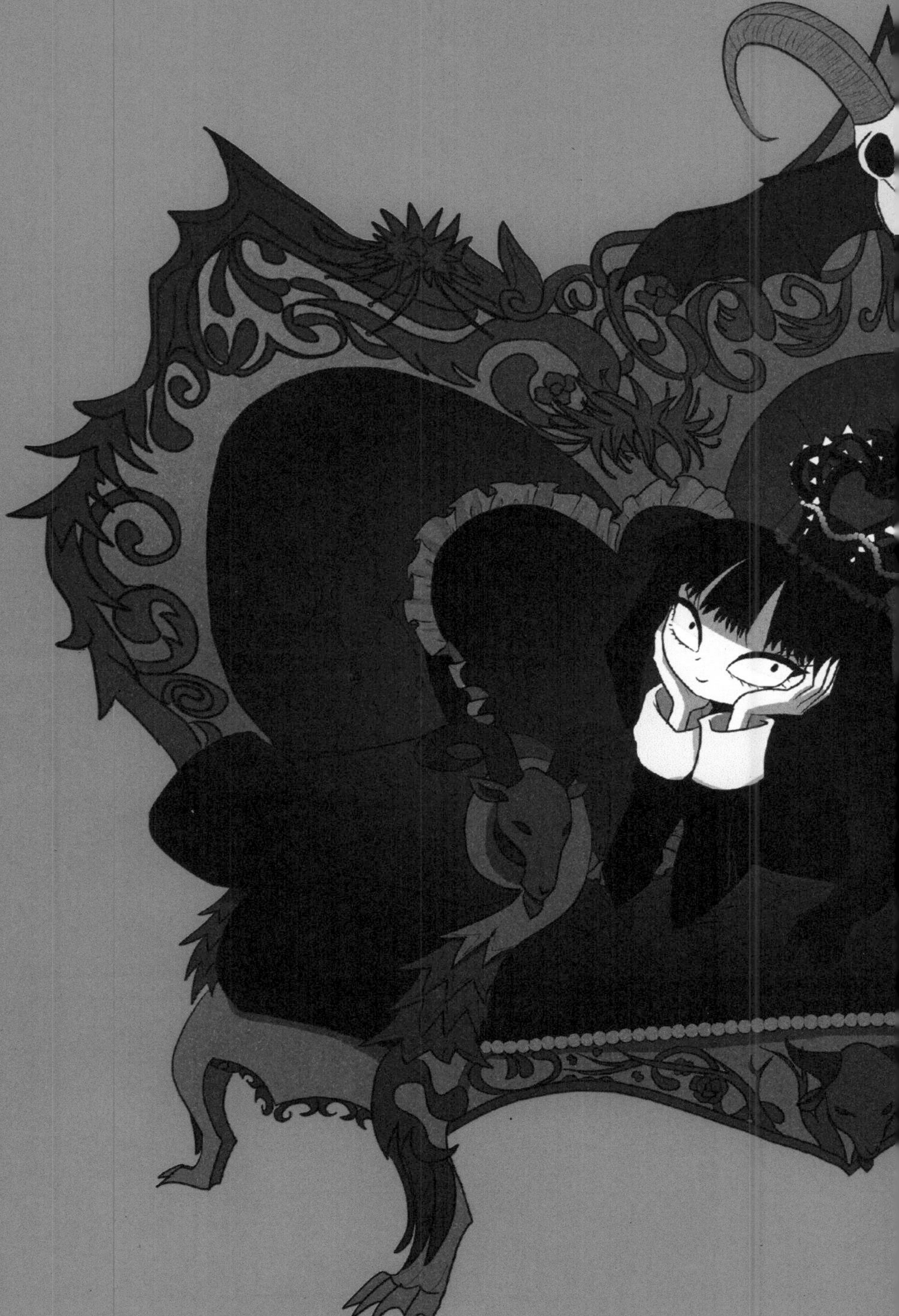

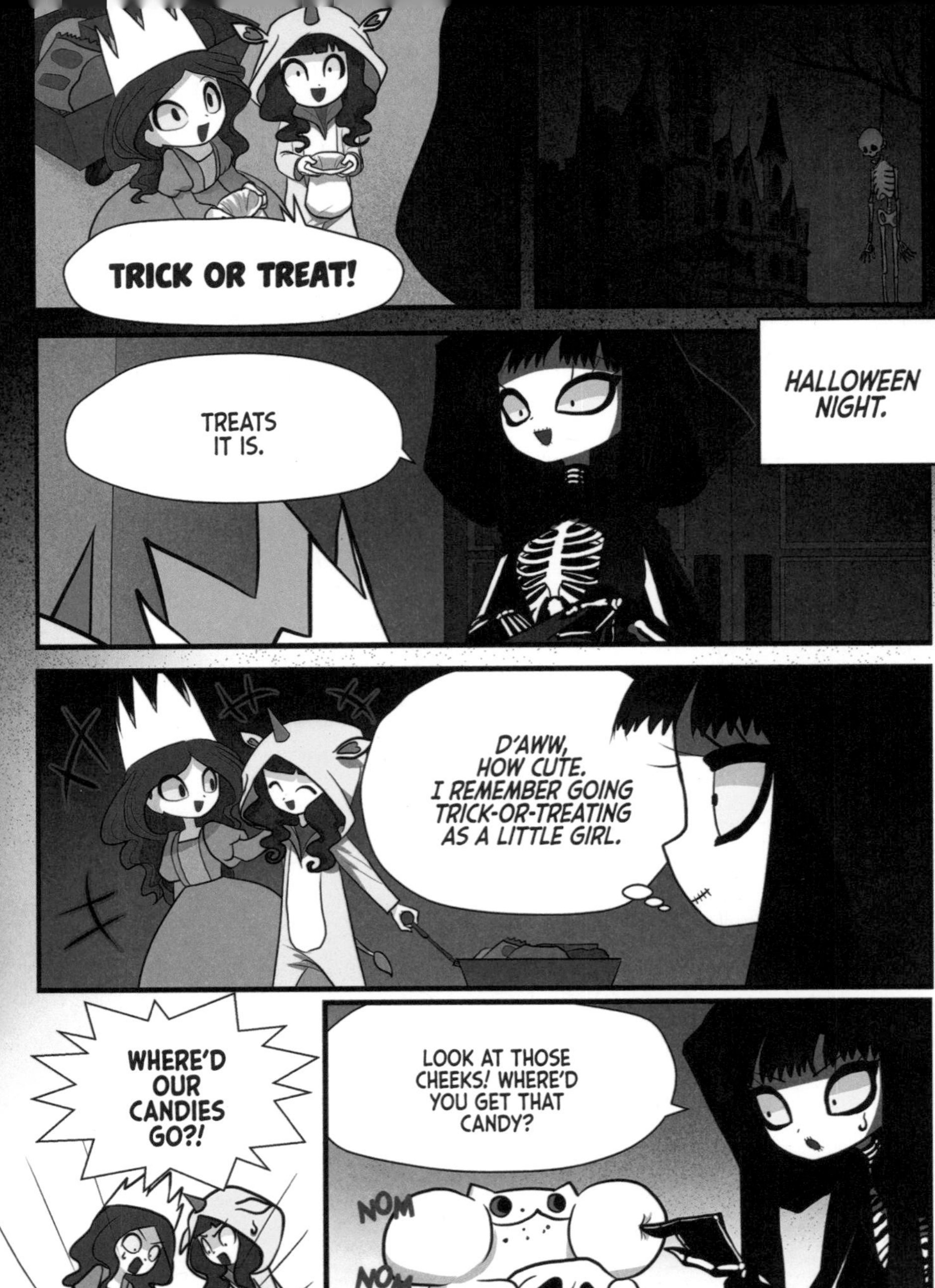

TRICK OR TREAT!
HALLOWEEN NIGHT.
TREATS IT IS.
D'AWW, HOW CUTE. I REMEMBER GOING TRICK-OR-TREATING AS A LITTLE GIRL.
WHERE'D OUR CANDIES GO?!
LOOK AT THOSE CHEEKS! WHERE'D YOU GET THAT CANDY?
NOM
NOM

EGGPLANT

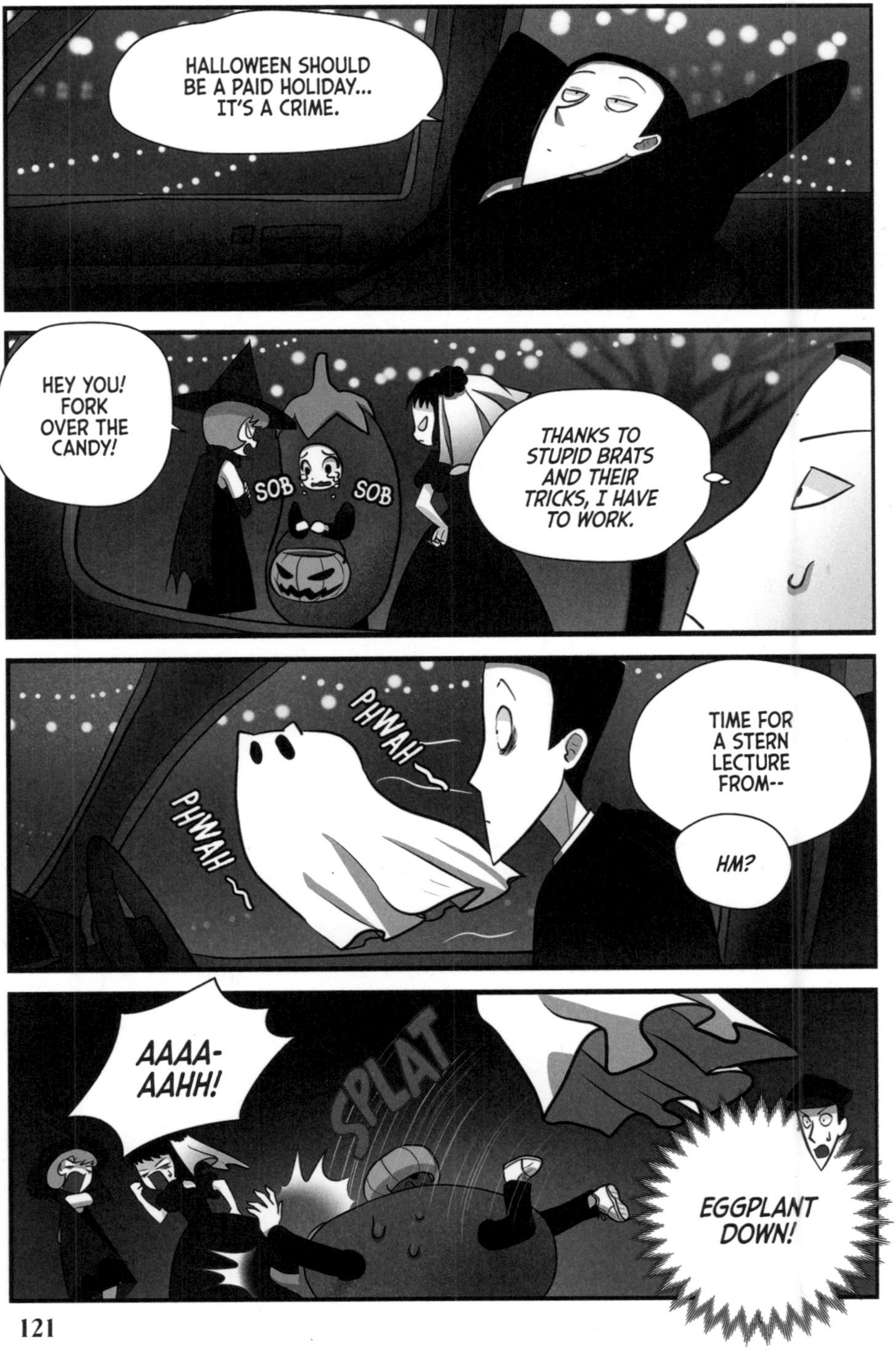

HALLOWEEN SHOULD BE A PAID HOLIDAY... IT'S A CRIME.
HEY YOU! FORK OVER THE CANDY!
SOB
SOB
THANKS TO STUPID BRATS AND THEIR TRICKS, I HAVE TO WORK.
PHWAH~
PHWAH~
TIME FOR A STERN LECTURE FROM--
HM?
AAAA-AAHH!
SPLAT
EGGPLANT DOWN!

THEFT

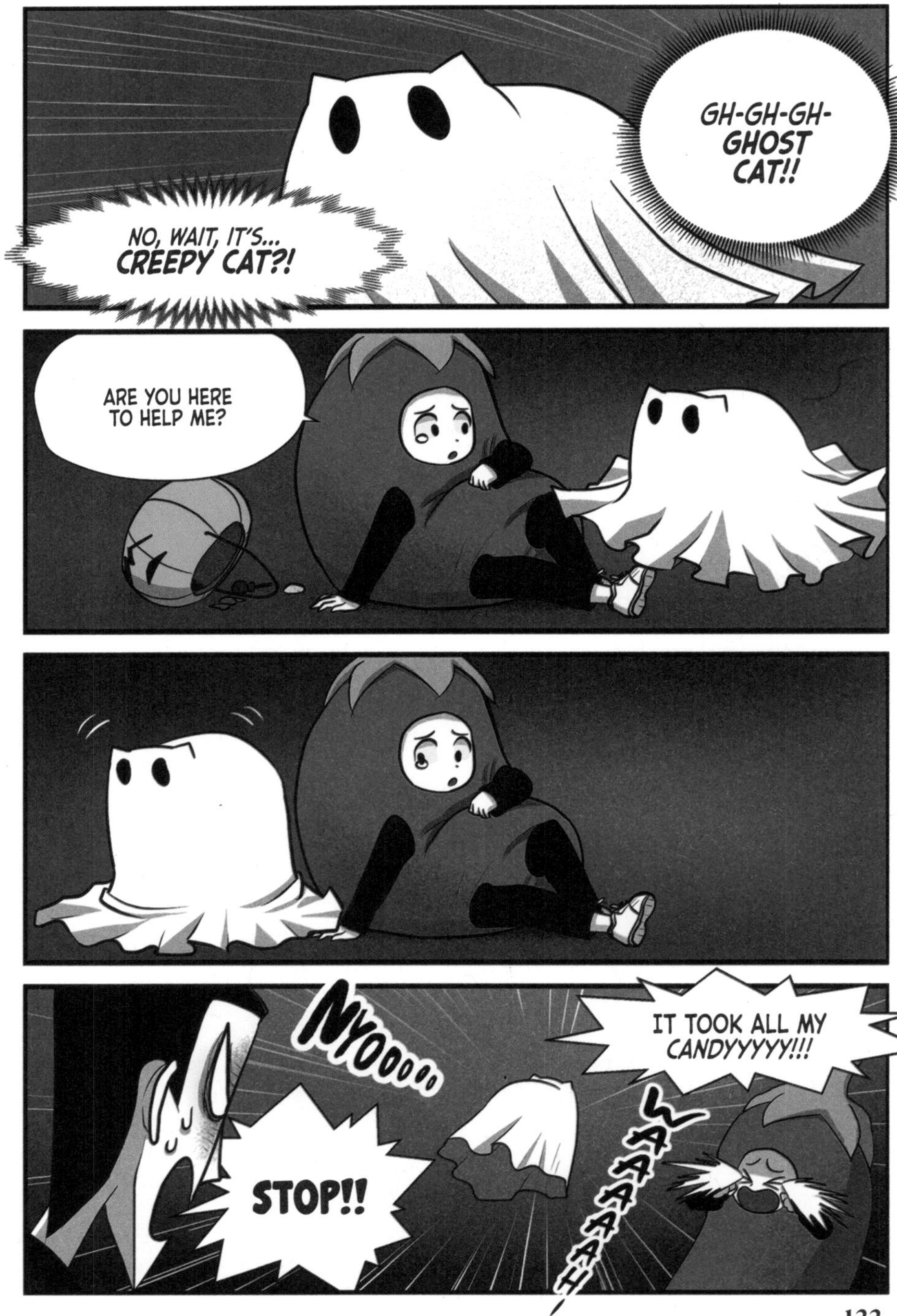

GH-GH-GH-GHOST CAT!!
NO, WAIT, IT'S... CREEPY CAT?!
ARE YOU HERE TO HELP ME?
NYOooo
STOP!!
IT TOOK ALL MY CANDYYYYY!!!
WAAAAAAAH!

RAGE

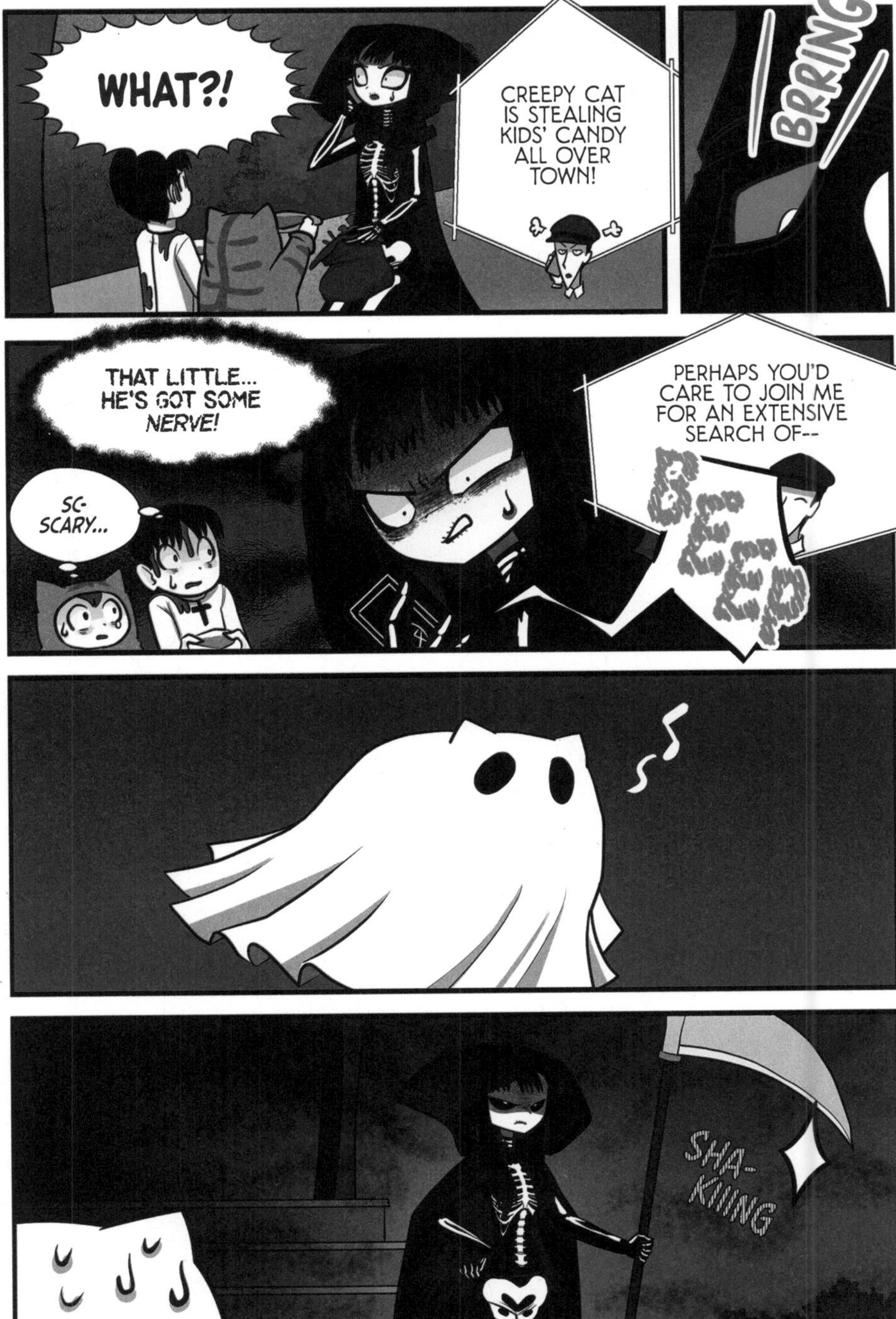

WHAT?!
CREEPY CAT IS STEALING KIDS' CANDY ALL OVER TOWN!
BRRING
THAT LITTLE... HE'S GOT SOME *NERVE!*
PERHAPS YOU'D CARE TO JOIN ME FOR AN EXTENSIVE SEARCH OF--
BEEP
SC-SCARY...
SHA-KIIING

TO THE FOREST

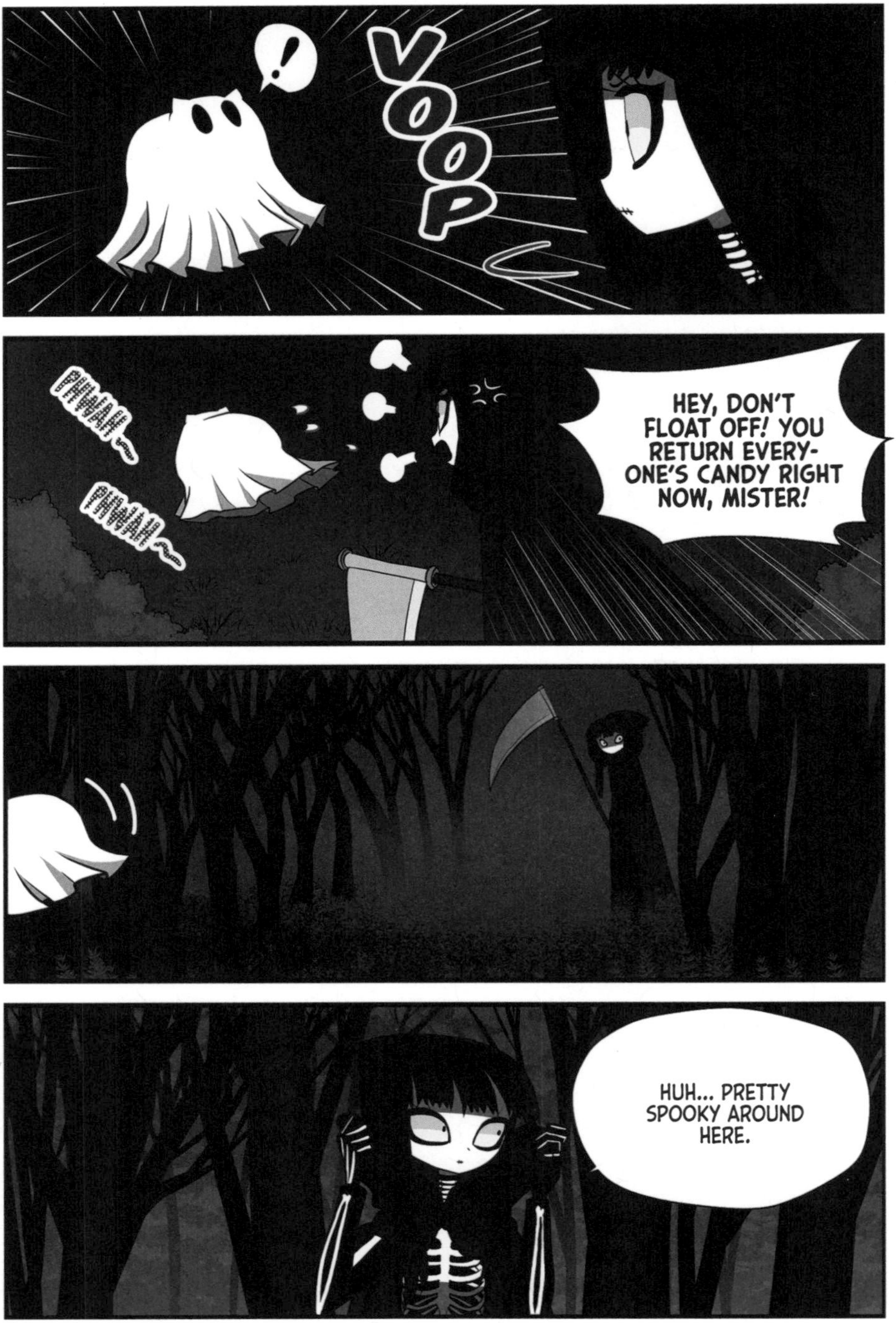
!
VOOP
HEY, DON'T FLOAT OFF! YOU RETURN EVERY-ONE'S CANDY RIGHT NOW, MISTER!
HUH... PRETTY SPOOKY AROUND HERE.

FULL MOON

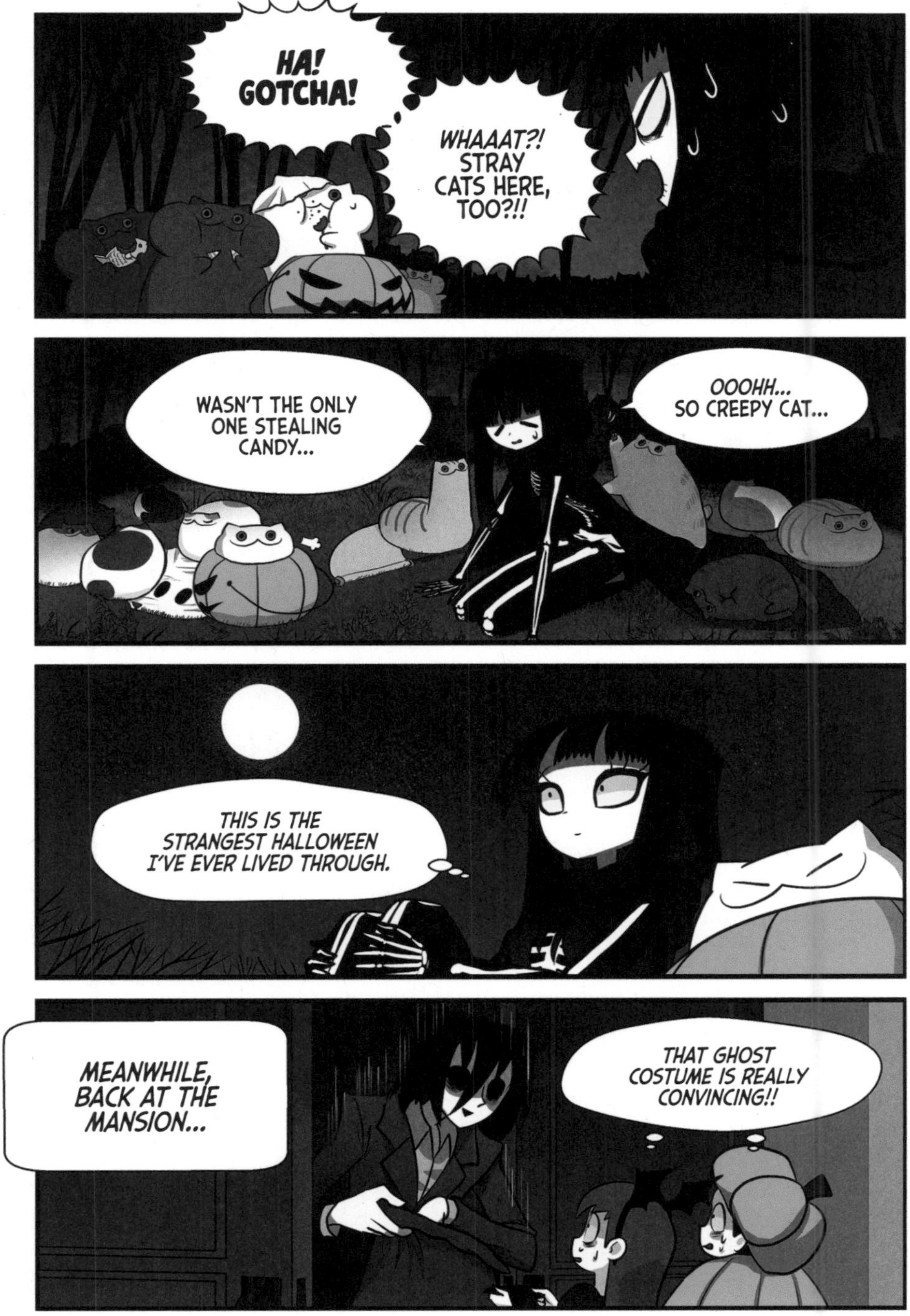
HA! GOTCHA!
WHAAAT?! STRAY CATS HERE, TOO?!!
WASN'T THE ONLY ONE STEALING CANDY...
OOOHH... SO CREEPY CAT...
THIS IS THE STRANGEST HALLOWEEN I'VE EVER LIVED THROUGH.
MEANWHILE, BACK AT THE MANSION...
THAT GHOST COSTUME IS REALLY CONVINCING!!

THE HISTORY OF COTTON VALENT

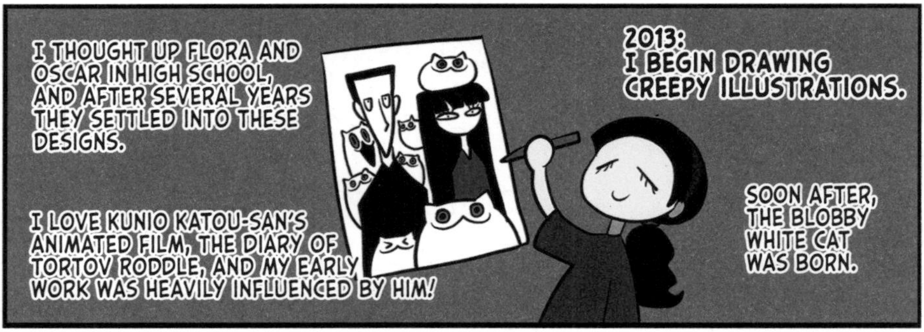

I THOUGHT UP FLORA AND OSCAR IN HIGH SCHOOL, AND AFTER SEVERAL YEARS THEY SETTLED INTO THESE DESIGNS.
2013: I BEGIN DRAWING CREEPY ILLUSTRATIONS.
I LOVE KUNIO KATOU-SAN'S ANIMATED FILM, THE DIARY OF TORTOV RODDLE, AND MY EARLY WORK WAS HEAVILY INFLUENCED BY HIM!
SOON AFTER, THE BLOBBY WHITE CAT WAS BORN.

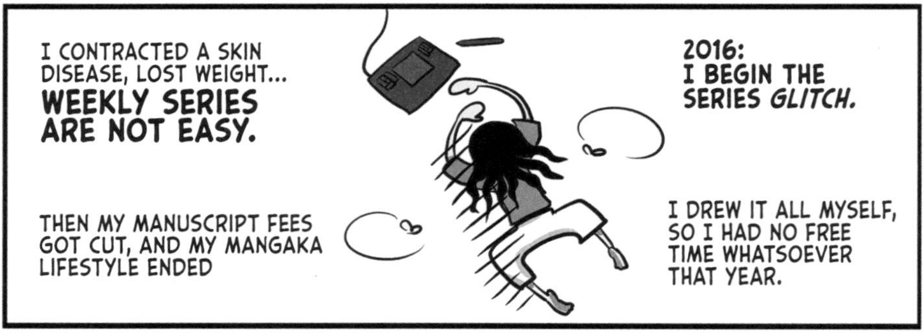

I CONTRACTED A SKIN DISEASE, LOST WEIGHT... WEEKLY SERIES ARE NOT EASY.
2016: I BEGIN THE SERIES GLITCH.
THEN MY MANUSCRIPT FEES GOT CUT, AND MY MANGAKA LIFESTYLE ENDED
I DREW IT ALL MYSELF, SO I HAD NO FREE TIME WHATSOEVER THAT YEAR.

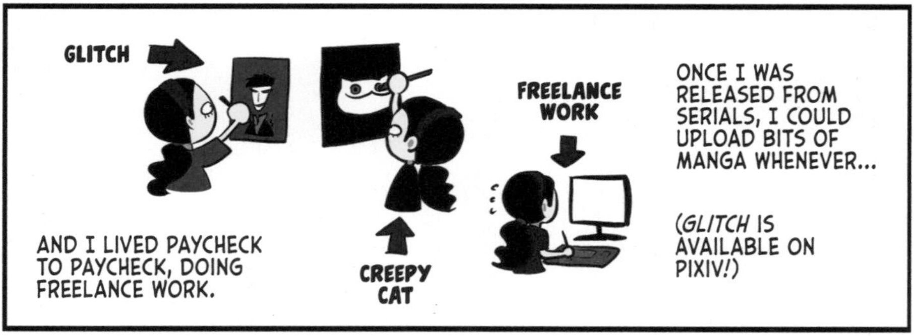

GLITCH
CREEPY CAT
FREELANCE WORK
ONCE I WAS RELEASED FROM SERIALS, I COULD UPLOAD BITS OF MANGA WHENEVER...
(GLITCH IS AVAILABLE ON PIXIV!)
AND I LIVED PAYCHECK TO PAYCHECK, DOING FREELANCE WORK.

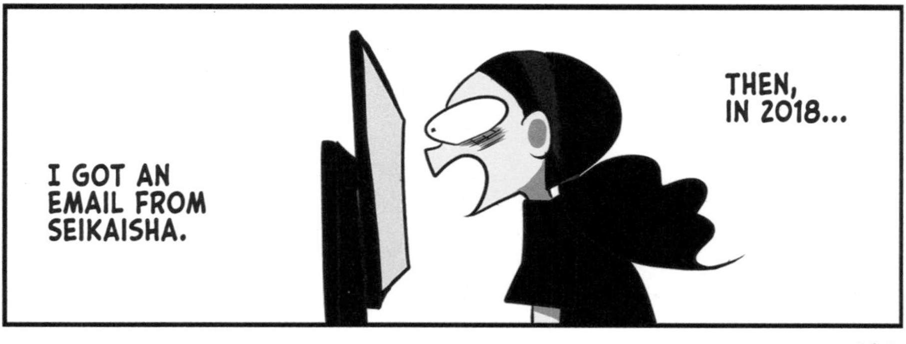

THEN, IN 2018...
I GOT AN EMAIL FROM SEIKAISHA.